POLITICS and
POLITICAL SYSTEMS

POLITICS and POLITICAL SYSTEMS

An Introduction to Political Science

John W. Ellsworth   Arthur A. Stahnke

Southern Illinois University at Edwardsville

McGraw-Hill Book Company

New York St. Louis San Francisco Auckland Düsseldorf
Johannesburg Kuala Lumpur London Mexico Montreal New Delhi Panama
Paris São Paulo Singapore Sydney Tokyo Toronto

**POLITICS AND
POLITICAL SYSTEMS**
An Introduction to Political Science

1234567890 KPKP 79876

This book was set in Helvetica by University Graphics, Inc.
The editors were Lyle Linder and John M. Morriss;
the designer was Anne Canevari Green;
the production supervisor was Sam Ratkewitch.
The drawings were done by Danmark & Michaels, Inc.
Kingsport Press, Inc., was printer and binder.

Library of Congress Cataloging in Publication Data
Ellsworth, John W
    Politics and political systems.

    Includes index.
    1. Political science.   2. Comparative government.
I. Stahnke, Arthur A., joint author.   II.   Title.
JA66.E55   320   75-34245
ISBN 0-07-019250-2

CONTENTS

PREFACE

From the beginning this book was conceived as a teaching instrument. The idea of writing the book and its general theoretical focus developed as we jointly taught the course "Introduction to Political Science." Over a period of two terms we debated, both in class and out, the proper focus and content for the introductory course, and the idea for this book was born. This open dialogue was possible because our academic interests were complementary, our egos were not unduly tender, and our mutual respect was not so great as to restrain expressions of honest disagreement.

As we defined the introductory course for ourselves and our students we found that existing texts did not fully suit our needs. Without fully comprehending the magnitude of the task, we set out to write the definitive text—theoretically elegant, comprehensive, erudite, integrated, and easy to read.

Of course this final product does not fully meet our initial expectations. But that is partly by later intention. As the book developed we came to strive for some characteristics, necessarily sacrificing others. The book is relatively brief and simple, not comprehensive, and encyclopedic. It is written for our students rather than our colleagues. It has an organizational coherence which is often missing from textbooks, but the frame of reference does not require readers to accept the authors' worldview.

The manuscript has met with the approval of our students who have used it over the past two years. We hope that our colleagues will share some measure of their, and our, enthusiasm for the book.

Many people have helped to form this volume. Ron Kissack, whose untimely death was a serious loss to both McGraw-Hill and us, was our first basic book editor; his toughminded determination to reach students at their level quickly made us realize that we were engaged in a difficult enterprise. More recently, the advice and help of Robert Rainier and Lyle Linder, both editors at McGraw-Hill, have been of substantial technical and substantive assistance. John Hendry, our basic book editor, showed a remarkable ability to sharpen our arguments and increase the clarity of our prose. Our colleagues at Southern Illinois University read, criticized, and sometimes used portions of our manuscript; they also goaded us to accelerate our progress on the project. Our students—who had little option in the matter—also gave us much useful feedback. Marian Miller and LaMora Sullivan were superbly efficient as they typed and retyped manuscript with speed and precision. Finally, Linda and Astrid, our wives, showed enough interest to provide continuing encouragement—and enough wisdom to direct their own professional interests elsewhere. With so much help, the book should have many merits; its limitations, we fear, must be entirely attributed to us.

John W. Ellsworth
Arthur A. Stahnke

POLITICS and POLITICAL SYSTEMS

CHAPTER ONE

POLITICS
The Management of Public Conflict

OVERVIEW **T**his chapter introduces politics as an activity which is rooted in human nature and in social activity. Pay particular attention to the notion of public conflict, and especially to the meaning of the word "public," which means different things to different people at different times. As you read this chapter, you should become aware that it is not easy to define the line between social activities which are political and those which are not.

It is also important for you to ask yourself why laws and rules are obeyed. How do rulers gain compliance from citizens? If rulers are to be obeyed, they must seek to create social conditions and to foster citizen attitudes which will gain compliance. The terms *authority, power,* and *force* are defined as the elements of political strength which public officials use to induce obedience.

Note that the emphasis is upon the complex relationships between officials and citizens. Politics involves webs of social interaction. In order to simplify the study of these complex human relationships you will be introduced to five functional

2 ☆

categories which form the basis for the organization of the first section of this book. Three of them are primarily concerned with describing the workings of political systems. The other two deal with broader social processes which influence political practices.

Be sure that you understand the following terms:

Politics	Political system
Social conflict	Decision making
Public conflict	Policy implementation
Authority	Issue definition
Power	Political socialization
Force	Political communication

LEARNING OBJECTIVES

After you have studied this chapter, you should be able to:*

1. Write the definition of politics given in the chapter.
2. Write a brief statement which differentiates between social conflict in general and conflict which is political.
3. Give examples of social conflict caused by cultural differences and economic factors.
4. Explain why any particular area of social conflict (for instance, religion) might be considered political in one time and place and not in another.
5. Identify examples of the use of authority, power, and force to gain compliance.
6. Explain the difference between authority, power, and force.
7. Analyze the usefulness of force for effective government, stressing both its merits and liabilities.
8. Label a diagram of a political system with the correct terms.
9. Identify definitions of decision making, policy implementation, issue development, political socialization, and political communication.

Politics is commonly viewed as both the most crass and the most exalted of arts, and citizens of modern nations commonly display mixed emotions

*If you are reading this text in a course, your instructor will probably expect you to be able to demonstrate your knowledge of text material besides what is covered in these learning objectives.

about political leaders and their activities. Their daily gossip often suggests that they endorse the half-century-old declaration of Finley Peter Dunne that politics is "the same old sport of highway robbery." At the same time, people pay high honor to the very politicians who are implicated as "highway robbers" by standing in line to hear or touch political candidates, Premiers, Presidents, and princes. Will Rogers spoke for much popular opinion in declaring that "all politics is applesauce" (a less polite phrase would be heard on the street corner); yet television, newspapers, magazines, and daily discussions are filled with accounts of politicians and their actions, testifying to a popular preoccupation with these matters. Politics is obviously a major concern of citizens, even if most of us react negatively to the political processes which affect us. We usually have some feelings that if only *someone* else would do *something* else with political power, things might be made better than they are.

Where do negative attitudes about politics and politicians originate? An examination of some common usages of the words "politics" and "political" may yield clues. A public official appoints a close friend or relative to a highly paid post and is accused of "playing politics" or dispensing a "political" favor. A contractor who made a contribution to a political candidate's campaign is awarded a contract to build a new city hall after the candidate takes office, and the contractor is charged with making "political" money. Or at the mundane level of sports, a football coach makes his own son quarterback of his team, and people say he made a "political" selection. In other words, "politics" and "political" often denote favoritism. This usage suggests that many people view politics as the exploitation of public office to promote private interests— or conversely, the unethical use of private influence to shape public policy for selfish ends.

But these same people often hold another, more favorable, view of politics at the same time; and they use other, more positive words to describe certain politicians and political actions. For instance, they adulate some public officials—most often dead ones—as "statesmen" (such as Abraham Lincoln, Winston Churchill, David Ben-Gurion). They also speak favorably, even reverently, about such political values as "justice," "law," and "freedom," even though they rarely agree on the precise meaning of these terms or on whether or not a given policy or action is in accord with such values.

Many citizens, then, have contradictory attitudes about politics and politicians. On the one hand, they often view politics as a dirty business in which ambitious persons misuse the public trust for their own ends. On the other hand, they believe that politics and politicians are at least potentially capable of contributing to the good life. It would seem that many people consider the daily business of politics to be a necessary evil at best, while simultaneously longing for political leaders who would be consistently selfless servants of the public good.

This popular ambivalence is understandable when we realize that politics is, by its very nature, controversial. In no society, past or present, has there ever been a total consensus on what is noble or just conduct. Societies are composed of individuals and groups with different values and different ways of viewing the social order. Politicians must make decisions which please some individuals and groups more than others, since all cannot be pleased equally. Even statesmen like Abraham Lincoln and John Kennedy were profoundly disliked in their own times. They were controversial men whose contemporaries did not unanimously agree that their policies and actions were in the best interests of the public they served. Since politicians cannot please everyone, they almost always disappoint or anger some citizens every time they act. Paraphrasing, we might say to politicians: "You can please most of the people some of the time, and some of the people all of the time, but you can't please all of the people all of the time."

POLITICS AS THE MANAGEMENT OF PUBLIC CONFLICT

Even when politicians are honest and selfless, then, it is to be expected that their actions will be controversial. They must choose between competing points of view, and decide between conflicting claims. David Easton has argued that the minimal function of government is to decide "who is to get what there is of desirable things."[1] And Harold Laswell has suggested that students of politics seek to determine "who gets what, when, and how."[2] Karl Friedrich views the "settling of disputes" as the "primordial function which a political order has to perform."[3] These three eminent political scientists underline a constant theme in the history of people's fascination with politics—the theme which maintains that politics arises out of human conflict in a social setting. In this context, politics must be seen as an important part of human social life, because governments and politicians are constantly involved in so many of the activities of citizens.

Politics may be broadly defined as the *management of public con-*

[1]David Easton, *The Political System* (New York: Knopf, 1953). p. 137.
[2]Harold D. Lasswell, *Politics: Who Gets What, When, How* (New York: Meridian Books, Inc., 1958).
[3]Carl J. Friedrich, *Man and His Government* (New York: McGraw-Hill, 1963), p. 423.

flict. As such, it is a social function which deals with the maintenance of social order and tranquility through the regulation of competition for valued items. Without such regulation this competition can lead to violence, disruption, and personal and social dislocation. Imagine a game of football in which the players do not obey or even recognize the same rules, and you will begin to perceive the problems that would beset a society without political means for regulating public conflict. Sandlot games played without umpires are plagued by endless arguments, but even these arguments are minor compared with those which might arise if opposing players refused to recognize the same general rules of the game.

Our game without rules points up two major aspects of political activity. Politics is, on the one hand, the means by which societies make rules (public policy) to govern social behavior. In this regard, politicians are similar to baseball or football commissioners: they lay down the rules for orderly conduct of the game. On the other hand, politics is also the process by which social rules are implemented and disputes under them are *decided.* In this regard, public officials act like umpires and referees, calling particular plays as they see them and thus overseeing the dispensing of rewards and punishments in the game.

Politics is not, of course, like baseball and football in all aspects; one big-city political boss noted this difference in his classic remark: "Politics ain't beanbag." But the basic comparison holds insofar as both sporting events and organized societies require regulation through rules and their enforcement. But games and politics are different in that game playing is confined to definite times, places, and conditions, whereas social conflict knows no set bounds; it occurs in almost endless forms wherever humans live in association with each other. And when social conflict comes to be considered as a public matter—that is, when it comes to be considered as *public conflict*—it becomes the root of political activity.

Politics and the "Public Interest"

Some people object to the definition of politics as the management of public conflict. They argue that such a definition fails to recognize the high moral purpose for which governments ought to strive. Arguing in the tradition of the great political and moral philosophers, some hold that political leaders rightly seek to discover a greater good, or public interest, which supersedes and subsumes the selfish interests which motivate most persons who compete in the public arena.

The importance of ethical and moral considerations for the study and practice of politics is clear. Attempts to define the public interest prompt discussion and debate which enhance the dignity of politics and of political science. But just as individuals and groups seldom agree upon the best economic policies for a government to pursue, so do they often disagree over the moral purposes of government and statecraft. In light of this persistent disagreement, it can be argued that debate over the content and character of the public interest is one of the elements of public conflict with which politicians must deal.

This last observation points to a fundamental distinction between social conflict and *public* conflict which will be discussed shortly. For now, it is sufficient to note that some conflict is obviously of public concern because of the attitudes and actions of large numbers of individuals or the actions of public officials. Issues such as the arms race, widespread poverty, and racial integration have attracted so much attention in recent times that there can be little doubt that the conflicts underlying them are of public, and therefore political, concern. The continuing debates over tax levies, crime rates, standards of public morality, and the use of natural resources are evidence that these matters, too, are of public—and therefore political—concern.

If the mere recognition that some conflicts gain widespread attention from citizens and politicians were enough for a thorough understanding of the political process, then political science would be almost superfluous. We could all retire to the newspaper and the six o'clock news for an understanding of politics. But political scientists seek to understand a number of questions which underlie the obvious manifestations of public concern and political action. They want to know how decisions concerning the public business are reached, and they want to understand the complexities of enforcing decisions and settling particular disputes which arise under general rules of conduct. Further, they are curious why particular matters come to be of political concern at all, and in the process, they seek to understand the human being as a social animal in conflict with other human beings.

Out of this desire to understand public conflict and its resolution, two immediate questions arise: What are the sources of social conflict? And when does social conflict become public conflict, thereby entering the domain of politics?

SOURCES OF SOCIAL CONFLICT

Social conflict is the product of differences between groups and individuals in society, and of the contending viewpoints which result from these differences. Large societies may have many different types of individuals whose characteristics and social situations differ in many ways. This diversity provides the basis for potential disagreement on virtually any question which becomes public business. To take an obvious example, business leaders and labor union officials have often disagreed over government policies designed to regulate labor-management relationships. Welfare recipients have come into conflict with middle-class taxpayers when they have requested benefits from the public treasury. And potential Vietnam draftees clashed with veterans groups and others who did not recognize the validity of protests against that war.

Such manifestations of social conflict over public issues result from differences between groups which are always *potentially* divisive, but may only surface in particular situations. Lower-class Catholics, Protestants, and Jews might agree on matters such as laws to provide a minimum wage, and only come into conflict when a question such as governmental aid to parochial schools arises. Citizens of various ideological persuasions might agree to support a given war, but disagree on questions of economic policy or taxation. That the possibilities for disagreement are almost endless can be seen in the case of prohibition, where the consumption of alcohol became a divisive issue, or more currently, in the dispute over the legalization of the use of marijuana. In these cases even personal habits led to public conflict and resulted in political action.

Cultural divisions in society

Virtually every modern nation contains a variety of *cultural* or ethnic groups which can come into conflict from time to time. The United States, while predominately "white," contains a large black minority of about 10 percent and sizable numbers of Mexican-Americans, Chinese, Japanese, and American Indians. Even the white majority contains a diversity of backgrounds based upon the cultures of the countries from which the forebears of present Americans emigrated. The Soviet Union contains

over 100 "nationalities," which include the predominant Russian population as well as Byelorussians, Lithuanians, Georgians, and many others.
Nigeria contains almost equal numbers of Yoruba, Hausa, and Ibo people,
as well as many smaller groups of diverse backgrounds.

Such differences in tradition and life-style are often viewed as
merely quaint or unusual to members of the dominant cultural group, but
they may be a very real source of concern for public officials. St. Patrick's
Day parades, "soul music," Hanukkah, Chinese New Year, Indian rain
dances, and other such manifestations of cultural diversity in the United
States are seen as colorful, educational, and fun. But the color of a ghetto
riot is red with fire and blood; militant Indians occupying Alcatraz or
Wounded Knee, South Dakota, are not seeking tourist applause; and the
struggle of various ethnic or cultural groups of the nation for equality and
a full share of America's riches is anything but child's play. These efforts
are intensely serious, and more often than not they become the business of
public officials who must deal with differences between competing cultural groups.

Intercultural tensions have, for example, created thorny problems
for those responsible for shaping educational policies in this country.
Since the 1954 Supreme Court decision outlawing racial segregation in
schools, a host of culturally related issues has arisen. Not only blacks, but
Mexican-Americans and Puerto Ricans have come to consider the educational system as biased in favor of white middle-class values. Middle-class
language usage, standardized tests which favor whites, textbooks which
exclude nonwhite culture, and other devices or features of the system, it
is argued, discriminate against those students who have learned to cope
with life in a way different from the predominant group of Americans. If a
student speaks Spanish at home, he may not learn to read, write, and
spell English as quickly at school. If a child learns to communicate in the
lively verbal style of the ghetto, he may not be able to handle the written
word as easily as a child who is continually exposed to books and
magazines. The discontent of American cultural minorities has had an
impact on public officials from the local school board to the White House.

Wherever cultural diversity exists, conflict is likely to occur at some
point. The Soviet Union has made great efforts to break down barriers
between the various nationalities it encompasses, but even now, more
than 50 years after the Russian Revolution, such groups as the Ukranians
resist Moscow and find themselves moved from one part of the country to
another. The long history of wars in Southeast Asia, including the American involvement in Vietnam, is partly based upon cultural differences
between such groups as the Viets, Thais, Khmers, Montagnards, and
Laotians. The recent civil war in Nigeria was clearly drawn on tribal lines

with the Ibo culture's survival at stake in the minds of the secessionist Biafran leaders. Not all such conflict can be attributed to cultural differences, but a close look at many controversies will reveal that they are either grounded in or aggravated by contrasting world views, traditions, and life-styles.

Economic divisions in society

As Adam Smith emphasized 200 years ago,[4] every society relies upon a division of labor in order to produce the goods and services needed by its people. Even simple societies assign different economic tasks to different persons. In some tribes, men are often responsible for hunting game and building shelter, while women gather roots, nuts, and fruit, and prepare the food. In medieval Europe, peasants were tied to the land and produced the food crops for the population, while feudal lords provided protection to the people. Auxiliary services such as the milling of grain were provided by trades people. Modern industrial societies are infinitely more complex in that virtually every person has specialized skills and tasks which contribute to the overall economic well-being of the society.

The specialization which is characteristic of industrial economies makes all individuals dependent upon many others for their material needs. City dwellers do not produce the food they eat, and farmers do not produce their own tractors and chemical fertilizer. Corporation executives seldom build their own homes, and trades people do not usually organize the massive business enterprises needed to produce automobiles, electrical appliances, and other conveniences. Because jobs have become so specialized, virtually no one is self-sufficient in an industrial, and so interdependent, society: even a strike of a few hundred tugboat operators or toolmakers can have profound effects on the lives of a thousand times as many other citizens. And the actions of bank presidents and corporation heads can determine whether millions of people will live in affluence or misery.

Due to this interdependence, economic issues tend to become governmental concerns in industrial states. When labor feels that it is being underpaid and cannot get what it wants from management, unions tend to ask public officials for help. If a strike shuts down a "vital" industry, management officials may ask the government to force workers

---

[4]Adam Smith, *The Wealth of Nations* (New York: The Modern Library, 1937), chaps. 1 and 2.

back to their jobs. When technology makes small farms and businesses unprofitable, the government is asked to subsidize the entrepreneurs affected. When medical costs increase greatly, as they have in recent years, patients may press for government insurance or guaranteed medical care. When major corporations fail, government loans or subsidies are often sought. Economic interdependence, then, produces conflicting demands upon public officials, demands resulting from the different economic positions of various members of society.

Karl Marx argued that all conflict was rooted in differences of viewpoint which resulted from economic arrangements.[5] He viewed the history of humanity as a battle between those who owned the tools or means of production and those who did not. Marx argued that modern industrial life produces an implacable struggle between the *bourgeois class* of property owners, business executives, and industrialists and the *proletarian class* of laborers and workers. According to him, each class views society from its own perspective and has its own ideology—capitalism for the bourgeoisie and communism for the proletariat. He reasoned that the proletariat would eventually tear down the state and the system of private property, and would produce a society in which all would share wealth in common. In this "classless" society, there would be no important economic differences between individuals.

The Marxian analysis need not be accepted in order to recognize that economic specialization produces differences in viewpoint which can lead to social conflict. Whether it appears as a struggle between agriculture and industry, rail transportation against trucking, steel against aluminum, or corporations against small businesses, it is easy to identify examples of social conflicts which arise when economic interests clash. Further, such interests can conflict with other values, as when conservationists seek to prohibit the owner of a redwood forest from cutting down his or her own trees.

Both cultural and economic differences are obvious sources of social conflict. Though they are only two general bases for the differences of opinion which arise between individuals, they are of prominent importance. As we have noted earlier, any number of other kinds of differences can also generate controversy, since any felt difference in social position can induce persons to seek different ends or to compete for the same valued resources. It is especially important to note that religious differences often produce conflict, as when Catholics clash with

[5]Karl Marx. *The Manifesto of the Communist Party* in *Basic Writings on Politics and Philosophy: Marx and Engels,* Lewis S. Feuer, ed. (Garden City, N.Y.: Doubleday Company, Inc., 1959). pp. 1–41.

Protestants in Northern Ireland, or when Buddhists and Catholics clash in South Vietnam, or when Jews and Arabs contend with each other in the Middle East.

But the point need not be belabored. The diversity of situations and viewpoints in contemporary societies gives rise to social conflict, and when that conflict becomes public, it enters the province of politics.

PUBLIC CONFLICT

Since politics is the management of *public* conflict, it is important to explore the difference between disagreements and disputes which are properly considered to be public business and those which are not. There are broad questions of policy which almost every state considers to be public business, and which almost everyone concedes are proper subjects for political action. Taxation, criminal laws against theft and murder, and the conduct of foreign relations are generally conceded to be public and therefore political concerns. These are matters in which virtually every citizen has a stake and which are usually considered public business. Few would contend that there should be no taxation (and therefore no government), or that individuals should be forced to defend their own property and person or conduct their own negotiations with foreign states. Thus, when large numbers of persons are concerned with a particular matter, or when public officials act or propose to act on it, it may become recognized as a proper political subject, as an item on the public agenda.

Other types of disputes are not usually considered to be public in character either because they involve too few people, are generally considered to be private quarrels, or are not regulated by public officers. Most arguments between husbands and wives, parents and children, or families in a neighborhood do not become subjects of public concern. Even larger-scale conflicts may be considered nonpublic, as when feuds between mountaineers in the Ozarks or Chinese clans in San Francisco were largely ignored a century ago. The key distinctions, then, are whether large numbers of people are involved in a conflict, and more importantly, whether a given society considers the subject of the conflict or the actions of the contestants to be of general public concern.

Individual rights and liberties versus public intervention

In Western countries there has been a strong tradition of individualism. Persons have guarded their privacy as a right, and have denied that most of their actions are proper concerns for public regulation. This can be seen in such everyday expressions as "a man's home is his castle," or "it's a free country." Philosophically, this emphasis on individual liberty finds eloquent expression in the writings of the nineteenth-century Englishman, John Stuart Mill, who defined liberty as "pursuing your own good in your own way," and maintained that the only justification for interfering with the liberty of another was "self-protection." Legally, it is common to find bills of rights written into the laws and constitutions of Western nations. For instance, the American Constitution specifically guarantees every individual virtually unlimited freedom of speech, press, religion, and peaceful assembly. And in practice, we find that individualistic traditions in countries such as France, Britain, and the United States have made citizens suspicious of attempts to regulate their lives or to pry into their daily affairs. The Western tradition has thus produced a situation in which every new attempt to regulate individual activity is likely to require broad public support and specific justification.

John Stuart Mill on the Proper Limits of Governmental Control over Individual Liberty

John Stuart Mill in his famous essay "On Liberty" set out the classic argument for the proper limits on governmental control over individual behavior:

> But there is a sphere of action in which society, as distinguished from the individual, has, if any, only an indirect interest; comprehending all that portion of a person's life and conduct which affects only himself, or if it also affects others, only with their free, voluntary, and undeceived consent and participation. . . . This, then, is the appropriate region of human liberty. It comprises, first, the inward domain of consciousness; demanding liberty of conscience, in the most comprehensive sense; liberty of thought and feeling; absolute freedom of opinion and sentiment on all subjects, practical or speculative, scientific, moral, or theological. The liberty of expressing and publishing opinions may seem to fall under a different principle, since it belongs to that part of the conduct of an individual which concerns other people; but, being almost of as much importance as the liberty of thought itself, and resting in great

part on the same reasons, is practically inseparable from it. Secondly, the principle requires liberty of tastes and pursuits; of framing the plan of our life to suit our own character; of doing as we like, subject to such consequences as may follow: without impediment from our fellow creatures, so long as what we do does not harm them, even though they should think our conduct foolish, perverse, or wrong. Thirdly, from this liberty of each individual, follows the liberty, within the same limits, of combination among individuals; freedom to unite, for any purpose not involving harm to others: the persons combining being supposed to be of full age, and not forced or deceived.

No society in which these liberties are not, on the whole, respected, is free, whatever may be its form of government; and none is completely free in which they do not exist absolute and unqualified. The only freedom which deserves the name, is that of pursuing our own good in our own way, so long as we do not attempt to deprive others of theirs, or impede their efforts to obtain it. Each is the proper guardian of his own health, whether bodily, or mental and spiritual. Mankind are greater gainers by suffering each other to live as seems good to themselves, than by compelling each to live as seems good to the rest. . . . [Reprinted in Carl Cohen (ed.), *Communism, Facism and Democracy* (New York: Random House, 1962), pp. 551–552.]

In recent decades, governmental activities in the West have grown increasingly broad, but this has been possible only because the development of industry and the crowding of people together into urban centers has led more and more individuals to realize that the actions of others affect them deeply. As long as it was possible to be physically isolated from other citizens and to avoid dependence upon others for the necessities of life, a large portion of an individual's life could easily be seen as outside the concern of others. But when only others can provide the job which a person needs or the specialized skills needed for the manufacture of a needed product (gasoline, electricity, medical care, shoes, and so on, ad infinitum), when a family cannot raise enough food in the backyard, when the antisocial habits of a neighbor can influence one's children or produce intolerable noise or property damage, *some* people tend to argue that *some* public agency should do *some*thing to ensure their welfare and provide protection from their fellow citizens. In fact, most people today feel they need a good deal of support and service from public officials and agencies.

This development can be expected whenever conditions (1) place people in close everyday contact with each other or (2) make people highly dependent on one another. Under crowded, economically and socially complex conditions, virtually everything a person does may affect someone else. It is at least likely that most individual actions will be perceived by some as having social consequences. As recently as 50 years ago, most Americans were free to use their guns for hunting or target practice almost without governmental regulations. In many localities today it is simply too dangerous to permit gun owners to shoot at bottles or rabbits in their own backyards; too many neighbors and their children are within rifle range. As a consequence, such sporting activities are now generally restricted. But social complexity—and thus social conflict and public intervention—need not depend on physical crowding. Many farmers live miles from their nearest neighbors and hundreds of miles from their customers. Yet they are just as dependent on these customers and on the industrial workers who produce the goods they need as city dwellers are dependent on them for food.

Thus, though individualism may act as a barrier to expanding the area of public concern, as people live together in closer contact the areas of life which are left untouched by public regulation tend to become fewer and smaller.

We have seen that social conflict arises from the diverse positions or perspectives which different individuals have on social affairs. One way in which these differences manifest themselves is in quarrels over the proper limits of public intervention. For instance, because of his or her own interest in producing goods as cheaply as possible, a business executive may dump raw industrial waste into a stream. Fishermen, finding that their own living is affected by the resulting reduction of the fish population, may argue that governmental regulation of the manufacturer is needed. From the business executive's point of view, the dumping of waste appears to be a private act. But the fishermen argue that it is a public matter because it affects them and the people they feed. If there are enough fishermen involved, or if they can get sufficient support from other citizens, they may make the dispute part of the public sphere by challenging the manufacturer in court, or by attempting to get legislation passed which would regulate the dumping of industrial waste. Whether the dispute is public or private is itself at issue. It may be resolved partly through the decisions of individual citizens, who may support one party or another, and partly through governmental action, since public officials will ultimately decide whether or not to act on the case.

Individual rights and liberties thus come into conflict and produce controversy both over the question of the proper limits of the public arena, and over the proper way to deal with a public question once it is so identified. Whereas one may believe that most of one's actions should not be subject to public concern and scrutiny, once brought into conflict with others, a variety of social and political forces and procedures will determine whether one will be subject to public regulation. Not all disputes over the limits of public interest reach courts, legislatures, or executive officers; many conflicts are regulated by social customs and informal procedures. But once public officials formally recognize a question, it becomes public conflict by our definition, at least until they reverse themselves.

Role of public officials

Up to this point, we have said relatively little about the role which public officials play in defining the difference between public and private matters. Competing group and individual viewpoints play an important part in the process, as we have just noted. But ultimately, governments decide which areas of social life they will regulate and which they will leave alone. In making decisions about the scope of their activities, public officials are constrained in part by the attitudes of the society they govern—a lone fisherman would not be likely to get official action against a water-polluting manufacturer unless he could get broad social support for his cause. On the other hand, most public officials have fairly well-defined ideas about the proper limits of their jurisdiction, ideas which may or may not accord with majority sentiment in society.

In the history of Western governments officials have differed over the extent to which questions of religion and economics were properly public business. Prior to the great Reformation, European princes considered themselves responsible for the faithfulness of their subjects, and they cooperated with the Church in suppressing heresy, collected taxes to support clerical activities, and supported schools and hospitals run by the clergy. As reformers such as Luther, Zwingli, Calvin, and Knox won converts to their versions of Christianity, various sovereigns took different sides in the struggle between Protestant sects and the mother church, and warred with each other for more than 100 years. Only with the treaty of Westphalia in 1648, were matters of religious faith left in the hands of individual rulers and governments. Still, public officials sought to enforce religious standards on their subjects, as in the infamous Salem witchcraft trials in colonial Massachusetts. And many states collected taxes to support an established church, whether it was the Anglican Church in England or the Roman Catholic Church in France or Spain. The United States Constitution of 1787 prohibited state involvement in religious matters, leaving faith to the conscience of individual believers; but even though contemporary governments generally remain aloof from religious disputes, public officials must sometimes deal with matters of faith which become public issues.

The Limits of Separation of Church and State in the United States

Though the principle of separation of church and state is firmly established as a principle in American politics, political controversies involving religious beliefs have occasionally erupted here. When they have, public officials have become involved and have been forced to make public decisions, as was shown in a recent textbook controversy in West Virginia. Public protests forced local officials to decide that certain textbooks could not be used in public schools because they offended the beliefs of many of the students' parents. The following *New York Times* story summarized the high points of the controversy:

Dept. of Book-Banning, W. Va. Division

Family rights and fundamentalist Christianity are strong strains in the mining people of West Virginia, and any attempt to go against them is sure to raise hackles. That's what has happened in a new book-banning controversy that has swept through Charleston and surrounding Kanawha County.

The controversy began at the opening of the school year when angry parents led by Fundamentalist preachers, protested the use by their children of new school textbooks, calling them "dirty," "anti-Christian," and "anti-American." The dispute got out of hand when it became entangled with labor issues.

The books in question are supplementary reading anthologies for use mainly in junior and senior high schools. They were approved by the County School Board, 3 to 2, upon recommendation of a teachers' committee.

As an example of material the protesters consider too sexually explicit and thus contrary to their parental teaching, the protesters cite a profile of the poet Allen Ginsberg in which Mr. Ginsberg is quoted as describing "a tall redheaded chick . . . mainly a whore, actually, with very expensive Johns, who would pay her $100 a shot." The profile originally appeared in the *New Yorker.*

The disputed book used in elementary schools reprints as a "fable" the story of Androcles and the lion, and in an accompanying teachers' manual suggests asking the students about other "myths" such as Daniel in the lion's den from the Bible. This is taken by the Fundamentalists as an attack on the literal truth of the Bible.

The protesters regard some works by militant blacks as anti-American because, they contend, the writings are critical of the police and whites.

The agreement that permitted the reopening of the schools called for a withdrawal of the books pending a review of their contents by a citizens' committee. The teachers' association saw the agreement as a setback for "academic integrity."

The controversy was complicated by the fact that some miners, who had joined their wives as pickets at the schools, reportedly saw an opportunity to press grievances against their employees and began to picket the mines as well. Their contract expires in November. The mines were closed because of the miners' traditional refusal to cross picket lines. [*New York Times*, Sept. 22, 1974.]

Just as attitudes toward the extent to which religion is a fit subject for public regulation have varied with the times, so have attitudes toward the proper extent of economic intervention by the state. During the sixteenth and seventeenth centuries, rulers accepted the doctrines of mercantilism, which held that all matters of trade were the business of the state. As commerce enlarged and the industrial age dawned, the capitalistic arguments of Adam Smith gained adherents. State interference in commerce and industry diminished as public officials were persuaded that a "laissez faire" or "hands-off" policy would best promote the public good. Since then the rise of complex economies and large-scale corporations has led to massive welfare programs, state regulation of commerce and industry, and even state ownership of major industries.

The crucial point is that public officials bring particular attitudes to their positions—attitudes which predispose them to view given types of disputes as either within or outside of the realm of public concern. These predispositions tend to reflect those of society at large, but may be partly personal. We find, consequently, that the effective definition of the public interest, and the consequent extent of state activities, varies from nation to nation in today's world. Whereas Soviet and Chinese leaders are inclined to view almost every matter as of public concern, British and American officials think of their responsibilities in more narrow terms. A Soviet painter or writer may be supported directly by the state. An American counterpart must rely on private patrons or buyers.

What then is the meaning of "public"? It should be clear that a precise and universal definition cannot be devised. The difference between public and nonpublic conflicts is continually redefined in the cauldron of social life and politics, and the proper limit of political intervention may be an important political issue in itself. Specific disputes are continually brought to the attention of political officials, who may or may not consider them to be public in character. And leaders may attempt to bring new areas under public management in spite of social resistance, as when Stalin forcibly collectivized Soviet agriculture over the sometimes violent resistance of peasants.

ELEMENTS OF POLITICAL STRENGTH

The management of public conflict involves the making of public policies, their enforcement, and the settlement of resulting disputes. We have seen that public officials find it virtually impossible to please everyone. Some people will resent almost any rule or the way that it is enforced, and when disputes must be settled by administrators and judges, those who lose will ordinarily feel resentment.

Since politicians cannot please everyone, it is necessary that they possess the means to enforce their decisions in spite of the resentments which might arise against them. In calm and untroubled times, or when political decisions play only a small part in social life, there may be little need for political strength. If, however, political decisions affect society greatly, or if they meet with widespread resistance, officials must have resources sufficient to make their decrees effective. We now turn to a discussion of the elements of political strength, which can in turn be seen as a discussion of how citizens are induced to obey the dictates of their governors.

Political strength may be seen in terms of three key elements: *authority, power,* and *force.* A seemingly universal tendency of people— *the habit of compliance*—also enters into any thoroughgoing consideration of political strength.

Authority

Authority is both the most efficient and the least obtrusive resource which a politician or regime can use. It is present when those who are commanded obey because they believe that it is right, just, and moral to do so—because they view the command as *legitimate.* The criminal who accepts his punishment as just retribution for his crime attributes authority to those who imprison him. The conscripted soldier who enters the armed services because he believes in the legitimacy of the order to go to war, recognizes that his draft board has authority over him. When we blame ourselves for violating the rules of the state; or when we believe that the state has a right to command us as it does, when we see compliance with orders from the state as our duty, we act as if the state and its officials have authority.

Thus viewed, authority is a psychological relationship between the governors and the governed. Authority rests upon the perceived legitimacy of those who give orders. It is a potent political tool because the governor has only to command and the citizen obeys. No threats, no force, no exercise of physical coercion is needed if, in the eyes of an individual, the public official who commands has the authority to do so. Authority is possessed by those who can issue commands and obtain compliance because they are perceived to have that right. Phrased differently, authority is possessed by those who are thought to have a *legitimate* right to make and enforce rules—it rests upon *legitimacy.*

Officials can acquire authority by virtue of holding public office; they may also build their authority through personal appeal and wise policy choices. A 1960 study of the United States by Gabriel Almond and Sidney Verba revealed that 85 per cent of American people claimed that they were proud of their political institutions.[6] A survey made by Albert

---

[6]Gabriel A. Almond and Sidney Verba, *The Civic Culture* (Boston: Little, Brown, 1965), p. 64.

Reiss, Jr., showed that six of the most respected occupations in America were governmental (e.g., Supreme Court justice, state governor, diplomat).[7] This would indicate that simply holding particular positions in the American government gives a public official high status. Of course, one's holding a political position is not, in itself, enough to guarantee that all or most citizens will view one's political commands as moral or just or legitimate. In addition, politicians seek to project themselves as personally honest, selflessly devoted to the public good, and consistently acting in the best interests of society. They utilize the rhetoric of nationalism and the words of religious and ideological teachings to persuade their followers that their "hearts are in the right place." And they take care to formulate policies which, when implemented, will gain widespread acceptance and produce results which will generate loyalty and adherence to themselves and to their public office.

Some men have been masters at the art of expanding their authority. Woodrow Wilson narrowly won reelection to the United States Presidency in 1916 on an antiwar platform and nonetheless persuaded his countrymen to work fervently to win a war "to make the world safe for democracy." Franklin Roosevelt led the Democratic party to smashing victories in the United States because he convinced large numbers of the people that his leadership was concerned with "the forgotten man," and offered a "New Deal for the American people." Adolph Hitler unified Germany because his followers became convinced that he could cure the social ills that besieged his nation and lead it back to greatness. Lenin and Stalin established their authority as unquestioned leaders of a proletarian revolution which would transform the lives of the Russian peoples first, and eventually all the working classes of the world. Such leaders are often said to be "charismatic" because the image of authority they convey is based not only on the offices they hold but also on personal qualities which win the loyalty of others.

Obviously not all public officials develop authority through their ability to inspire respect and to win the loyalties of others. Often citizens obey because of the office a person occupies, apart from his or her personal strengths or weaknesses. Suppose a citizen pays a $15 fine to an arrogant, unshaven, none-too-sober justice of the peace because he or she did not see the "No Parking" sign in front of the drugstore (which also happens to be the J.P.'s office). The citizen might pay because of a fear of losing a driver's license or spending a night in jail. But quite possibly the citizen will pay because he or she believes the justice of the

[7]Albert J. Reiss, Jr., *Occupations and Social Status* (New York: Free Press, 1961), p. 54.

peace has authority, regardless of personally obnoxious characteristics or the questionable character of the "justice" dispensed. The office alone may suffice to confer legitimacy upon the acts of its occupant.

Habit of compliance   We have said that people obey public officials because they recognize that those officials have authority over them. But they also obey rules and directions because they have a general *habit of compliance.* This is an important resource for leaders which complements their authority. Individuals *do* obey laws and specific commands because they have been trained to do so. They do not view traffic lights as improper restraints upon their moral rights, and they generally make their social security payments without so much as a second thought. This habit of compliance makes the task of governors easier, but there are times when people neither perceive a command as just, nor obey it simply because they are habituated to comply. In such situations the *power* of the state may become decisive.

Power

Whereas citizens comply with state directives because of an image of *legitimacy* when *authority* is present, they respond to an image of *strength* when *power* is the prevailing influence. Faced with a situation in which the state or its officials are thought not to have the right to command, a citizen may obey because of a fear of the consequences of disobedience: the citizen knows (or thinks) that the state has the strength to enforce its commands. Conscripted soldiers who go to war for fear of imprisonment by the courts or a loss of social status are responding to power rather than authority. They believe they will be more miserable if they disobey that if they do not. Of course, it is possible for them to feel that the state commands them by right, and also to have reasons to avoid induction. In that case, their decision to obey results from both a sense of duty and a fear of the consequences of defiance.

It is easy to underestimate the importance of power as a political resource. How many people come to a full stop at a stop sign on a deserted street, not because they think it is necessary or right, or because it is habit, but because they might get a traffic ticket if they don't? How many potential shoplifters are deterred by fear of apprehension rather than by moral considerations? How much cheating on income tax returns is curtailed by fear of a tax audit and accompanying penalties?

Power, then, is a vital element of political strength. Indeed, it is tempting to agree with Aristotle's rather pessimistic declaration that most men "are naturally apt to be swayed by fear rather than by reverence, and to refrain from evil rather because of the punishment that it brings, than because of its own foulness." The fear of punishment by a strong state is a means of providing order in society, order which may or may not be related to feelings about the morality or justice of state activities. Thus, the image of strength which public officials project to the citizenry enables them to secure compliance in spite of the resentments that any portion of the populace might feel toward particular policies or policy-makers.

Both power and authority are rather delicately rooted in the attitudes of those who are asked to comply with political decisions. In a very real sense, perceptions of strength or legitimacy are more important, in many cases, than "objective strengths" as might be determined by an outside observer. This aspect of political reality has been clearly understood by men like J. Edgar Hoover, the late head of the Federal Bureau of Investigation, who managed to convince Americans that his small force of investigators was so skillful, efficient, and honest that those who might violate federal laws within its jurisdiction would almost surely be caught. In promoting this image, he stressed not only actual performance in catching and convicting criminals, but also favorable publicity about his agency. Similarly, the Internal Revenue Service has regularly publicized improvements in its tax collection procedures. The clear intent is to convince each taxpayer that cheating on a tax return will result in certain punishment.

Force

If power relies upon an image of strength, force is the application of it. In its simplest form, force is coercion. Mao Tse-tung said that "political power flows from the barrel of a gun." His statement asserts that *force* is the key political resource. Certainly this accords with Chairman Mao's experience; he successfully led a revolutionary army against the standing regime of Chiang Kai-shek. Mao was by no means naïve, however, and his army was mobilized more by persuasion and discipline than by coercion. And China is not currently governed by the continual use of armaments. Instead, the Chinese are schooled in Maoist doctrine, which stresses the legitimacy and justness of state policies (see inset below). They are also continually reminded of the unpleasant consequences which will follow if they refuse to comply with the orders of public offcials. Perhaps Mao's point is that the ultimate credibility of political power rests upon the ability of a leader to monopolize the guns and use them if need be, not that power and authority depend on a repeated pulling of the trigger.

Establishing Authority: Chairman Mao on the Well-Being of the Masses

The writings of Chairman Mao contain many statements urging the Communist party to unite with the people. In 1934, in the midst of the struggle between Communists and the Kuomintang, Mao delivered a speech before a Congress of Workers' and Peasants' Representatives in which he stressed the need to be concerned with the well-being of the masses:

> If we only mobilize the people to carry on the war and do nothing else, can we succeed in defeating the enemy? Of course not. If we want to win, we must do a great deal more. We must lead the peasants' struggle for land and distribute the land to them, heighten their labour enthusiasm and increase agricultural production, safeguard the interests of the workers, establish co-operatives, develop trade with outside areas, and solve the problems facing the masses—food, shelter and clothing, fuel, rice, cooking oil and salt, sickness and hygiene, and marriage. In short, all the practical problems in the masses' everyday life should claim our attention. If we attend to these problems, solve them and satisfy the needs of the masses, we shall really become organizers of the well-being of the masses, and they will truly rally round us and give us their warm support. . . . [*Selected Readings from the Works of Mao Tse-tung*, vol. I(Peking: Foreign Languages Press, 1967), pp. 147–148.]

In a sense, the use of force by state agents is a confession that authority and power have failed, for if citizens believed either that the state was right (legitimate) or that it would punish them violently, it would be unnecessary to use force. This statement covers a complex range of situations, and it deserves some explanation. Students who stage a sit-in in a public building are defying the *authority* of the state; they accept the virtual certainty that the state has sufficient strength to punish them. Burglars who try to elude the law are, in contrast, defying the *power* of the state—they take a chance that the police are not strong enough to catch them. They may or may not feel that the laws against burglary are just. Guerilla forces and revolutionary armies defy *both* the *authority* and *power* of the regimes they seek to unseat. They declare the injustice of existing policies, and gamble that they are stronger than the state as well. In each of these three examples, violence must be used by the state because either the justness or the power of public officials is called into question.

No state can survive indefinitely when it must use force against a major portion of its citizenry over long periods of time. The brutality of such conditions erodes confidence in the ability of public officials to regulate the society in an acceptable way. Mahatma Gandhi and Martin Luther King were particularly sensitive to this aspect of politics. Both sought to challenge the authority of existing officials and laws by goading the state into the use of force against peaceful violators of civil orders. Gandhi began his long campaign for Indian independence by walking down to the Indian Ocean with a band of followers, gathering a few pinches of salt. He invited arrest by the British Colonial government, and was arrested because he violated a salt-tax law. Both Gandhi and King were jailed many times. Their followers were beaten, killed, and imprisoned. But in the process, these men made the state employ force in such a way that the justness of its policies was called into open question in the minds of many members of society. The more dramatic actions of American blacks who have rioted in cities such as Detroit, Newark, and Watts, as well as waged undeclared war against the police in the slums of American cities, have also made government officials display open force. They have created a crisis in the confidence Americans have long had in the ability of their political order to survive.

It is true that passive resistance has little chance of success against authorities who are sufficiently strong and ruthless to use force massively and repeatedly. Mahatma Gandhi and Martin Luther King would almost surely have been quickly shot in Hitler's Germany or Stalin's Russia. Their followers, too, would have come to speedy ends under regimes where force was viewed as the legitimate antidote to dissent. Nevertheless, open and repeated use of force may purchase obedience at the expense of resentment—resentment which can fester into open rebellion and civil war. Subjugated citizens have risen against oppressive rulers repeatedly, from provincial uprisings against Ancient Rome to peasant rebellions in various countries in the current century. Whether or not such rebellions are crushed, an open and forceful clash between parts of a society leaves a heritage of bitterness which undermines the basis for orderly regulation of society by government.

Political regimes may ultimately rest upon force, but it is a most expensive resource. It may produce social instability which can undermine confidence in officials and laws. Open force is generally destructive of the sense of legitimacy necessary for authority to exist, and unless dissent is decisively and overwhelmingly suppressed, force undermines the image of strength necessary for political power as well.

OFFICIALS AND CITIZENS: A SYSTEMS MODEL

The goals of citizens and public officials are both complementary and competing. Every society needs agents who make and enforce policies which manage public conflict. However, concrete questions arise concerning which activities should be politically regulated, which rules should regulate them, and which enforcement procedures should be used to those ends. These questions divide citizens into competing camps and sometimes pit members of society against public officials. Further, it is not uncommon for individuals to want to be left alone to pursue their own goals. There is a tendency to want the strength of the state to be limited, at least insofar as that strength affects us personally.

Public officials, on the other hand, are concerned with maintaining the power and authority they judge necessary to preserve their effectiveness. The need for political strength thus may place officials in conflict with citizens. While there may be agreement that governments are necessary, citizens also may differ as to what they think governments should do.

Any adequate explanation of political activity must account for the complex relationship between public officials and individuals in society. The great political thinkers, from Plato to the present, have done this in a variety of ways, and consequently there are numerous approaches which can be utilized to introduce students to the study of politics. An introductory textbook cannot possibly do justice to every such approach, and some difficult choices must be made.

For instance, should the *personalities* of great politicians be stressed, or, alternatively, the *social* and *historical forces* within which they must operate? Should the requirements of an *ideal* state be outlined, or an attempt made to convey a sense of the variety of political arrangements which *actually* exist? Should *ideologies* such as fascism, communism, and democracy be the main theme, or should the *actual behavior* of public officials and the reactions of citizens to them be the central focus? Should *contemporary issues* of public policy be highlighted, or should particular stress be placed instead on *historical developments?* Not all of these options are mutually exclusive. Nevertheless, some overall framework should be utilized, a framework which will convey the excitement, complexity, and variety of political life and exclude as little of importance as is possible in an introductory textbook.

Several important considerations have led us to use a framework which is commonly called the "systems" approach to politics. First, this approach attempts to describe the relationships of political activity to other aspects of social life. Second, it does not prejudge the relative merits of various types of political arrangements which societies have devised. Third, with this approach it is possible to relate the discipline of political science to other social sciences such as sociology, economics, psychology, and anthropology. And finally, the approach permits the division of the subject matter into convenient "functional" topics. The political activities of public officials and citizens can be studied under separate topical headings which nonetheless form an integrated picture of society and politics.

Political system

The central proposition of the systems approach is that all social, including political, phenomena are interrelated—they affect each other. At the outset then, the systems approach assumes that it is not possible to understand one part of society in isolation from the other parts which affect its operation. For example, if we want to comprehend fully how laws are made, we must study more than just the legislative machinery; we must also examine such factors as the pressures applied to decision makers and the way in which they think a given law may affect the citizenry. If we want to know why a police officer behaves in a certain manner, we must know what orders the superiors gave, what social forces motivate the superiors, how the police officer views the citizens with whom he or she deals, and what citizens themselves might do as a result of the officer's actions. Any political question, properly understood, must be related to a broader social context.

Earlier we broadly defined politics as the management of public conflict. Now, in keeping with our systems approach, we can sharpen that definition a little and say that we shall consider politics as a *system* for the management of public conflict. But let us be very clear on one point here: our systems approach meaning covers *all types of* political systems— republican or representative, monarchical, socialist, communist, fascist, or whatever. As we noted in the last section, the systems approach enables us to divide our subject matter into convenient *functional* topics; and these topics are equally useful in the study of all types of political systems.

In its broadest sense, the term "system" denotes any set of interrelated elements. The human circulatory system, for instance, consists of the interaction of the heart, arteries, veins, capillaries, and blood. The respiratory system includes the working of breathing passages and lungs. If a human being were viewed as a system, all the active elements of the body would be included as parts of the system, including the circulatory and respiratory systems, which could then be considered to be *sub*systems. An automobile may be viewed as a mechanical system composed of its various parts (and of such subsystems as the ignition and exhaust systems). We commonly speak of a city "school system," which includes all the buildings, teachers, pupils, administrators, and supporting personnel and machinery to conduct elementary and secondary education.

Like biological, mechanical, educational, and other systems, the political system is defined according to its *function.* The circulatory system is composed of those biological interactions which function to distribute food and collect waste within the organism. A school system consists of those activities which function to educate the young of the community. Similarly, a political system consists of those social activities and interactions which manage public conflict for a society.

Further, the political system, like any complex system, is composed of subsystems which perform specialized functions which are part of the overall functioning. An automobile will not run if the ignition system does not work, and a government cannot manage conflict if it cannot reach decisions or enforce them. In the case of politics, there are any number of ways in which one could divide the system into functions. The particular division we have used is not meant to offer final definitions of the "real" functions of political systems. Rather, our functional categories are intended as a device to help the student gain a clear understanding of fundamental political processes.

A political system may be rather simply mapped as in Figure 1-1. In this diagram, the political system is shown generating rules and decisions ("outputs") which affect all society. Those who make the rules are affected by demands and support from their fellow citizens ("inputs").

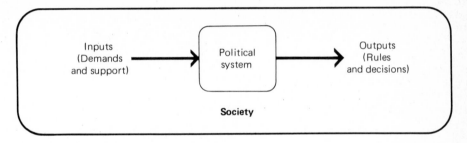

Figure 1-1. A simplified diagram of a political system.

In a simple way, this picture of a system conveys the notion that public officials must consider the broad social consequence of their actions.

Obviously this diagram leaves much to be explained. A few lines on a piece of paper cannot convey the intricacies of a subject matter as complex as politics. It serves as a point of departure, by emphasizing the need to relate parts of society to the whole. In using it as a guide we will be less likely to study politicians to the exclusion of citizens in our attempts to understand political phenomena.

Political functions

The actual activities of public officials, which are undifferentiated in Figure 1-1, may be represented by a box divided into three parts, as in Figure 1-2. The center represents the activity of making public policy and is labeled *decision making.* Not all public officials are included, but only those persons who resolve general policy issues for all society. It is not shown as a closed box because different people may be involved in the activity only from time to time. A group of Presidential advisers might, for example, call upon the military Chiefs of Staff to participate in their deliberations one day, and Under Secretaries of State the next.

The point may be further clarified by expanding the example. A President may consider a proposal to revise the draft law. He knows it cannot be revised without the approval of Congress and the cooperation of the bureaucracy. He also knows that acceptance of the law by the citizenry will enhance its effectiveness. As a consequence the President may call in representatives and senators in order to solicit their opinion. He may also determine current public reaction to the draft. When he does this, he engages in the activity or function we call *issue definition.* That is, the process by which citizens and groups express their preferences,

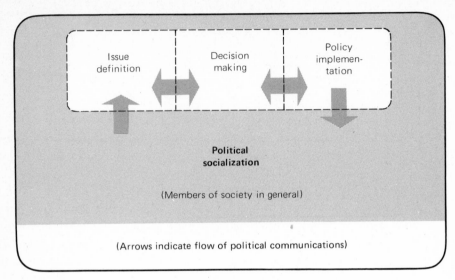

Figure 1-2. A functional representation of a political system.

make demands and counterdemands, and offer policy alternatives. A prudent President might also seek the opinions of the local draft board and law- enforcement officials as to the feasibility of enforcing the modification. In so doing, he relates his decision to the function of *policy implementation*—the processes which will be taken to implement his decision.

None of these activities or functions is independent of the other. A political system should be viewed as a set of activities bounded by broken lines. This reflects the interdependence of the actors and their activities. The arrows which cross from one set of broken lines to the other are meant to illustrate that none of the activities of the system can be successful without extensive exchange of information. The importance of the function called *political communication* is thereby noted.

Finally, *political socialization* is identified as a function crucial to the understanding of politics. It is the process which affects the political life of a society by shaping attitudes toward authority and public officials. The attitudes produced by the socialization of a people limit and condition the mode of operation of their public officials.

In the following five chapters we examine each of the five functions we have just identified:

Decision making
Policy implementation

Issue definition
Political communication
Political socialization

SUMMARY

Politics is a social activity which manages public conflict. Citizens may become resentful of political actions because public officials must make choices between conflicting points of view, and their decisions cannot please all the people all the time. Conflicting viewpoints arise from the diverse social and economic characteristics of different individuals. While variations in social position need not produce conflict, specific issues can divide societies along lines of sex, class, economic status, cultural background, ideological predisposition, and any number of other differences.

The extent to which political regulation penetrates society varies from time to time, depending upon the attitudes of both citizens and public officials, and upon the prevailing social situation. This makes it desirable to study politics in its larger social context. One way to do this is to employ the systems approach which views politics as the activities and structures of a system. Within that system, demands and conditions are imposed upon, or presented to, the political leaders by the members of society. Leaders, in turn, make general policy decisions and oversee their enforcement. As policies are enforced, members of society and public officials alike evaluate the consequences, and new demands may be formulated. Throughout, communication takes place between the parts of the entire system.

This approach is only one of several alternatives which could be used in the study of politics. But it has the utility of providing an orderly scheme which accounts for most of the complex realities of political life in a wide variety of social settings. We shall, therefore, employ the systems approach in this book.

SUGGESTED READINGS

Charlesworth, James C. (ed.): *Contemporary Political Analysis* (New York: Free Press, 1967). A book of readings for students of academic political science. Introduces some of the basic approaches

to the study of politics, and some fundamental disagreements between political scientists.

Easton, David: *The Political System* (New York: Knopf, 1953). Together
with Professor Easton's later books, *A Framework for Political Analysis* (1965) and *A Systems Analysis of Political Life* (1965), the most
authoritative exposition on politics as an input-output system.

Lasswell, Harold D.: *Politics: Who Gets What, When, How* (New York:
Meridian Books, Inc., 1958). A now classic analysis of politics as
"the study of influence and the influential." The focus is upon how
elites distribute deference, income, and safety, and upon the various
forms which influence takes.

The following three short books provide a stimulating introduction to the
history of political ideas.

Plato, *The Republic.* A forceful argument for the moral basis of the state
and for rule by the best men—the philosopher-kings.

Machiavelli, Niccolo, *The Prince.* Generally read as a handbook in the ruthless use of political power, without respect for morals.

Marx, Karl, *The Manifesto of the Communist Party.* Written as a pamphlet
designed to gain adherents to communist ideology.

CENTRAL PARK

CHAPTER TWO

DECISION MAKING
Formulation of Public Policy

OVERVIEW

In this chapter, we examine decision making—the first of the five basic political functions outlined at the end of Chapter 1. Note that only decisions of general importance for society are under consideration, not personal decisions or interpretations of major policies. The questions to be answered are (1) *Who* makes general policy decisions? (2) *What motivates* the decision makers to make policy? (3) *What influences* policy choices; or what are the elements of the *context* of decision making? (4) What are the major *types of decisions* and what are the characteristics of each?

You should note that even as decision makers "inside the system" are discussed, it is necessary to refer to other people and other aspects of social life to explain their actions. This points up the important fact that all social actions are interrelated; the impact of various actions and actors on each other must be taken into account as any particular process is studied. This chapter points out that the authorities attempt to anticipate the consequences of their policy decisions, thus taking the reactions of others into account. Further, general social processes shape the attitudes of decision makers as well as citizens; therefore a knowledge of a state's social condition is necessary to an intelligent analysis of its modes and centers of decision making. Finally, influentials bring pressure from centers of power and wealth to bear on policymakers, and authorities must consider their constituencies as they deliberate.

As the three major types of policy decisions are discussed, carefully note the differences in the way they are reached and in their probable impact on society. Emergency decisions are unique in that there are relatively few decision makers involved, they are made quickly, and it is very clear who is responsible for the policy chosen. Routine decisions and nondecisions typically involve less risk, more people, more predictable outcomes, and less clear responsibility.

Be sure that you understand the following terms:

Authorities	Socialization
Influentials	Constituencies
Formal elites	Role
General rules	Emergency decisions
Power elite	Routine decisions
Stress	Nondecisions
Regime norms	

LEARNING OBJECTIVES

After you have studied this chapter, you should be able to:

1. Define and differentiate between formal elites, influentials, and authorities.
2. Identify the sources of stress and explain the relevance of stress to the decision-making process.
3. Define and explain the significance of each of the elements of the context in which decisions are made: regime norms, socialization of authorities, constituencies, consistency, and information.
4. Identify the major characteristics of emergency decisions, routine decisions, and nondecisions.

On July 15, 1971, President Richard Nixon announced that he would visit China before May of the following year. As a longtime friend of the

Nationalist Chinese regime on Taiwan, and a stern opponent of the People's Republic of China, his declaration was surprising to all, alarming some, and praiseworthy to others. Since then, observers the world over have witnessed the drama of two longtime mutually hostile states cautiously edging toward "normalization of relations."

Before these public events took place, Nixon had ordered a complete reassessment of United States policy toward China. When the results were in and fully considered, *general policy decisions* on China were reached which ultimately made the President's dramatic announcement possible. This previous step—the reassessment—was not much publicized. But if it had not occurred, the President's flight to Peking would not have taken place.

In every society there are some individuals, like the American President in ours, who are expected to make crucial public decisions. Through directing the energies of the public and through using public authority, power, and coercion (force), these individuals attempt to bring about and maintain the public safety and well-being. They have the responsibility to set rules for distributing or allocating the things which their societies value, whether these be limited to material wealth and personal safety or are extended to include religious morality, national greatness, or imperial expansion. Some public leaders may exercise very little discretion as they make important decisions: the rules which govern their society may be so rigidly detailed that departures from tradition would not be accepted by their people. Other leaders appear to have much greater discretion in making policy choices. Even a dictator as powerful as Adolph Hitler could be brought down if policy decisions required more resources for successful implementation than the government or its people could command. This is exactly what happened in Hitler's Third Reich. His long-range policy decisions (to attack Russia and England, etc.) had proved disastrous, and even his short-range policy decisions (no retreat in the defense of Berlin, etc.) had been to no avail. Hitler did of course commit suicide, but it is clear that his earlier policy decisions—which required more resources than the German people commanded—had brought him down.

In this chapter we are concerned with those individuals who make general policy choices for a society and with the processes by which choices are made. We shall call these policymakers the *authorities.* Their social task is to make general rules for their societies while resolving issues which arise from domestic conflict or from situations produced by contact with other, external political systems. It should be emphasized that we will not be interested in every instance of policymaking. The fact that a local sheriff issues an extraordinary number of traffic tickets as part of the fight against crime reflects a policy decision on the sheriff's part. Yet this decision and subsequent actions are too particular and too trivial for serious analysis here. Rather, we shall focus on public decisions which affect all or most members of society. The establishment of a national health insurance program in the United States, or a Japanese decision to revalue the yen, are examples which fit these conditions.

WHO MAKES THE POLICY DECISIONS

At first glance, to ask who makes policy decisions may seem a search for the obvious. After all, any high school civics student "knows" that in America the President, the Congress, and the Supreme Court make the laws and enforce them. Elsewhere, Prime Ministers and Parliaments, or Emperors and Councils, "obviously" do the same.

But things are not really as simple as that. The question of who governs has long fascinated students of politics, and they have come up with conflicting answers. For example, some writers contend that the United States is really governed by a "power elite"[1] or a "military-industrial complex."[2] Others are equally insistent that the power to govern is divided among a great number of competing groups, each of which plays a limited part in decision making.[3]

Formal elites

In searching for the "real" decision makers, it is usually appropriate to begin by examining the formal arrangements as found in constitutions or basic laws. These ordinarily spell out, at least in general terms, who or what bodies *should* make policy—i.e., are constitutionally responsible. In many cases, in fact, constitutions provide a rather accurate picture of reality. Even when the difference between *who decides* and who *should decide* is substantial, the actual decision makers ordinarily want their policies to be legitimized by the formal political leaders.

Identifying *formal elites* (or those who are "officially" powerful) is thus an important first step in identifying the actual policymakers. But it is

[1]C. Wright Mills, *The Power Elite* (New York: Oxford University Press, 1956).

[2]The phrase "military-industrial complex" was made popular by President Eisenhower, who warned against its evils in his farewell address of 1961.

[3]Robert A. Dahl, *Who Governs?* (New Haven, Conn.: Yale, 1961).

no more than that. Even a very lengthy constitution will omit some important details that have a bearing on our question. For example, in the United States Congress, the heads of the standing committees sometimes have life-or-death control over the enactment of legislation which comes before their respective bodies; invariably they are influential within their sphere of competence. Yet about these congressional leaders the Constitution says only that "each house may determine the rules of its proceedings" and that each house shall choose its own officers (other than the presiding officer of the Senate). As a result an understanding of the roles played by committee leaders requires much more than a reading of the Constitution. Internal rules, customary practices, and personal influence are also clearly relevant.

Constitutions not only have gaps; at times they also may be vague or inconsistent. What is one to make of the provisions of the 1958 French Constitution which designate the President as the "guarantor" of national independence and the integrity of the territory (Article 5), while the Prime Minister is "responsible" for national defense (Article 21)? Or what is the precise definition of the phrase "republican form of government" which the United States national government is to "guarantee" to each of the states? Even the apparently categorical phrase "Congress shall make no law," with which the First Amendment to the United States Constitution begins, has consistently been interpreted to mean: "Congress shall make no law *except* in certain justifiable cases."

Justice Black on the First Amendment

The late Justice Hugo Black was one proponent of the view that the First Amendment of the United States Constitution means exactly what it says. In a dissenting opinion in the case of *Barenblatt V. United States* (360 U.S. 109) he wrote:

> To apply the Court's balancing test . . . is to read the First Amendment to say "Congress shall pass no law abridging freedom of speech, press, assembly and petition unless Congress and the Supreme Court reach the joint conclusion that on balance the interests of the Government in stifling these freedoms is greater than the interests of the people in having them exercised." Not only does this violate the genius of our written

Constitution, but it runs expressly counter to the injunction to the Court and Congress made by Madison when he introduced the Bill of Rights. . . . Unless we return to his view of our judicial function, unless we once again accept the notion that the Bill of Rights means what it says and that the Court must enforce its meaning, I am of the opinion that our great charter of liberty will be more honored in the breach than in the observance.

Finally, constitutional provisions may be ignored or perverted by the powerful to cloak their real character. Orthodox Marxist-Leninists, for example, call Western "democratic" constitutions a sham because they cloak the commanding position of capitalists in "bourgeois" societies.[4] Likewise, Western scholars have noted that the Soviet constitution of 1936, while hailed as "the most democratic in the world," did nothing to curtail the dictatorial powers of Stalin.[5] Both assertions have merit, and political leaders of other states have often hidden behind a facade of "constitutionalism" as they ruled more or less autocratically.

Influentials

If it is necessary to look beyond the fundamental written norms of a political system to determine who governs, where does one search next? Often, clues can be obtained by identifying and observing the privileged persons and groups in a given society. It is they who control most of society's wealth, who enjoy great prestige or status, or who are most favored by existing government policy. Whether they are business executives, military leaders, or landed aristocrats, they are usually not difficult to identify.

[4]Wrote one eminent Soviet jurist: "Look at any parliamentary country you like, from America to Switzerland, from France to England, Norway, and so on. The real state work is done behind the scenes and carried out by departments, chancelleries and staffs. In parliaments they merely babble—with the special purpose of fooling 'simple folk.'" Andrei Y. Vyshinsky, *The Law of the Soviet State* (New York: Macmillan, 1948), pp. 314-315.

[5]For example, Gwendolyn M. Carter in her treatment of the Soviet political system writes: "The Soviet Constitution describes what is in fact a facade behind and through which operates the Communist Party," in *The Government of the Soviet Union* (New York: Harcourt Brace Jovanovich, 1972), p. 19.

Nevertheless, their identification is important, for they have *an interest* in preserving their positions, and the governmental order which makes those positions advantageous. Moreover, those who prosper most in a political system are apt to have resources of substantial importance to those who hold office. Wealth, expertise, and status are among their most important assets, and each is of crucial importance to the ability of a ruling elite to govern effectively. As a result the privileged are apt to have considerable leverage with those who govern. They can contribute or withhold needed support.

Of course, not every wealthy industrialist, military leader, or otherwise privileged individual need be, or is even likely to be, actively involved in the political process. Yet some of them—those who speak for their own interests and for those who are similarly placed—are very likely to advise, suggest, or even pressure the decision makers. These persons can appropriately be labeled *influentials.*

Authorities

The *authorities* are those individuals who actually maĸe policy decisions for a society. It is they who govern. The easy assumption is that the authorities are the formal elite, since the formal elite is officially empowered to make public policy. However, this easy assumption is not always a safe one. The authorities are sometimes members of the formal elite, sometimes powerful influentials, and sometimes combinations of both.

It was noted earlier that the question "who governs?" is difficult to answer. In part this is because the line between influencing decisions and making them is very thin. In theory, there is a clear-cut difference. The influentials are persons who promise, threaten, advise, beg, or bribe but do not decide. Only when they *order* and obtain compliance are they the authorities. Yet in actual cases, the influentials do, in fact, sometimes force the decision. When a mugger says, "Your money or your life!" does the victim "decide"—does he or she really have any choice? Public officers are also sometimes "under the gun," and when they are or feel they are, they lack real decision-making power.

Those who argue that there is a power elite or a military-industrial complex in the United States assert that the formal elites have become the tools of private groups, that influentials have usurped the functions of the formal elites and have effectively become the authorities. Those who deny the accuracy of this view contend that military, business, and other elites in the United States are merely influential. Is there any way to determine which thesis is the more valid?

Much can be learned by looking at the specific relationships between influentials and formal elites. Do the same individuals or groups always have the access, or do different influentials have access on different issues? In what ways is influence exerted? Are proposals backed by cogent supporting evidence or by threats of retaliatory action if they are not favorably acted upon? Are policy recommendations by one influential or a single group of influentials countered by conflicting recommendations from other influentials? And how often are the policy recommendations of a given group of influentials modified or rejected by the formal elite?

To the extent that many influentials with separable interests put forward recommendations on their merits and present several contending views before policies are finalized, and to the degree that recommendations are regularly and substantively modified and even sometimes rejected before policy is finally made, it is safe to assume that the influentials are no more than that. On the other hand, to the extent that the same few individuals or groups invariably put forward uncontested recommendations which are accepted as public policy without alteration, to that extent it is likely that the influentials have become the de facto policy makers.

We see, then, that the question of who governs can be answered by studying actual cases. But the question nevertheless remains in dispute. Its investigation is hampered by the understandable desire of formal elites and influentials to keep their ties at least partially concealed. There are always substantial reasons for each to claim that their relationships are exactly as the terms imply: that influentials influence the formal elites as the latter govern.

STRESS: SPUR TO DECISION

Policy decisions are made in large part because the authorities respond to, or wish to avoid, stress. *Stress* may be defined as the impairment of the authorities' ability to govern. Stress can endanger a single authority's tenure in office, or threaten a regime. If it becomes so great as to cause a breakdown of the political order, it can even overthrow the whole political system. The most severe manifestations of stress include widespread civil disobedience, great economic crises, and major defeats in warfare. As

"Stress" as the Result of Poor Politics

The word "stress" is an analytical tool, not a description of a tangible or commonsense social phenomenon. It is used in the "systems" approach to encompass a wide variety of public problems which can undermine support for public officials, regimes, and communities.

In terms of the discussion in Chapter 1, stress might be seen to result from poor politics—from inadequate management of public conflict. If police cannot deter criminals, if selfish interests block popular public projects, if foreign powers appear to dominate domestic affairs, or if for any reason citizens lose confidence in the ability of their officials to regulate the social order, support can wane and governmental effectiveness decline.

There are two obvious examples of the point. First, societies make laws to manage conflicts which are expected to occur over and over again, such as disputes over land ownership. Governments are expected to have regular means to settle such disputes. If disputes over property result in repeated, disruptive outbreaks of violence, citizens are apt to lose confidence in the ability of their government to do its job. Something like this seems to have been happening in American cities recently, where citizens have been arming themselves in the face of rising crime rates.

A second obvious example occurs when the authorities prove unable to handle emergency conflict. A government which loses a major foreign war typically falls. Internal strife, too, can produce a new set of governors or a new form of government. A society must have the ability to meet emergency conflict or it will most likely be either dominated by outsiders or destructively split by internal insurgencies.

As we shall discuss in Chapter 4, however, political decisions are responses to social problems; and for now we can consider such problems as capable of producing stress.

stress increases, public confidence in the authorities and sometimes even in the existing political arrangements can be badly shaken. Wise authorities therefore attempt to deal with potential disturbances in a routine manner before they become so serious as to impair their ability to govern.

Stress can result from developments in the domestic environment over which the authorities have exercised little or no control. The Great Depression in the United States resulted partly because the government had not actively intervened to ensure high levels of production and employment. But as things got worse, more and more of the unemployed looked to the government for aid. Thus, the Great Depression placed stress on the American political system; eventually change in economic policies resulted, and stress was reduced.

Stress also may develop because the authorities take actions which produce dissatisfaction. For example, the British subjects who inhabited the thirteen American colonies rejected policies designed to tie them more closely to the mother country. When King George's government attempted to obtain compliance by imposing sanctions against Boston in the "Intolerable Acts" of 1775, open rebellion ensued, and its later attempts to appease the colonists failed. Thus, a series of British policy decisions ultimately produced dissatisfaction so severe that King George could no longer govern the colonists.

Foreign policy decisions or decisions by foreign states may also produce severe stress. The Russian Revolution of 1917 came in the aftermath of repeated military defeat. Russian authorities made every effort to maintain public confidence in their ability to defend their land. As they failed again and again, popular dissatisfaction rose until it was impossible for them to control domestic affairs.

Of course, stress need not be so severe as these examples might suggest. But when it is, authorities must respond promptly. Their policy alternatives must be judged in terms of whether they will strengthen or weaken confidence in, and support for, themselves and the political system.

The authorities of a political system are thus charged with a heavy responsibility: They must not only attempt to satisfy the social needs of the moment but must anticipate future conditions as well. They must weigh the consequences of their policy decisions, taking care that they do not sacrifice too much short-run gain for possible future benefits. Given the fact that policymakers make errors, and given the complexity of directing societies and managing public conflict, it is not surprising that the careers of many contemporary public officials are relatively short, and that in chaotic times whole systems of government are changed with regularity.

FACTORS INFLUENCING POLICY DECISIONS

We have said that policy decisions are made to minimize or reduce stress in political systems. Wise authorities seek to enhance their popular and organized support, to conserve public resources, and to satisfy expressed or perceived social needs. Yet these are not always easy tasks. How does one go about winning and maintaining popular support in "normal" times, let alone in periods of great crisis? How are economic catastrophes to be met or domestic social controversies resolved?

Regime norms

The most fundamental factor which shapes the decision-making process is the set of general and fundamental *standards* or *norms* which define authority roles. These are called *regime norms.* They establish: (1) the area appropriate for public involvement, that is, for political action and (2) the powers and procedures that may or may not be utilized in such action. These, in turn, determine (3) the relationships of authority positions or roles to each other. Taken together, regime norms define the areas of social life in which the authorities may act—they define the mode of official operation—and prescribe relationships between various public officials as well.

Regime norms are based upon norms in the larger society. Consequently, the extent of public power and the standards and appropriate mode of conduct of officials varies from one society to another. For instance, the constitutional guarantee that Americans shall be protected against "unreasonable" searches and seizure rests upon American social values which prize privacy and private property. Where there is not the same societal emphasis on personal privacy and property, as in the Soviet Union, it is not surprising to find that regime norms permit public officials to search the persons and habitations of citizens almost at will. It is easier for a military leader to establish a personalized, autocratic regime in a country like Spain, which has a cultural tradition of seeking a strong "man on horseback," than in nations where such a tradition is absent.

Regime norms draw a line between those matters which are public, and those which are not. One of the most important regime norms enshrined in the United States Constitution is that of "limited government." According to this principle, certain areas of personal and social life are properly beyond the reach of governmental regulation or jurisdiction. The First Amendment, for example, forbids government interference with religious practice, free speech, the press, and free assembly. It places real constraints on American policymakers who might wish to censor newspapers or to prohibit religious groups from performing their rites of worship. In other states, similar limitations on the authorities are effectively established by laws or administrative decisions. In nearly every political system, the "rules of the game" define a part of social life as nonpublic in the sense of being beyond the jurisdiction of governmental authority.

Regime Norms and the Definition of Politics

Much of the literature of political philosophy is concerned with defining the appropriate relationship between citizens and rulers. From the seventeenth and eighteenth centuries the United States inherited a tradition of limited government which held that subjects should obey their rulers only when the rulers acted within the limits of legitimate political authority. Thus, the American Declaration of Independence declares that governments are established to preserve life, liberty, and the pursuit of happiness, and that when they cease to do so they should be overthrown. The American Bill of Rights declares certain areas of the life of the citizen to be beyond the reach of government.

Other political traditions, most notably that of fascism, have produced regimes with norms which either tacitly or explicitly held that all individual interests were subordinate to the state.

Regime norms can thus play an important part in defining "politics" for any given state. By establishing what is appropriately "public" business, they effectively place more or less restricting limits upon what is considered political. In the People's Republic of China the norms of the regime thus include control of the news media, while in the United States conflict between the media and the government is not to be publicly managed.

Regime norms do more than delimit the appropriate areas for political regulation. They also define the manner in which various political actors are expected to participate in public life. British authorities, for example, are expected to consult freely and regularly with those who may be affected by their policies and to be publicly answerable for their decisions. This is the case in the United States as well. However, British regime norms structure the government in such a way that it would be unseemly for a Prime Minister to rebuke the Parliament for acting against his wishes. American Presidents, on the other hand, are expected to seek direct public support as they struggle with the Congress. The Shah of Iran embodies the social traditions of a society stretching from ancient Persia to the present and is admired by his subjects from afar and with reverence. In contrast, the democratic norms of many contemporary societies require leaders to have a "common touch" and to be seen and touched periodically by crowds of admiring citizens.

Finally, regime norms define the relationships of authority roles to each other. They may determine whether one person or many have authorization to decide on an issue. For example, Chief Executives sometimes have sole power to decide, as when President Ford pardoned ex-President Nixon. On the other hand, legislators must ordinarily act collectively, resolving their differences in order to reach a decision. Regime norms also may determine whether responsibility is to be shared, as when the American Senate must ratify treaties and Executive appointments. If policymaking competence is shared, differences must be compromised and alternatives examined. On the other hand, an unequal distribution of power tends to permit the more powerful to make public policy over the objections of the others.

All told, then, regime norms play an important part in determining the processes and the final products of decision making. They are the rules of the game, power or force is less likely to be needed.
conform to regime norms. They do so in order to cloak their policies with the mantle of authority. For if their actions are perceived to be within the rules of the game, power or force is less likely to be needed.

Socialization of the authorities

In a commonsense way, we all assume that a person's actions will reflect his or her experiences and personality. We expect a lawyer to use the same cold logic in an argument with her husband as she would employ in preparing a client's brief. A preacher seems likely to be a moralistic parent and a bookie, by reputation, would give odds on the probability of his son's being drafted.

In recent years, political scientists have explored the relationships between a person's political acts and the social and psychological antecedents of those acts. In fact, these relationships are the central focus of a branch of political science known as *political socialization.* Scholars are beginning to find out (1) when persons develop certain kinds of political attitudes, (2) what agents (e.g., school, family, churches, etc.) are crucial in that attitude formation, and (3) what kinds of attitudes typically lead to certain types of political behavior. In Chapter 5 these questions will be discussed in more detail.

The effect socialization has on specific decisions is usually unclear. Franklin Roosevelt was a wealthy gentleman from a respected New York family, and a direct connection between that background and the economic reforms of his New Deal would be difficult to infer. Indeed, he was labeled a "traitor" to his class by other upper-class Americans. Socialization conditions people, but only broad tendencies are likely to be predictable from a leader's background. Leadership roles impose new pressures and norms which may sometimes produce decisions which differ from those one might predict on the basis of past socialization.

Yet, in other cases, the ties between past socialization and present political action are clear, and it is becoming apparent that knowledge of the socialization of decision makers can be valuable to the political analyst. Like the rest of us, decision makers often show sensitivity to their past associates and group affiliations. The person who has been a farmer, a labor union leader, or a business executive is not apt to forget old friends upon reaching high public office. Thus by identifying the dominant educational and occupational patterns of a nation's political elite, clues can be derived about the substance and process of decision making.

Also important is the fact that decision makers resolve questions in ways that have been successful in the past and avoid the repetition of past failures. When they identify and evaluate a problem, or when they define success and failure, their judgments are usually colored by their past experience. For a revolutionary leader like Lenin, politics was seen as a dog-eat-dog proposition, a case of *Kto—Kovo* ("who crushes whom"); for most satisfied, middle-class Americans, on the other hand, politics involves more subtle and less final questions. Either view, when held by a political leader, influences the manner in which he or she approaches a political decision as well as the substance of the decision itself. Similarly, one's perceptions of political leaders and institutions prior to one's own acceptance of authority roles shape one's subsequent policy decisions. A government of bankers or bureaucrats can be expected to behave differently from one composed of warriors or shamen. Each group would bring to politics the expertise, the experience, and the blinders characteristic of its interests and past activities.

Constituencies

It was just noted that political leaders remember past groups and friendships when they assume public office. Yet there are instances where a particular decision will lead to the cry of "betrayal" by the erstwhile friends of a President, Prime Minister, or judge. In the United States, for example, Lyndon Johnson was selected by John Kennedy as a vice-presidential running mate because of his ties to the South. Yet after he became President, Johnson incurred Southern wrath because he supported the most thorough and far-reaching civil rights bill ever enacted into law. In 1958, Charles de Gaulle, a lifetime military leader, was made the virtual dictator of France, thanks in good part to the support of the French military elite. Yet he shortly alienated much of the French officer corps when he negotiated the French withdrawal from Algeria.

Neither of these apparent turnabouts is as surprising as might at first be supposed. When Lyndon Johnson became President, he had to cultivate a national constituency if he was to be an effective Chief Executive. Likewise, de Gaulle was no longer just a general, even a general who had led the French liberation forces during the Nazi occupation. Rather, his concerns after 1958 included the entire spectrum of political, economic, and military problems in France. To deal with them, he had to split with his comrades-in-arms over the war in North Africa. Other constituents had gained access to the general, and had won the day.

Each of these examples was taken from nations usually said to have governments "responsive to the people." As a result, it is not difficult to suppose that leaders in these cases were somehow bound to comply with demands made by some segment of society. It may be somewhat more surprising that dictators or autocrats also carefully weigh the demands of their constituents, whether foreign or domestic. South Vietnamese President Thieu, for example, was particularly attentive to the "advice" of the United States Ambassador in Saigon during the American involvement there. East German leaders have likewise been especially mindful of Soviet views on issues of importance to the Warsaw Pact nations. The fact is that *any* political leader, be it Stalin, Hitler, or Calvin Coolidge, achieves and holds a position of power only with the help of others; one of the fastest ways of losing that position is to ignore or forget the indispensable helpers.

Beyond this generalization, it should be noted that the variety of relationships between constituents and leaders is great. In some instances a relationship might be relatively permanent. Thus, candidates running for office in the United States must always heed those who will finance their next campaign, as well as those who might vote for them. On the other hand, a leader might find a certain constituency to be only of temporary importance. Marshall Zhukov and the military interests he represented were a major factor in Khrushchev's struggle against a Soviet "antiparty" group in 1957. But once he had won that struggle, Comrade Zhukov was removed from high office and the Army's interests were de-emphasized. Likewise, Senator McGovern gained the Democratic presidential nomination in 1972 as a proponent of liberal causes. Yet once he was nominated, he moved to the right on some issues, thereby angering some of his earliest supporters. The Senator was looking for new constituents—unsuccessfully, as it turned out.

Leader-constituency ties vary in intensity as well as duration. In seeking support, an official usually weighs the significance of the benefits a given person or group can supply, in taking their views into account. An individual vote, for example, is relatively less important in a political campaign than is an endorsement by a prestigious civic leader. Consequently, a candidate is more likely to tailor policy positions to the liking of a civic leader than to a single voter.

Finally, the leader and constituent relationships may be established either voluntarily or under duress. Surprisingly, in many cases, neither party is totally free to join or leave an alliance. A President cannot really quit his political party. A white, Deep-South senator cannot—yet—represent the National Association for the Advancement of Colored People. Only a voter can be "independent," since in that case the commitment is minimal.

All this suggests that authority-constituent relationships are complex. Decision makers must weigh the relative interests of all affected parties, the utility of their continued support, and the probable intensity of their reactions as they make policy. It is easy indeed for a leader to make a mistake in these estimates.

Need for consistency

As dissent in the United States over involvement in Vietnam increased in the 1960s, one of the standard Johnson administration arguments for continuing the war was that past commitments had to be honored.

Others, like the influential Senate Armed Forces Committee Chairman, John Stennis, asserted that since the original decision to go into Vietnam had been made, it was necessary to continue the war to a victorious conclusion. In both cases, the argument rested upon the proposition that decisions of today must support, and be supported by, the decisions of yesterday. Years later—in early 1975—President Ford made the same argument when he asked Congress for more aid to the embattled Saigon government.

Whether the hawks or the doves were "right" on Vietnam, there can be no serious dispute over the desirability of a degree of consistency in decision making. Erratic behavior, based upon mutually contradictory decisions, is a luxury a government can seldom afford. Even a supreme autocrat like Adolph Hitler found that pressures for consistency often outweighed his power to issue just any order. There are several reasons for this.

First, in politics, as in other things, the consequences of almost any decision foreclose some subsequent options. The Soviet commitment to rapid industrialization precluded the simultaneous investment of limited resources into agriculture. Likewise, the American commitment to a "free enterprise" economy has precluded the nationalization of industry as a strategy for coping with economic problems. In common parlance, political leaders, like the rest of us, must sometimes choose between eating or having the cake.

Further, the full consequences of a policy are typically apparent only after time passes and events unfold. As a result, one decision might in time force a second upon an almost unsuspecting policymaker. British leaders during the 1930s did not foresee the implications of their foreign policy of appeasing Hitler's Germany. Senator Eugene McCarthy's decision to oppose the incumbent President of his own party in 1968 was not intended initially to make him a serious candidate. Because previous choices so restrict later options, one leading student of politics, Charles Lindblom, has suggested that most decisions are "incremental."[6] That is, no policymaker begins with a clean slate; invariably the policymaker will need to complete half-finished projects, scuttle past failures, and avert impending disasters.

Politically, constituency support usually requires leaders to act with overall consistency. President Nixon's clients, the "silent majority," had

[6]Charles E. Lindblom, "The Science of 'Muddling Through,'" *Public Administration Review*, vol. 18, pp.79–88, June 1959.

to see continuing evidence that he shared their concerns about "law and order," preserving America's "honor" in Vietnam, and negotiating for a peaceful world. From their vantage points one "bad" decision could be forgiven and forgotten. But had he set a pattern markedly inconsistent with the old, he would have risked losing his precious supporters without allaying suspicions of his old political foes. In fact, President Nixon temporarily forsook his "Southern strategy" in mid-1970 when he announced his administration's intention to desegregate the last of the Southern schools. Shortly thereafter, Senator Thurmond, a key Southern supporter, attacked his administration for its alleged "liberalness." Though the President received positive reactions from a few liberal columnists, he gained little permanent support from the left. As a result, he was faced with the political necessity of reasserting the old positions his supporters wanted to hear.

Incrementalism

The tendency for policy decisions to reflect relatively minor changes in existing arrangements is particularly noticeable in government budgeting.

However issues of public policy may be debated in the press or in political campaigns, public expenditures tend to change by small increments from year to year. Changes in leadership can result in changed emphases, or can lead to expansion of one department and contraction of another. But agency budgets usually increase drastically only in times of emergency, as when defense expenditures increase in time of war. And they usually decrease drastically only if the agency loses the support of vital constituencies (or the constituencies lose their clout), as when the Nixon administration effectively dismantled the Office of Economic Opportunity.

When governmental agencies are established to implement decisions, they tend to develop their own constituencies and bases of support. Consequently, a decision maker must be cautious in adjusting agency budgets, lest support be needlessly lost in the process.

In a similar vein, both citizens and subordinate elites respond badly to authorities who fail to be largely *predictable* in their decisions. It appears that the predictability of the authorities may, in many cases, be more important than their actual policies. People want to be able to count on the rules, even when they dislike or resent them. This is particularly true of those subordinate elites who must implement policy. If they are repeatedly told to switch directions, they may find that their task is unworkable. In such cases subordinates have been known to develop opposition to the authorities on the grounds that they are disrupting the government with their unpredictability.

This point relates directly to the technical requirements for efficient governmental operation. Lower-level officials who execute the policies of a President or a Parliament must understand them and coordinate them with previous and later decisions. Executive-level decisions to enforce antitrust legislation vigorously or to establish strong legal sanctions against polluters have a fundamental impact on enforcement agencies. If a department or bureau is to act effectively, its assigned tasks cannot be revised abruptly. In fact, even impending shifts in purpose can have serious negative consequences for administrative bodies. In a sense, they are like speeding autos which cannot change direction or stop instantaneously.

Information

Authorities cannot afford to make decisions in ignorance. They must receive accurate information if they are to make rational decisions. As a result, contemporary governments devote considerable effort to the collection and evaluation of information. Information on economic activities, education, crime, and countless other domestic subjects are collected and stored in sophisticated data banks. Foreign governments are monitored by large intelligence agencies which use complex (and devious) techniques.

But despite these massive efforts, serious questions are often decided with only a meager informational base. For one thing, decision makers face serious time constraints. If one particular issue is not pressing, ten others probably are, and very often the issue which requires greatest thought and deliberation is not recognized until the time needed has already been lost. By the time the President or Prime Minister is made aware of a problem, action, any action, is required.

The nearly impossible task of pulling the crucial data out of the great mass of accumulated raw information is another constriction. In part, this can be an organization problem: needed information might be squirreled away—a little here, a little there—in the files of several autonomous departments. In this case, the decision maker is like students who know that the needed information is in the library—if only they can find it. To illustrate, the Japanese attack on Pearl Harbor in 1941 would not have been a surprise if information gathered by United States intelligence sources had been understood and relayed to the President. However, it wasn't and the alert for an approaching attack was not given.

Sorting relevant from irrelevant information is also an intellectual problem. Authorities must be like wise detectives who can quickly ascertain the significance of every possible clue. And like detectives, they deal with others who may deliberately try to confuse or misinform them.

Finally, well-informed national decisions are often difficult because the decision makers do not know real meanings—the full implications— of the information on which their decisions are based. For example, it is helpful for American foreign policymakers to know how many rubles the Soviets spend for defense, how many troops they have in uniform, and what capabilities their strategic military services have. But in addition to these bits of "hard" information, it is highly desirable to know what they signify about Soviet intentions: do the Russians seek to dominate the world, or are their objectives less grandiose? Chinese leaders had a similar problem trying to assess the motives behind the United States involvement in Vietnam: were American forces there to maintain a presence in Asia, to threaten China's territorial integrity, or to protect a friendly government from aggression? Often, the best answers possible to questions about motive or intention are mere "educated guesses."

Because of these obstacles authorities often cannot move beyond playing hunches. No one can claim to understand the full range of cause and effect which produces changing social conditions, and attempts to control political developments are always tinged with uncertainty. Good information cannot eliminate this problem, but it can provide authorities with a better basis for making decisions than would a lottery or a Ouija board.

TYPES OF DECISIONS

Several elements are known to affect both the content of general decisions and the procedure by which they are made. It would, however, be a mistake to assume that authorities invariably utilize the same procedures to decide issues, or that factors such as social background or regime norms influence each final decision equally. Even so, decisions may be divided into three general types.

Emergency decisions

Almost all political decisions are made under some pressure, if only that associated with the need to avert possible problems in the future. But some decisions must be made more *quickly* than others if catastrophic consequences are to be avoided. For example, when floods occur or when a state is under military attack, fast decisions are imperative. The 1962 Cuban missile crisis was an emergency situation for President John Kennedy, and the procedures he followed illustrate the manner in which emergencies are usually met.

In the first place, since emergencies are important by definition, time need not—indeed cannot—be spent establishing the need to act. All routine matters are set aside until the emergency has passed or been resolved. President Kennedy was stumping for votes for his congressional supporters in the 1962 elections when he was called back to Washington to examine sobering intelligence reports of Soviet missile installations in Cuba. For the 13 days during which the crisis existed, he treated both the upcoming election and all other issues as secondary.

Secondly, the structure of the decision-making body is also apt to be more simple than usual, and less consultation with others is likely to take place. President Kennedy did not involve the Congress or the lower echelons of the bureaucracy in the missile crisis. Nor did he consult the many nongovernmental bodies which ordinarily participate in the political process. Rather, he gathered a small group of his most trusted advisers (some with no official responsibility in the foreign policy area) and together they weighed the merits of each possible alternative. The need for both speedy action and secrecy precluded the enlargement of the decision-making apparatus.

Thirdly, responsibility for making a decision in emergency cases is unusually clear. There could be no question that it was President Kennedy who decided to place Cuba in "quarantine." His advisers, to be sure, may have persuaded him to adopt that decision, but the responsibility was his and he fully understood its implications. In more routine cases of decision making, responsibility is often more diffuse and is sometimes even confused—at times intentionally (as when a decision is likely to offend more voters than it pleases).

All these attributes suggest that emergency decision making is highly streamlined, explicit, and biased toward action. The alternative of letting things ride, of decision making by default, is seldom acceptable.

Routine decisions

Most decisions by authorities are routine in that they (1) treat recurring or ongoing problems and (2) are considered according to prearranged schedules and procedures. But note that routine questions are not necessarily trivial; for example, all political systems make periodic allocations of public resources, and such budgeting for governmental programs is clearly of great importance.

Decision making in routine matters tends to be complex and time-consuming. It can be so because the authorities involved can predict with considerable accuracy the development of potential stress their decisions are designed to alleviate. They know, for example, that defense allocations must be made before previous funding has been totally expended. Legislation can be renewed at any time before it expires and still remain in effect. The number of welfare clients an agency will handle in a given year can be estimated from past experience. Since lengthy and painstaking deliberation can take place without adverse consequences, it is obviously desirable since it affords an opportunity to try for the best possible decision—and the broadest possible support.

Routine decision making also tends to be complicated and time-consuming because authorities must obtain soundings from many groups and individuals. In so-called representative political systems, elected officials seek out the views of interest group representatives and specialists or risk being rejected when campaign funds and votes are needed at the next election. Even where competitive elections are not conducted, however, authorities are usually solicitous of the views of those who will execute the policy, or will benefit or be governed by it. Soviet authorities, for example, supervise a continuing dialogue with their subordinates on both the drafting and execution of their 5-year plans. They need expert advice on program feasibility, likely consequences of alternative levels of spending, and probable reactions of affected groups, just as do their American or British counterparts.

Because routine decision making tends to be complex, responsibility for decisions once taken is often diffused. In the United States, the President, high-level bureaucrats, and the Congress (or some of its individual members) all play important but varying roles in the expenditure of federal funds. At times determining the extent of responsibility each has had is difficult. In more centralized states, responsibility is somewhat easier to pinpoint, though subordinates often can, like their American counterparts, obtain policies they prefer by skillfully marshaling the available evidence to support them.

Finally, since routine decisions are not made speedily, authorities cannot afford to give them exclusive attention. Rather, the processing of at least several routine matters may go on simultaneously. Decision makers, as a result, must divide their time and attention accordingly. This in turn tends to diffuse responsibility for making decisions even further. Though only Congress can enact laws, members of Congress very often must defer to the opinion of acknowledged experts on the bills up for consideration: they simply do not have time to study the whole gamut of public issues, from foreign affairs to agricultural subsidies, and from environmental control to social security benefits. Presidents or Premiers are similarly unable to concentrate on all routine topics and so must rely on advisers and specialists. Thus, lower-level officials, outside advisers, "pressure groups," and even ordinary citizens have a heavier involvement in routine than in emergency decisions.

In summary, routine decisions are arrived at by a quite different process from that utilized in emergency cases. Yet good decisions in either case will serve to reduce and avoid stress on the political system, and viable systems must have mechanisms both for solving emergencies and for handling routine business.

Nondecisions

Each of us has experienced what is sometimes called the "put-off." Parents sometimes tell their children that they will "explain later" when the latter become too inquisitive, and professors have been known to hide behind the standard response: "We'll take that question up later in the term." Such replies are often deceitful, for behind the pretense that a more opportune time will come, there may be the hope that the question will be forgotten.

Governmental bodies and officials also use this technique in response to popular or organized pressures. Lobbyists may be told, "I'm 100 percent behind your bill, but I can't do anything until after the election"; and politicians tell their people that at some indefinite date in the future their needs will be better served. In fact, the put-off as a technique for avoiding pressure to make decisions has been greatly refined by government leaders, and it may be used when demands are thought to be ill-defined, frivolous, or too controversial.

One means to avoid decisions is to control access to decision makers. It is not easy to obtain an audience with Presidents or Premiers. Even members of Congress, members of Parliaments, or Ministers have assistants through whom entreaties must be channeled; most of the mail sent to government officials is answered, if at all, by staff personnel. Only the exceptional messages are actually seen by the person to whom they are sent, and usually even they get only brief attention.

Second, the elaborate procedures which characterize routine decision making are used to avoid action on many demands or requests. In political systems where legislatures are important decision-making bodies, parliamentary procedures are typically so cumbersome as to cause wonder that any issues are resolved. In the U.S. Congress, no more than one proposed bill in twenty is enacted into law, while most of the rest are "killed in committees." In other countries, where executive bodies exercise more rule-making authority, similar procedural niceties may be fatal obstacles to proposals: agendas may be arranged to exclude certain items from consideration or delays may occur while position papers are prepared.

Once a decision has been successfully avoided, it may never be reconsidered. In other cases persistent efforts may force reconsideration and decisions. Advocates for legalized abortion refused to stop their crusade when few authorities would even speak publicly on the issue; ultimately the Supreme Court agreed to decide the issue.

In some cases the avoidance of a decision by the authorities may force or permit lower-level governmental officials to resolve a given problem or conflict. During the period of the Fourth Republic in France (1946–1958) the avoidance of decisions by the Cabinet and Parliament greatly strengthened the roles of top officials in the several government ministries. In the absence of direction from above, bureaucrats in many cases had a virtually free hand to make policies within their areas of jurisdiction. The consequences of avoiding decisions may thus vary greatly, from killing all chances of action, to merely delaying the inevitable, to effectively delegating decision-making authority by default.

SUMMARY AND CONCLUSION

In our analysis of decision making we have raised the questions: Who decides or governs? Why are decisions made? What factors and/or considerations shape the processes and substance of decision making? And what regularized patterns of decision making characterize the political processes of contemporary systems? In almost every case we have hedged on our answers.

This reflects the fact, which is unfortunate from the analyst's point of view, that decision making usually takes place behind at least a partial cloud of secrecy created by the individuals involved. The revelations of the Watergate scandals pointed up the degree to which authorities and influentials rely upon secrecy, and only served to emphasize the informal influences which operate to sway formal decision making bodies such as the Federal Trade Commission and the Department of Agriculture. No matter what reforms are taken in efforts to achieve more openness in American government, the nature of politics dictates that some secrecy will always obscure the public view of the discussions and dealings of the very powerful.

To secrecy, the problem of complexity must be added. Many factors, each with many components, impinge upon each of the many decisions the authorities of any political system must make. Each of these factors affects the decisions differently in each case. Small wonder then that with a sense of frustration some political scientists have labeled the decision making structure "a mysterious black box," thus suggesting the enigmatic properties of our topic.

But, as has been shown, there is considerable knowledge about decision making. It is even possible to make some rather general predictions about tendencies in decision making though, of course, with much less certainty than those which could be offered about the inevitability of death and taxes. Here, as in most cases of concern to social scientists, we are at a point somewhere between complete ignorance and sufficient knowledge of the subject.

SUGGESTED READINGS

Dahl, Robert: *Who Governs?* (New Haven, Conn.: Yale, 1961). Dahl disputes the Hunter thesis and argues that power is distributed in multiple centers.

Hunter, Floyd: *Community Power Structure* (Chapel Hill: University of North Carolina Press, 1953). An important study which concludes that the "real" political leadership of a community is often not exercised by formally elected, visible public officials.

Kennedy, Robert F.: *Thirteen Days* (New York: Norton, 1969). An inside account of the decisions taken by the Kennedy administration during the Cuban missile crisis of 1962.

Mills, C. Wright: *The Power Elite* (New York: Oxford University Press, 1956). A classic, sometimes polemical study of decision making in the United States. Mills argues that military and industrial leaders, together with top-level bureaucrats, make the significant decisions.

Neustadt, Richard E.: *Presidential Power* (New York: Wiley, 1960). An important study of the informal as well as the formal means by which Presidents attempt to achieve their policy objectives.

CHAPTER THREE

POLICY IMPLEMENTA- TION
Bureaucrats and Bureaucracy

OVERVIEW

This chapter deals with the difficult and complicated problems associated with the implementation of policy decisions. Public administrators, or bureaucrats, are charged with this function, and they are found wherever large governments are encountered.

Policy implementation requires organizations which will respond to commands from the authorities. Take special note of the characteristics of bureaucratic organizations which promote this responsiveness. Also note the importance of expertise and specialization for bureaucracies. It is a two-edged sword which provides the capacity to both implement policy and influence the authorities.

As with other political relationships, interdependence characterizes interaction between authorities and administrators. Though the authorities have considerable latitude in appointing and transferring personnel, in reorganizing the bureaucracy, and in using supplemental agencies for advice and information, they are ultimately dependent upon bureaucratic loyalty and performance for their own effectiveness. This two-way relationship should be kept in mind as we discuss the problems which authorities and administrators create for each other and the resources available to each to deal with these problems.

This chapter should provide you with some sympathetic insights into the problems of administration. It is easy to malign bureaucracy, but we have yet to invent a more effective type of organizational structure to implement policy—and that applies to private as well as to public management.

Be sure that you understand the following terms:

Bureaucrat   Specialization of roles
Bureaucracy   Impersonality in administration
Lines of responsibility

LEARNING OBJECTIVES

After you have studied this chapter, you should be able to:

1. Identify and differentiate between examples of the following characteristics of bureaucratic organizations: (a) clear lines of responsibility, (b) specialization of function, (c) impersonal administration.
2. Identify the major problems encountered in keeping organizations responsive to their clientele.
3. Identify the major problems encountered in keeping bureaucrats responsive to the authorities.
4. List the major resources and strategies available to the authorities in their efforts to keep bureaucrats responsive to their assigned missions and their clients.
5. Identify the major resources and strategies available to bureaucrats in their efforts to exert influence upon the authorities.
6. Identify the influences which encourage cooperation between authorities and bureaucrats, instead of one-sided domination by the authorities.

We are all familiar with the difference between making a decision and implementing it. Who hasn't resolved to lose weight, to be nicer to mother-in-law, or to stop biting fingernails—only to find that the firmest initial resolve quickly fades. Smokers who quit their habit daily or weekly know all too well how firm decisions can go up in smoke at the first sign of stress. In politics, too, policymaking guarantees little if commitment to a policy is not continuing or if inadequate resources are committed to achieving results. Lyndon Johnson declared "war on poverty" in 1964; but when he left office in 1969, the war had not yet been won, and some alleged that it had never even been waged.

Policies do not implement themselves. Between the announcement of a decision and the realization of the goals which prompted it, many actions must be taken and many persons other than general decision makers become involved. The policy of the Allied Powers to oppose the Axis coalition in World War II required the commitment of millions of persons and the expenditure of tremendous material resources for its ultimate success. In the process of achieving military victory, millions of words of exhortation were delivered in many languages, the economies of the involved nations were transformed, the personal energies of millions of citizens were mobilized to the task, and over 30 million persons in Allied countries lost their lives. In order to implement the general decision to wage war in quest of victory, many auxiliary and corroborating decisions had to be made from the highest to the lowest levels of vast organizations. While most policy decisions are less dramatic than this example, they all require organization and resources in order to be implemented.

In this chapter we will focus on the administrative organization of government and on the problems which the authorities and administrators face as they attempt to implement general rules. It should be noted that authorities (policymakers), as well as administrators, play an important part in policy implementation: their range of interest extends to all aspects of politics.

ADMINISTRATIVE ORGANIZATION

Those who make general policy decisions seldom enforce them directly. The Soviet Politburo may set the general production norms for the Soviet economy, but subordinates all the way down to the factory manager or *kolkhoz* (collective farm) chairman must see that actions are taken to fulfill them. And Congress may cooperate with the President by enacting welfare legislation, but the Department of Health, Education, and Welfare draws up guidelines, and state and local agencies write the checks. Given this division of labor, policymakers have a fundamental interest in recruiting and organizing those who will administer or enforce a policy by applying it to specific cases. Effectively organized and talented administrators are an essential resource; without them, the authorities could announce policies to their heart's content, but they would have no means to enforce them. Generals don't win battles *without sergeants and privates* who will, in fact, faithfully execute their orders.

Policy Making Is More than Decision Making

David Easton underscores the importance of policy implementation for policy making.

A decision alone is of course not a policy; to decide what to do does not mean that the thing is done. A decision is only a selection among alternatives that expresses the intention of the person or group making the choice. Arriving at a decision is the formal phase of establishing a policy; it is not the whole policy in relation to a particular problem. A legislature can decide to punish monopolists; this is the intention. But an administrator can destroy or reformulate the decision by failing either to discover offenders or to prosecute them vigorously.

If the law directs that all prices shall be subject to a specified form of control but black markets take root and the appropriate officials and the society as a whole accept their existence, the actual policy is not one of price control alone. It also includes the acceptance of black markets. . . . Similarly, if the formal policy of an educational system forbids discrimination against Negroes but local school boards or administrators so zone school attendance that Negroes are segregated in a few schools, both the impartial law and the discriminatory practices must be considered part of the policy. [David Easton, *The Political System: An Inquiry into the State of Political Science* (New York: Knopf, 1953), p. 130.]

The basic characteristics of effective administrative organization include (1) clear lines of responsibility, (2) specialization, and (3) impersonality.

Clear lines of responsibility

Authorities usually attempt to create and maintain clear lines of responsibility in the agencies they establish to implement their decisions. Such lines require that administrative officers know from whom orders are to be taken and for whose performance they are responsible. Positions in these organizations thus assume patterns of dominance and subordination. The extreme example is a military organization, in which there is a "chain of command" running from the commander to the lowest-ranking privates; each knows who his or her superiors and subordinates are. This stratified structure of roles makes responsibility for the transmission and execution of orders and decisions clear from the top to the bottom of the organization. It provides a structure through which the actions of all members of the organization can normally be controlled by those at the top.

Specialization

Contemporary organizations are highly complex and perform many specialized functions. As a consequence, they need specialized personnel who report through differentiated chains of command. The crew of a large warship, for example, has many specialists: helmsmen, navigators, radar technicians, gunners, fire-control officers, doctors, cooks, barbers, and intelligence analysts, to name a few. The specific responsibilities of each are normally beyond the concern of others. Where their responsibilities overlap, their relationship is coordinated by a single superior.

Policy implementers have relatively specialized competencies or jurisdictions. A Foreign Ministry is responsible for executing foreign policy, while a Ministry of Justice enforces domestic laws. And within each there will be many specialized public agencies with differentiated responsibilities. The advantages of such specialization are clear—and differ little from the principles of mass production. Procedures and duties for each position can be made explicit and routinized, thus promoting efficiency and control. Those who occupy administrative positions can thereby become expert in their own sphere, and contribute to the organizational effort without comprehending either the whole or all of its other component parts.

Impersonality

As agencies are created or reorganized, standardized rules of operation are established. Each position within the organization is likely to be given a job description. In these ways the impact of the personal traits of administrators is minimized. Individual employees, with their unique talents or limitations, are of slight concern in charting an organization. Rather, tasks are largely determined by organizational needs and goals. It is expected that duties will be exercised in the same way by whoever is assigned the responsibility accruing to a particular job. Though this impersonal character of rule-enforcing agencies can, and sometimes does, lead to a failure to utilize special skills and insights of personnel, the advantages of standardization and permanence are clear. If roles are impersonally defined, the organization reduces its dependence on particular individuals, in two ways. First, the organization can replace individuals more easily. Second, employees can deal with each other more or less exclusively in terms of their job functions rather than their personal characteristics. For example, Jones may not like Smith's attitude, manner, politics, face, or tie color, and Smith may feel likewise about Jones. But the impersonality of their organizational roles *usually* means that Jones can work effectively with Smith in their respective organizational roles of chief clerk and office manager.

The impersonality of administrative agencies is also reflected in the practice of judging, rewarding, and punishing employees for job performance rather than for personal qualities or private behavior. According to most administrative norms, personnel are not ordinarily to be judged for private activity. Only if their "private" actions interfere with their organizational performance, or are so outrageous as to become public issues, are they to be given formal attention by superiors.

Qualities of the administrators

The qualities expected of administrators may be largely inferred from the principles outlined above. They must be efficient and competent, they should understand and accept the objectives of their organizations, and they should execute directives given from above. Taken altogether, they should be professional in ability, training, and orientation, and should ordinarily be recruited through processes which adequately determine the possession of these qualities. It is standard to set educational attainments and technical skills as necessary, but not sufficient, prerequisites for obtaining a given administrative position. To ensure competence, many governments employ standardized examinations (usually called civil ser-

Max Weber's Principles of Bureaucratic Organization

The classic statement of the principles of bureaucratic organization was made by the great sociologist Max Weber. He used the term "rational legal authority" to designate bureaucracy, and attributed the following principles to it:

1. A continuous organization of official functions bound by rules. . . .
2. A specified sphere of competence. . . .
3. The organization of offices follows the principle of hierarchy; that is, each lower office is under the control of a higher one. . . .
4. The rules which regulate the conduct of an office may be technical rules or norms. . . .
5. . . . It is a matter of principle that the members of the administrative staff should be completely separated from ownership of the means of the production or administration. . . .
6. . . . There is also a complete absence of appropriation of his official position by the incumbent. . . .
7. Administrative acts, decisions, and rules are formulated and recorded in writing, even in cases where oral discussion is the rule or is even mandatory. Talcott Parsons (ed.), *The Theory of Social and Economic Organization* (New York: Free Press, 1947), pp. 329–330.]

vice examinations in this country) to regulate the employment and promotion of administrative personnel.

PROBLEMS OF BUREAUCRACY

Administrative organizations adhering to the principles just outlined are called *bureaucracies*, and the administrators who work in them are commonly referred to as "bureaucrats." (What are usually called "departments" or "agencies" in the United States are often called "bureaus" in Europe. Indeed, that term is sometimes used in this country, as in the Federal *Bureau* of Investigation.) The utilities of enforcing policies through rational (that is, logical), professional, complex, efficient agencies—through bureaucracies—are so widely accepted that virtually all contemporary political systems have created organizations of this kind. Every state has its bureaucrats—and it should be noted that almost every large private organization does too. The administrative machinery of General Motors is a form of bureaucracy; so is that of the Roman Catholic Church. It is generally accepted among students of organization that bureaucracy is the most efficient type of organization known. That is why the administrative structures of almost all contemporary political systems are fundamentally similar.

That bureaucratic administration has real advantages may come as a surprising fact, for nearly everywhere bureaucrats are regarded with hostility and disdain. Even within administrative bodies, one administrator may admonish another not to "behave like a bureaucrat." In the United States, "bureaucrats in Washington" are attacked in virtually every political campaign. In the Soviet Union and the People's Republic of China, with perhaps the most extensive bureaucracies in the world, "bureaucratism" has been lumped with corruption and waste as practices to be eradicated by all possible means. These negative attitudes suggest that bureaucracies are not an unmixed blessing, and the negative aspects of bureaucracies, as well as their advantages, should be considered.

In essence, the problems of bureaucracy stem from the tendency of any human organization to develop its own sense of self-interest apart from the reasons for which it was originally created. Once real people are placed in organizational slots, they tend to think of the organization as an end in itself, rather than as a means toward an end. It becomes important to them to preserve the organization and their own positions in it, regardless of outside pressures and influences. Thus, bureaucracies tend to develop a kind of insulation from the publics or clientele they are created to serve or regulate. They may also resist control by the authorities, particularly where changes in organization or procedures may be involved. Phrased differently, it might be said that bureaucracies tend to develop *problems in responsiveness* (1) to the citizens who are their clientele and (2) to the authorities. It should also be noted that bureaucrats utilize the authority of their superiors when they deal with their clients. They may also cite their closer relationships with their clients to influence the authorities.

Responsiveness to clientele

One of the most common criticisms of bureaucracies is that they stress *procedure* at the expense of achieving their objectives. People complain that "red tape" makes it difficult if not impossible to accomplish anything. For example, when authorities decide to provide medical aid for the elderly or relief to small-business owners or farmers, bureaucrats supposedly require so many different forms in so many copies that the hapless farmers or aged patients may feel they will be bankrupt or dead before the needed help arrives.

The bureaucrat's preoccupation with procedural correctness may at times even cause him or her to decide that the person seeking aid cannot be helped at all, because the formal responsibility for such aid lies elsewhere. ("I'm sorry—I can't help you," is an answer people all too often get from bureaucrats.) One of the authors witnessed a suicide attempt which succeeded because public officials were unable to decide who was responsible for carrying out a rescue operation. A man jumped off a bridge into a river which separated two cities. The rescue squad of one city argued that their counterparts should save him because he had jumped from the other side. The second group argued that the first crew should get into action since the man had floated to the other side of the river. Unfortunately, the question was soon beside the point.

Bureaucrats are commonly criticized for developing a greater commitment to the preservation of their organizations than to the accomplishment of the ends for which they were created. The Air Force general who opposes the development of a new bomber, whatever its utility, is unusual, and the Secretary or Minister who voluntarily recommends a substantial cut in the budget is similarly uncommon. The development of "departmental interest" has been studied in some detail, and it has been found that once the objectives of an organization are achieved, its leaders search for—and ordinarily find—new ends toward which the organization should work.

This can also be seen in private organizations. The March of Dimes is a case in point. It was founded to fight poliomyelitis. When vaccines for infantile paralysis were found, the organization was not dissolved; instead it turned its attention to other diseases. The goals or aims of the organization may have justified its original creation, but once the organization was established, it generated a new rationale and broader goals.

Responsiveness to authorities

The authorities have another problem with bureaucrats because they often develop stronger ties to the objects of their policy enforcement than to their superiors. The Secretary of the local Soviet Communist party primary organization in a factory is responsible to his superior in the party for the successful performance of that industrial unit. In practice, however, it is apparently common for him to "cooperate" with the factory manager in showing the plant's performance in a highly favorable light. That is, he and the factory manager may enter into a kind of informal partnership to make each other look good. As a consequence, the party leadership can no longer obtain the independently derived, accurate information it seeks. In other states as well, "watchdog" agencies have often become little more than puppets of the "private" organizations they are supposed to oversee. Here, at home, the Interstate Commerce Commission, the Food and Drug Administration, and other regulatory agencies have frequently been accused of this failing.

It is sometimes very difficult for authorities to see to it that bureaucrats promote the authorities' goals instead of their own. Bureaucratic organizations are rational (efficient) and staffed with "experts" or specialists who usually "know" more about "it" than their superiors or their critics, and this expertise means that they can often successfully promote their own goals, for better or for worse. When an Air Force general argues that a new bomber is needed, what novice in military affairs can debate the point on even terms? Or when a team of British economists presents a study of the likely consequences of their government's entry into the European Common Market, how many average voters can make a serious evaluation or criticism of their argument?

Bureaucrats Do Not Automatically Obey Authorities

As President Harry S. Truman sat in the Oval Office and thought about General Dwight D. Eisenhower becoming President, he is quoted as saying, "He'll sit here and he'll say, 'Do this! Do that!' *And nothing will happen.* Poor Ike—it won't be a bit like the Army. He'll find it very frustrating."

Truman is also said to have remarked of his own White House experience, "I sit here all day trying to persuade people to do the things they ought to have sense enough to do without my persuading them. . . . That's all the powers of the President amount to." [Richard E. Neustadt, *Presidential Power: The Politics of Leadership* (New York: Wiley, 1960), pp. 9–10.]

Countermeasures: mastering the bureaucracy

Each of us has probably had some experiences with bureaucratic "red tape," and we have all heard other people complain about it. Authorities too are very much aware of the difficulties caused by such bureaucratic "dysfunctions" as lack of responsiveness, and they seek to reduce their occurrence and to minimize the adverse consequences which result.

One tactic authorities use to control these dysfunctionalities is the *regular transfer of personnel.* It is common practice to assign bureaucrats to new locations and new positions periodically, and to rotate supervisory personnel. In the U.S. Foreign Service, and in the military as well, assignments ordinarily run for no longer than 2 or 3 years.

There are positive benefits for administrators in periodic transfers. Gaining experience in a variety of situations is an important means of increasing one's range of competence. But beyond that, the authorities seek to use transfers to break down informal patterns of interaction which may have developed, and which are sometimes used to circumvent or obstruct the purposes of the authorities. At the very least, those who are transferred ordinarily feel that they must "prove themselves" again, and are almost certain to be highly motivated for at least a time.

A second method of controlling bureaucratic organizations is to *reorganize or to modify the structures themselves.* Over time, bureaucratic agencies tend to develop vested interests and precedents which cloud or reduce the options available to the authorities. When Khrushchev assumed the dominant position in the U.S.S.R., he drastically overhauled the state bureaucracy, in good part because the old structures would not implement his reforms. And by reorganizing, he was able to transfer from Moscow the personnel who constituted one of his biggest political threats.

Finally, authorities may increase their control over bureaucracies by *creating special bureaus or ad hoc bodies with watchdog responsibilities.* The Government Accounting Office in the United States watches over the activities of the federal bureaucracy. The secret police in the Soviet Union monitor the responsiveness of administrators to the authorities. These are ongoing agencies, but "Royal Commissions," "Presidential Commissions," and more informally organized personal advisers often perform the same function.

The advantages of such independent, outside agencies or groups stem from the fact that the persons involved do not have to reflect the interests of any operational bureau. Ad hoc groups have the further advantage that they need not justify past mistakes nor be consistent with past appraisals. Rather, they can take a free and fresh look at the subject of their concern and suggest alternatives exclusively on the basis of their evaluations. Needless to say, they are only as good as their judgments, and wise authorities play them off against the bureaucrats.

Our argument thus far can be summarized as follows: Policy implementation does not take place automatically, and authorities must rely upon administrators to accomplish their objectives. Because they cannot do the job themselves, they create organizations to act as their agents, and they typically have found that bureaucracy has been the most appropriate organizational form for that task. Nevertheless, bureaucracies also create problems for authorities, which, in turn, are met by transferring personnel, reorganizing organization structures, and creating watchdog agencies.

BUREAUCRATIC DILEMMAS AND RESOURCES

To this point we have looked at policy implementation from the perspective of the authorities, and have stressed the obstacles they face and must overcome if the bureaucracy is to be kept responsive. But there is another viewpoint to be considered: that of the bureaucrats. They too are confronted with serious and even fundamental dilemmas as they seek to implement policy decisions—even when they agree with those decisions. And they too have resources they can use to protect their own interests and promote their own objectives.

Dilemmas

Bureaucrats regularly face four troublesome dilemmas: those arising from (1) ambiguity, (2) inconsistency, (3) insufficient resources, and (4) ignorance in high places. One recurring source of difficulty for bureaucrats at every level is the problem of *ambiguity*. No matter how comprehensive, detailed, and precise a general policy is, problems almost always arise in its implementation. General policies rarely provide for all possible contingencies; if they did, they would be so rigid as to create serious problems. Rather, discretionary authority (to decide how the policy will work in particular cases) is typically delegated to the operations level, with only overall guidelines and objectives set out in the general policy statement. As a result, administrators do not know precisely how the authorities would have them act in every case. Should they decide to allocate funds for an airport in St. Louis or for one in Seattle? Should they renew a license to operate a commercial radio station, or grant one to a new group which seeks to replace the corporation requesting the renewal? "Wrong" decisions may lead to political stress, as the bureaucrat finds out only after the fact.

In most cases, the problem of ambiguity is related to a second dilemma—*inconsistencies* between general policies. These may be readily apparent and direct, or quite beneath the surface.

Early in World War II, President Franklin Roosevelt decided to rely upon the Nationalist Chinese government to act as a check against the Japanese in Asia once the war was over. To that end, China was identified as one of the major allies, with the right to participate in the planning of the postwar world order.

The Chinese leader, Generalissimo Chiang Kai-shek, understandably took this to mean that the United States would pursue wartime policies designed to realize that long-term objective. The Chinese theater of operations, for example, would receive a high priority rating in the general plan for achieving victory. In addition the United States would provide the Nationalists with the aid necessary for them to consolidate their domestic position so that they could assume their designated place in world affairs.

Unfortunately, for the Chinese government at least, President Roosevelt also decided to support a military strategy which placed a top priority on winning the war in Europe first, and which relied upon the progressive encirclement of Japan by capturing the islands it controlled in the Pacific. The net result of this two-pronged strategy was to reduce the Chinese theater to secondary importance and to divert to "more important" tasks the supplies which Chiang thought he would get. If China ever had a chance to assume "great power" status under the Nationalists, as Roosevelt had proclaimed as his goal, it was lost in part because of United States war strategy. American representatives in China, particularly General "Vinegar Joe" Stillwell, had the impossible task of placating the Nationalist government while implementing a policy that ran contrary to its interests. Though "Vinegar Joe" was hardly a diplomatic person, his problem was basically one of policy inconsistencies—his leaders wanted to achieve mutually incompatible objectives.

Conflicts within one policy area or between several general policies also occur at more mundane levels. A high school principal is directed by the school board to develop a highly innovative curriculum while he is denied permission to recruit a teaching staff qualified to make the new program a success. The result is apt to be "new math" taught in "the good old-fashioned way."

Administrators also commonly face the prospect of attempting to implement policies despite *insufficient resources.* During the final weeks of the Nazi regime in Germany, Hitler issued numerous orders to his troop commanders which were simply impossible to realize, given the depleted state of his armies. In the same vein, Stalin ordered the collectivization of the Soviet peasantry in the 1930s without much regard to the dilemmas this forced on his local agents. According to the experience of one,

> The day begins with uninterrupted bombardment on the telephone and special requests on paper. "We ask you at 10 o'clock to send your 'responsible' representative to the Oblast Land Aministration;" "at 10 o'clock you must also go to the Oblast Land Administration and at 12—to the same place;" "immediately sent . . . to the Oblast Planning Commission, to the Consumers Cooperative;" we are reorganizing . . . sent a representative to the League of. . . .
>   When you . . . listen on the phone, you feel like screaming "Help, they assault us, they pull us apart, they deprive us of our individuality . . . and don't let us work!"[1]

For many of the newly independent states, insufficiencies of administrative resources have been a particularly serious problem. While they have passed laws calling for comprehensive educational opportunities or other services, the educational facilities or human talent available have not always been adequate.

Finally, administrators are constantly confronted with the problem of relative *ignorance in high places.* As specialists, they are usually more knowledgeable about the needs and opportunities within their areas of competence than are the generalists above them. Because they are constantly involved in the single problem area, they tend to magnify it and to belittle or ignore other matters outside their concern. George Kennan has been one of America's most learned and well-known diplomats in recent years. Yet his specialist's view comes through repeatedly in his memoirs, particularly when he recalls the actions of his superiors. Why did they make him look foolish before the Portuguese rulers in 1942, or why didn't they ever understand the concept of "containment" which he had introduced as the basis for a foreign policy toward the Soviet Union? Seldom did he admit that his own frame of reference was necessarily different from the that of his President.[2]

Kennan is not unique in this respect. Generals commonly feel that

[1]See Merle Fainsod, *Smolensk under Soviet Rule* (Cambridge, Mass.: Harvard, 1958, p. 256.
[2]George F. Kennan, *Memoirs* (Boston: Little, Brown, 1967).

their civilian superiors do not "really" understand military problems, and show a similar frustration with them. It is a frustration shared with physicians, scientists, professors, engineers, and lawyers who hold positions in bureaucracies.

Resources

It was noted earlier that authorities have considerable resources at their disposal which can be used to obtain desired ends from their subordinates. For example, they can create or reorganize government agencies, dismiss personnel or transfer them from one position to another, or utilize special agents or groups. But bureaucrats also have resources with which to protect their interests and promote their objectives. In fact, it sometimes appears that the bureaucrats are the real movers in a society. Their effectiveness in dealing with their superiors rests on (1) their *technical expertise,* (2) their *organizational expertise,* (3) their *proximity* or direct involvement with actual policy implementation, and (4) their *delegated authority.*

When the average person goes to a lawyer, doctor, or auto mechanic, it is ordinarily to seek *expert advice* on the best course of action. While the person might "decide" whether to plead guilty to a criminal charge, submit to an operation, or have the automobile transmission overhauled, the decision is almost certain to be based on the information obtained from the appropriate expert. But if this person does not like the choices (or has lost confidence in the "expert"), he or she can only go to *another* expert for a second assessment and set of options. Of course we are usually not totally at the mercy of specialists. Many of us can spot a crooked auto mechanic as soon as the latter tries to sell us a new battery to improve our car's gas mileage. Presidents and other authorities usually know more about matters of public policy than most patients do about the mysteries of medical practice. Yet the difference is a matter of degree rather than kind, for authorities cannot be as knowledgeable as their bureaucratic specialists without becoming specialists themselves.

The discretion of a subordinate is illustrated in the events which led to the resignation of former Vice President Agnew. Attorney General Elliot Richardson was not responsible for the initiation of the Agnew investigation. A Baltimore district attorney began the work, and by the time Richardson and the President were told about the developing evidence, they felt compelled to support the investigation despite the embarrassing implications. Had the district attorney not gathered and pre-

Technical Expertise as a Bureaucratic Resource

It is a questionable, though sometimes fashionable, assumption that technocrats in the Soviet Union, Europe, the United States, and elsewhere control politicians, or that politicians control the technocrats. There may never be a clear victory either for those who generate or defend a political ideology or for those who claim that their access to knowledge permits them to displace or eliminate the importance of ideology. Each depends on the other, and this mutual dependency sharply limits the power of either side.

In fact, both politicians and technocrats are genuinely confused about the nature of their respective roles. The current belief is that the domain of politics is the exclusive responsibility of the politician, while the expert is exclusively concerned with rationality. But the actual behavior of experts is more complex and does not fit these expectations. We find in practice that experts do exercise power of their own. A modern Prince does not completely control his experts, even though they depend on him since he hires and fires them. But there exist many subtle ways to evade and influence a Prince, and these subtleties are not unknown to the successful planner (bureaucrat). [Guy Benveniste, *The Politics of Expertise* (Berkeley, Calif.: Glendessary Press, 1972), pp. 5–6.]

sented the information so vigorously and effectively, Mr. Agnew might still be active in politics.

But it is possible to overstate the opportunities open to lower-level bureaucrats as they seek to obtain a desired outcome. This is particularly so when the authorities clearly state and strongly enforce their own preferences, even in the face of failure. For example, during "the Great Leap Forward," Chinese authorities told their subordinates to rely upon human resources to increase production levels dramatically. Local officials entrusted with the actual implementation of "the great leap" could see the human and technical failures of the policy. Nevertheless, they generally reported tremendous increases in output in order to avoid the displeasure of their superiors. They could not change the policy, and because of the strong commitment of Peking to it, both the authorities and the bureaucrats failed.

The same phenomenon occurs in all political systems. President Lyndon Johnson refused to accept interpretations of the Vietnam war which included gloomy forecasts; over the years, official reports increasingly described events as the President desired.

A fourth important factor which increases the influence of bureaucrats is the *delegated or formal responsibility* assigned to the positions they hold. When authorities create positions or roles, they ordinarily describe the responsibilities attached. The director of the Office of Management and Budget, for example, has the general task of overseeing the drafting of the annual executive budget for its submission to the Congress; to that end, the director has been given comprehensive guidelines for the execution of the bureau's task. So long as they are followed, the director is relatively invulnerable to pressure from above.

The strength of the bureaucrats' position, so long as they execute their formal responsibilities and follow standard operating procedures in doing so, is best illustrated by instances where they and their superiors fundamentally disagree over the disposition of a matter. Special Prosecutor Archibald Cox was appointed by President Nixon to investigate the Watergate break-in and related matters. He did so, vigorously, even to the extent of seeking subpoenas for the President's tapes and other documents. Nixon's displeasure was evident when he ordered Cox to stop his efforts to obtain further court orders. The Special Prosecutor refused on grounds that that was an essential part of his responsibility. Though he was fired, his successor continued the work, even to the point of keeping the same staff together and seeking the same evidence. Of course, either could have "followed orders" if he had been so inclined. But when they chose not to, they had a powerful argument in the fact that they were "doing their job."

COOPERATION: KEY TO SUCCESSFUL POLICY IMPLEMENTATION

Thus far problems and conflicts in relationships between policymakers and administrators have been emphasized. Usually, however, the two types of public officials work cooperatively; governments, after all, tend to be ongoing despite recurrent or even persistent elements of tension. It is, therefore, appropriate to conclude by examining the factors which make cooperation between authorities and bureaucrats a normal state of affairs.

Common objectives

Cooperation between policymakers and administrators is most likely to occur when there is general agreement over the objectives to be pursued. City fathers, for example, can expect maximum support from their police force if there is a common understanding of the proper role of law-enforcement agencies in the control of crime.

In most cases the range of agreement over objectives far outweighs points of difference. One reason for this is that the authorities create administrative organizations, establish their objectives, and recruit the necessary personnel. Bureaucrats typically understand and accept the organizational goals when they assume their positions. Thus, military forces are established for purposes of defense, and persons who fill the ranks indicate that they assent by following orders and accepting their pay. Similarly, Foreign Service officers, Department of Agriculture employees, and nearly all civil servants show a willingness to accomplish their agencies' objectives. And once appointed, loyalty to their agencies is usually strengthened as they come to know departmental norms. As a result, they either follow directions and serve whoever happens to be their superior, or they seek a new assignment or resign.

Nevertheless, bureaucrats may occasionally revolt because they object to agency objectives. A new administration might come to power and change priorities to such an extent that the missions of some agencies are altered beyond recognition. Such changes may provoke bureaucratic resistance. Seymour Martin Lipset found that the professional civil service in Saskatchewan, Canada, resisted implementation of a radical program of change announced by the ruling Cooperative Commonwealth Federation.[3] In the extreme case, military officers (who are part of the bureaucracy) have overthrown the existing authorities and assumed their roles. Though open resistance by bureaucrats is sensational, it occurs relatively infrequently.

Balanced resources

A second condition which fosters cooperation between authorities and bureaucrats is a relative balance of political and organizational resources between them. The authorities must be able to exercise reasonable control over the bureaucracy. Likewise, policy implementation goes forward most efficiently when administrators have resources sufficient to bring their knowledge and expertise to bear on problems with some

[3]Semour M. Lipset, *Agrarian Socialism: The Cooperative Commonwealth Federation in Saskatchewan* (Berkeley: University of California Press, 1959), especially pp. 255–276.

independence and flexibility. A kind of balance of power between decision makers and bureaucrats optimizes the policy-implementation process.

When President Nixon was reelected by a landslide in 1972, his political resources were at a peak. In addition to a broad base of public support, he had the active cooperation of business organizations and labor unions, and of course he had vast powers under the Constitution and the laws of the land. With these resources, he was able to exercise iron control in the formation and implementation of public policy. His Cabinet-level subordinates could not effectively oppose him, even if they were so inclined. They, in turn, were not likely to be undermined by their own underlings. Though military leaders and others may not have agreed that better relations with China were desirable, for instance, they were powerless to resist the execution of the President's policy. The result was that the entire administration spoke with one voice, and higher- and lower-level government employees worked in concert. There was little opportunity for criticism from the field to influence policy.

By mid-1974, President Nixon's resources had been greatly reduced. A majority of citizens wanted him removed from office by impeachment or resignation. His former allies in labor, business, and the professions became increasingly critical, and some joined the call for impeachment. Some of his most avid supporters sadly questioned his capacity to govern. As the President's resources were reduced, conflicts within the federal bureaucracy increased. Sharp disagreements surfaced over the steps the government should take to cure the nation's economic ills. Former Governor John Love of Colorado resigned from his position as energy chief because he could not agree with the President's policy on fuel allocation. Stories of conflict between State and Defense Department officials over foreign policy questions became increasingly common. Subordinates came to believe they could resist directives from above because their superiors' resources had been drastically diminished. Effective administration and coordination were thus made difficult by the weakness of the authorities.

At times, officials take steps to ensure that their subordinates do not have excessive resources. When John Kennedy was elected President in 1960, Adlai Stevenson was the most prominently mentioned prospective Secretary of State. He had been an articulate supporter of liberal positions in foreign affairs; he had been the presidential candidate of the Democratic party in the previous two campaigns; and he had a large, loyal public following. President-elect Kennedy, however, bypassed Stevenson and selected the relatively unknown Dean Rusk. One of the major reasons for this decision was his wish to avoid conflict within his administration over the conduct of foreign policy. He viewed Stevenson's independent political resources as a potential threat to his own freedom of action. On the other hand, Rusk's anonymity—and lack of a resource base—were viewed as pluses. He would be likely to faithfully carry out the President's policies. In fact, he did just that.

Finally, it should be noted that when the authorities have greater resources than their responsibilities require or permit, the difficulties are not likely to take the form of conflicts; bureaucrats like almost everyone else seldom fight hopeless causes. The unhealthy consequence of this imbalance is rather the undermining of the morale and the initiative of administrators. They cannot provide expert criticism if their independent judgment is not allowed; they cannot maintain their commitment if they believe they are consistently being abused, their prerogatives are being usurped, and their expertise ignored. With such conditions, if bureaucrats do not resign, their performance is apt to be perfunctory. For somewhat different reasons than those indicated in our earlier discussion, they have insufficient resources to perform their tasks.

Adequate and precise measures of balance of resources are difficult to obtain. Nevertheless, it is reasonable to assume that in viable, ongoing political systems, effective resources are allocated to both general decision makers and policy implementers in amounts roughly commensurate with the responsibilities they are assigned; if such is not the case, the performance of government will suffer.

Precisely defined relationships

Critics of "progressive education" have registered many complaints about that general philosophy of education. Their usual theme is that students are given excessive freedom rather than the order and discipline they should have. It is not unusual for critics to cite personal experience in which they laud a third- or fourth-grade teacher who was strict but good: "She was a real disciplinarian, but at least you always knew where she stood."

There are advantages to knowing "where you stand." Uncertainty in our relationships with others, when we are acting in our capacities as parents, children, or friends, can produce both anxieties and bad decisions. If children do not feel they can confide in their parents, there is a real—and widening—generation gap. And if students cannot trust their instructors, the probabilities that they will benefit from their classes are surely reduced.

The web of relationships between authorities and administrators is more formalized than those between parent and child or student and instructor. As a result, there is an even greater need for explicitness in defining them; instead of "understanding" there must be rules. And while cooperation within a family or a classroom can be based in good part on affection and/or personal ties, in bureaucracies the use of impersonal sanctions must play an important, if not a dominant, role.

The problem of defining roles precisely, of allocating authority and responsibility in clear-cut, workable terms, is that *precision* can become *rigidity.* Just as proponents of progressive education are correct in noting that children need to have freedom to explore that which interests them and to develop their own resourcefulness, so there is a corresponding need for public officials at all levels to have the freedom to assess and decide questions as they arise. If they are bound by overly precise rules, they cannot treat each problem with the sensitivity needed for its solution. Somehow, a compromise must be made between certainty, precision, and clarity on the one hand, and flexibility, adaptability, and even ambiguity on the other.

Successful accommodation of these opposites must include precise *delegation of authority.* The rules of the bureaucracy should stipulate who can decide what—who can arrest a criminal suspect, who can authorize the payment of a welfare check, or who can dismiss an employee. Precision should also govern the *procedures* by which decisions will be made. Arrests should be made only when certain acts have been committed and in a certain way; authorizations for payment of benefits or dismissals of employees should be given only when the determinations have been made by approved means. If responsibilities and the procedures for their exercise are precisely defined, the authorities ordinarily can safely permit their subordinates to use independent judgment as they apply the rules to individual cases. Subordinates will know what they are expected to do and how they are expected to do it. They can also be confident that by acting within defined limits the further trust of their superiors can be earned by good performance.

Though authorities almost always understand the benefits of precision in the definition of their relationships with bureaucrats, they sometimes fail to act on their knowledge. They may neglect to act on it because they are more concerned with other needs. During the Stalinist era Soviet legal procedures were notoriously vague. Courts could punish persons for acts which were not specifically defined as criminal under the law. It was sufficient if they were "analogous" to other acts which were. How legal cadres should determine when the principle of analogy applied was far from clear. In this case the bureaucrats needed precise legal guidelines, but the authorities placed a higher priority on their own "need" for great flexibility in their intimidation of a potentially hostile citizenry. So the Soviet authorities were willing to sacrifice legal precision because its absence helped them achieve their overriding goal of effective intimidation.

A more recent example from the United States can also be cited. Theodore Lowi has noted a tendency for Congress to be increasingly imprecise in its delegation of authority. He cites a draft of a 1964 law that declared "war on poverty" and stated that a community action program is one:

1. Which mobilizes and utilizes resources, public or private, of any urban or rural, or combined urban and rural, geographical area, including but not limited to a state, metropolitan area, county, city, town, multicity unit, or multi-county unit in an attack on poverty;
2. Which provides services, assistance, and other activities of sufficient scope and size to give promise of progress toward elimination of poverty or a cause or causes of poverty through developing employment opportunities, improving human performance, motivation, and productivity, or bettering the conditions under which people live, learn and work;
3. Which is developed, conducted, and administered with the maximum feasible participation of residents of the area and members of the groups served; and
4. Which is conducted, administered, or coordinated by a public or private nonprofit agency which is broadly representative of the community.[4]

How were the administrators charged with the duty of establishing centers of this description to decide how they would operate and what they would actually do? Congress's desire to deal with the vicious cycle of poverty seemed to supersede the requirements of stable, rational administration.

As desirable as either the Soviet or the American congressional objective might have been, in both cases there was a price to be paid: in uneven administration of justice and abuse of authority in one case, and in waste and inefficiency in the other.

[4]Theodore J. Lowi, *The End of liberalism* (New York: Norton, 1969), pp. 235–236.

SUMMARY AND CONCLUSION

In contemporary political life, authorities generally rely upon bureaucracies to implement their general policy decisions. Consequently, certain steps must be taken to ensure that bureaucrats remain responsive to the goals of the authorities and sensitive to the citizens affected by their actions. Administrators must act to ensure that the operational implications of policy choices are clear to decision makers and that resources adequate to the task at hand are assigned by the authorities. Both authorities and administrators have advantages as they deal with each other, and there must be a balance of strength between them as well as an appropriate degree of precision in the definition of administrative authority and procedures. In the end, policy implementation rests upon the joint efforts of all public officials involved—authorities and bureaucrats alike. The relationship of superior to subordinate is not purely hierarchical since either superiors or subordinates can effectively thwart the efforts of the other.

When authorities and administrators work together, governments can function remarkably well. As specific political systems are examined in later chapters, it will be clear that there are stable and efficient governments in today's world—the Soviet Union, Britain, and the United States being examples. In these and in numerous other cases, authorities and administrators overcome their differences in background, perspective, and expertise to translate the needs and demands of their citizens into the implementation of workable policies.

SUGGESTED READINGS

Blau, Peter M.: *Bureaucracy in Modern Society,* 2d ed. (New York: Random House, 1971). A short but important contemporary study of bureaucracy.

Frankel, Charles: *High on Foggy Bottom* (New York: Harper and Row, 1968) An irreverent memoir of a former Assistant Secretary in the Johnson administration.

Lindblom, Charles E.: *The Policy Making Process,* (Englewood Cliffs, N.J.: Prentice-Hall, 1968). A systematic statement of policymaking by increments.

Mosher, Frederick C.: *Democracy and the Public Service* (New York: Oxford University Press, 1968). A study of the tensions inherent in a democratic society with a professionalized civil service.

Ready, R. K.: *The Administrator's Job: Issues and Delemmas* (New York: McGraw-Hill, 1967). A study of organizational behavior from the administrator's point of view.

Simon, Herbert: *Administrative Behavior,* 2d ed. (New York: Macmillan, 1957). A landmark treatment of decision making. Simon attempts to make the study of administration "scientific."

Weber, Max: "Bureaucracy" The classic statement of the nature of bureaucracy. Written over 100 years ago, it is still worthy of careful study today.

CHAPTER FOUR

ORIGINS OF PUBLIC POLICY
Defining the Issues

In this chapter we close the circle between social problems and policy decisions. Issues result, in part, from consequences of past action or inaction by the authorities. Past policies thus produce results which give feedback upon which new policies may be based. If there are exceptions to this rule, they lie in areas where unexpected or unforeseen events provoke the need for policy decisions.

Note that both the *intended* and the *unintended* results of policy may make new decisions necessary. Also note that there is a difference between issues which result from the implementation of past policy decisions and past failure to take action. Further, while failure to act may be a deliberate choice or nondecision, other issues result because nature and foreign powers act independently of the authorities.

Note that as social problems are shaped into policy choices, those seeking political action try to maximize potential support and minimize opposition to their proposals. The attempt to achieve maximum levels of agreement and support is characteristic of all forms of government, from those commonly considered dictatorial to those thought to be democratic.

Associational groups, institutional groups, and political parties are identified as important agencies in issue definition. Be sure you understand the difference between *groups* and *parties,* and between *associational groups* and *institutional groups.*

Note that the authorities themselves seek to influence the development of policy proposals: they do not passively wait while groups and parties draw up alternative policies.

Be sure that you understand the following terms:

Wants
Demands
Issues
Associational groups
Institutional groups
Political parties

LEARNING OBJECTIVES

After you have studied this chapter, you should be able to:

1. Identify the sources of policy demands and explain the differences between them.
2. Differentiate between wants, demands, and issues, and explain their relative usefulness to the authorities.
3. Distinguish between associational and institutional groups, and explain their relevance to, and differential impact upon, the definition of issues.
4. Differentiate between the roles played by political parties and those played by other social groups in defining issues.
5. Describe the differences between foreign and domestic policy issues, and explain the significance of those differences.

In 1945, Los Angeles, California, discovered the meaning of a new word— smog. Fog, mixed with smoke from industries, and exhaust fumes from automobiles, hung low over suburbs and orange groves. At first it was only a minor irritant and something of a joke. But smog eventually made environmental protection a concern of millions of Americans—and this

widespread public concern gave birth to policy proposals of major importance.

There was no immediate demand for governmental action from Los
Angelenos when they first found that their air was periodically fouled by
noxious fumes. But over time, smog became a more common occurrence. News of "killer" fogs (actually, smog that made eyes smart and
water, and that did indeed kill some elderly people with chronic respiratory ailments) in London and Pittsburgh added to general concern.
Demands that something be done increased until the matter became a
public issue that the authorities had to deal with; studies of the problem
were initiated, proposals for corrective actions were made, and finally
laws banning or restricting polluting activities were enacted.

The case of smog in Los Angeles illustrates the process by which
public policy is made. A significant problem is perceived by private
citizens, public officials, or perhaps both. It is viewed as appropriate for
governmental attention, and demands are made that public authorities
"Do something!" The demands are publicized to generate additional
support. Often countergroups form and make counterdemands. In this
dialogue, alternatives—along with their benefits and costs—are considered and refined. As a result, the decision makers receive information
about the technical, political, and social implications of the alternative
decisions under consideration. This process, which can be called *issue
definition,* provides the authorities with the basis for informed decisions.

In theory, it is easy to identify the steps of this process. But in actual
cases it is often more like a maze without beginning or end; some policies
are constantly being refined and redefined. In our smog example it soon
became clear that the use of petroleum and coal as energy sources and
the disposal of trash by burning were the most important causes of air
pollution. But the automobiles and factories which burned the polluting
fuels were an essential part of the life-style Californians had become
accustomed to. Even trash disposal by means other than burning was
more expensive and inconvenient than letting it go up in smoke. And of
course the problem could only get worse as the westward migration of
thousands of Americans continued after the war.

Since 1945, policy alternatives to deal with air pollution have been
proposed and opposed by various public and private groups at all levels
of government. Representatives of a major countergroup, the automobile
industry, first argued that they lacked the technology necessary to make
the internal-combustion engine "clean"; later they argued that it could be
done, but only at an unacceptably high cost. Other industries have

contended that the costs of smokestack emission controls and the use of clean-burning natural gas would force them into bankruptcy. Taxpayer groups have fought measures that would raise government budgets. Truckers, highway construction contractors, automobile associations, and even state highway departments have all actively opposed mass-transit systems. Not surprisingly, perhaps, smog remains a serious problem, and continuing redefinitions of the issues and restatements of public policy remain on the political agenda.

As we examine this process of issue definition or clarification, three major topics or questions will be discussed: (1) What activates the process of issue definition? (2) By what processes do "problems" become issues? (3) What agents or groups participate in refining demands and needs into issues?

INITIATING THE PROCESS: PRESSURE OF A PROBLEM

What leads people to make policy proposals, indeed often to feel compelled to make them? A variety of answers could be given, but fundamentally, issues begin with problems—that is, situations that cause dissatisfaction. As in the case of air pollution, demands for policy changes come from people (often organized into groups) who feel that something is amiss and that corrective public action should be taken. But demands for no change, or slower change, or a different kind of change may be voiced by other persons or groups. Demands for new policies almost invariably provoke opposition from those who would be adversely affected by them. Thus air pollution stimulates some people to demand controls on smoke emissions, and such demands activate others to oppose policies which would change their business practices or life-styles.

Circumstances which produce dissatisfaction can develop in many ways. Some problems can be traced to the effects of past policies upon society. For example, the problem of smog can be traced, in part, to the long-established federal, state, and local policies of encouraging automotive transportation—often at the expense of less-polluting transportation modes such as railroads—by massive highway construction programs. Policies generally are made for particular purposes, but their consequences often affect more than the specific problems for which they were made. Both the anticipated and the unanticipated consequences of policy can create new problems requiring further attention. Here is another example, from French politics:

During the First World War the French government required large quantities of alcohol for use in the manufacture of gunpowder. To ensure that sufficient alcohol would be produced, a new state agency was established with monopoly powers to buy alcohol at high prices. As a consequence, it became highly profitable to grow sugar beets from which alcohol could be distilled. The manufacture of wine was also encouraged since it, too, could be a source of alcohol.

The policy had the anticipated effect of encouraging the manufacture of alcohol. It had unanticipated effects as well. When the war ended and less alcohol was needed, the government could not repeal the alcohol laws without losing needed public support—too many French farmers benefited from the subsidy program. On the other hand, there was a growing surplus of alcohol and an overabundance of wine on the market.

New policies were needed to deal with these altered social conditions. Accordingly, the government periodically required the addition of alcohol to all gasoline sold in France (at additional expense to the taxpayer as well as the gasoline buyer), and conducted occasional campaigns designed to wean French people from their wine. Thus, a policy which resolved one problem produced conditions which required new policy measures.

Agricultural subsidies in the United States provide a similar example. In this case, as in the politics of alcohol in France, a government program provided incentives for high levels of production. As in France, surpluses developed and had to be stored at high cost to the government and the subsidies were difficult to end. Consequently, further policies had to be devised in order to encourage consumption and/or discourage production. Food was provided for school lunch programs, food stamps were distributed to the poor, exports of grain were negotiated by the government, and farmers were paid not to grow surplus crops.

In each of these examples, the policies were successful; each policy achieved the purpose of stimulating production. Additionally, however, each of these policies produced *unanticipated consequences* which necessitated further measures to deal with them. Thus, even "successful" policies can create new problems for the authorities.

At times, the *anticipated consequences* of policies can also lead to demands for change. When medical care was first supplied to the aged under the social security system in the United States, the benefits were deliberately set at a low level. According to plan, the hospitals were not overcrowded and physicians were not overtaxed by the new recipients of government aid. But low benefits also produced new dissatisfactions.

Citizen groups, the Social Security Administration, and members of Congress insistently demanded higher benefits. Proposals were developed which progressively gained support, and the laws were modified over the objections of those who opposed spending more money.

In the case of Medicare, then, the anticipated consequences produced new demands. These new demands were predictable, and were in fact themselves anticipated by proponents of governmentally financed health care. They knew that once a program of public services, payments, or subsidies is begun, it is difficult to keep it from expanding. The initial health program was a "foot in the door" which would create increasing demands that more people be covered and that the level of benefits be raised.

Past policy decisions are thus important sources of current issues since they produce consequences which may stimulate new demands for action. But they are not, however, the only source of issues. Some developments are beyond the control of the authorities or are outside their immediate concerns. When independent or unforeseen developments create problems, new policy issues can be raised.

In 1957 the Soviet Union launched Sputnik I, the first man-made orbiting earth satellite. For many, the image of America as the preeminent world power in technology was shattered. This unexpected Russian breakthrough triggered a series of wide-ranging debates within the United States over the level of military spending required, the need for funding and organizing a crash program for space exploration, new priorities for the development of military weapons systems, and the steps needed to improve the nation's technological capabilities. These debates culminated in the creation of the National Aeronautics and Space Administration (NASA), accelerated development of intercontinental ballistics missiles (ICBMs), and related delivery systems, and massive subsidies for the education of scientists and engineers and for science education generally. All these policies had consequences which affected American society and politics well beyond the specific programs initially implemented.

The launching of Sputnik I illustrates how an event independent of the control of the authorities (and even unexpected) can generate domestic demands. Had Americans not been preoccupied with being "number one," had the 1950s not been marked by hostility and suspicion between the United States and the Soviet Union, no change in policy need necessarily have resulted. But in the cold war context, a national debate was begun, policy proposals were made, and decisions were reached.

"Natural" developments can also provoke demands and result in policy issues. Unusually heavy flood damage along the Mississippi River and its tributaries in 1973, for instance, led to demands for government-sponsored flood insurance. Policy alternatives were quickly developed and debated and a program was adopted within months. Demands may develop and issues crystallize because serious social or economic changes within a nation go undealt with for a time: there is *no* policy for dealing with them. Great Britain's Labour party became the political agent for the nationalization of heavy industry because both existing parties, the Conservatives and the Liberals, refused to meet the demands of the laboring class in the late nineteenth and early twentieth centuries. The heavy impact of the Great Depression in the United States was partly due to previous ignorance about the consequences of industrialization. No policies had been developed to cope with widespread business failures and unemployment. In these cases stress resulted from an absence of policy, and ultimately led to corrective action.

Whether problems develop because of past policies or because of independent or unforeseen developments, or because the only policy is a "policy of drift," they can generate demands for policy changes. Proponents of such changes usually confront opposition from those who are benefited by, or are comfortable with, the status quo. In clashes between advocates and opponents of new policy, issues are clarified and related to the interests and opinions of influential groups and individuals. Thus the basis for decision making is laid.

Issues as Signals of Stress

Since issues arise because citizens and groups have competing notions of what the government should or should not do, demands and issues can be seen as signals providing information about stress to the authorities.

In our discussion of policymaking in Chapter 2, we pointed out that stress was the "spur" to policy decisions. We used stress as a convenient shorthand for all the potential and actual dissatisfactions with officials and governments which make it difficult for the authorities to govern effectively. At that time we noted that Chapter 4 would deal with the basis for policy decisions in more detail.

As we discuss the process of issue definition, we will explore the chief ways in which the authorities are alerted to actual and potential public problems. Debates over demands and policy proposals provide important information about the opinions, interests, and feelings of citizens and groups. As they complain, propose, and oppose, the participants in issue definition give indications of how much clout they have. Knowledge about this aspect of social reality is most important to the authorities as they formulate policy decisions.

CONTINUING THE PROCESS: FROM PROBLEMS TO ISSUES

Though issues ordinarily develop and are acted upon to meet the needs of at least a part of a given society, a complex process of combining and refining individual wants or expectations must take place before issues are decided. The range of individual wants and hopes in any society is enormous. We aspire to perpetual youth; we desire wealth and power; we want challenging employment and many other things.

Most of these wants are too individualized or too grandiose, or too vaguely defined, for governments to act upon them. They may not even be articulated among intimate friends. But people recognize some of their wants as *important,* or of *general concern,* and *as appropriate for a public response;* they then become *political demands.* When people need jobs, or price relief, or protection from foreign enemies, they generally feel these needs strongly enough to demand government action.

Even such fundamental demands for political action do not ordinarily begin as fully articulated proposals for new policies. Rather, they resemble a cry for help. When a detailed plan to change a specific tax levy is proposed, it is likely to have been drafted in response to more generalized complaints about existing tax levels or forms. A law regulating sewage disposal might have its origins in protests over contaminated rivers or lakes. Thus, demands tend to highlight problem areas; they are indicators of real or potential stress; and they are the incentives for authoritative action.

Not all demands can be met. Some may not be seen as of sufficient importance by the authorities. For instance, college students and their parents have long called for tax relief on income spent on tuition. To date, there has been little governmental response to this demand. Some demands are fundamentally inconsistent with others: public officials may heed one side or the other, but not both. Some may be grouped together or be met with a single response: as when a general agricultural subsidy program may be established to meet the needs of grain producers, tobacco growers, and dairy workers. Still other demands are met by compromise: labor demands for a $3 per hour minimum wage, countered by business pressures for $1.75, might result in a law setting the minimum at $2.25.

The process of refining demands into policy proposals is typically very complex. As we noted earlier, demands ordinarily stimulate active opposition from groups which might be adversely affected. Several decades ago when black citizens and civil rights groups called for "equal protection under the law" and for racial integration, white supremacists responded virgorously and organized to protect their social and political advantages. Since all the demands and counterdemands could not be satisfied, government leaders were forced to compromise some and to refuse others, to delay on some and to give others high priority for consideration and action.

The process of refining demands is also made complex because of the wide variety of groups and individuals who participate in it. Government officials, private individuals, newspaper and television editorialists, and a broad range of private bodies all voice their opinions on public issues from time to time. Each typically brings to bear a unique mix of influence, level of interest, knowledge, and support; the authorities who must decide can only estimate how each will react to alternative policy decisions. The range of groups and the parts they play in defining issues will be examined in the next section.

Debates over health care policy in the United States can illustrate the various ways demands may be refined into policies. In 1945 President Harry S. Truman announced his "Fair Deal" program, which included a plan for national health insurance. Though his program was supported by organized labor, it was almost immediately pigeonholed in the Congress, while interested persons and groups worked on the preparation of alternative policy positions. The demand that the government assume responsibility for a basic level of health care was rejected. Instead, the position of most physicians and private insurance companies prevailed—public agencies were not to supervise and finance health care delivery. Medical services were not to be provided through federal financing, but medical schools, research, and hospital construction were to be subsidized by the federal government. Physicians and speakers on behalf of medical schools argued that these measures would satisfy the need for improved health care, and their arguments prevailed at the time.

In the years that followed, two groups of people became increasingly effective in gaining a hearing for government-supported health care: the poor and the aged. While their demands were combined and received increasing support from congressional leaders, another also became a part of the final compromise: the demand that the federal government not run the program directly. The policy alternative which won out in 1959 provided that states would receive subsidies from the federal government if they instituted medical programs for the poor and the elderly.

This example points up the two overriding concerns of persons and groups who participate in the process of translating demands into policy proposals: (1) to offer an alternative which will maximize the satisfaction of their demands and (2) the need to simultaneously win broad enough support to obtain favorable action from the authorities. Thus, President Truman's proposal for national health insurance was set aside because it lacked sufficient support. A less drastic proposal which spoke to the

---

From Problems to Policy Proposals: Summarizing the Process

The processes whereby social problems become policy proposals are too complex to be neatly summarized—any summary will oversimplify and distort. Nevertheless, the following is a convenient, if oversimplified, way to think about issue definition:

1. A situation (such as smog) is perceived by some people to constitute or to create a *problem.*
2. If the problem seems important, of general concern, and appropriate for public response, the concerned people will made *demands.*
3. Demands generate counterdemands, and an *issue* develops.
4. If public officials think an issue is serious enough, the demands and counterdemands are weighed, combined, compromised, and some are eliminated as *policy proposals* are developed to deal with them.
5. When "raw problems" have been thus refined into policy proposals, the issue has been *defined* sufficiently well that the authorities can then resolve the issue with a policy decision (the process discussed in Chapter 2).

same problem was formulated. It gained more general support, and it ultimately became public policy.

Sometimes winning broad support is less urgent than neutralizing potential opposition. In such circumstances the question becomes, "What acceptable policy will arouse the opposition of the fewest influential people?" By tabling President Truman's plan, and meeting the objections of speakers for the medical profession and insurance companies, the corollary objective of improving and increasing health care facilities and benefits for the poor and aged was realized. And the proposal became law only after considerable time had elapsed, time during which more people became informed, the needs became more pronounced, and the beneficiaries became better-organized. The process was incremental: delay, compromise, coalesce, educate, and finally, convince the authorities to act.

PARTICIPANTS IN THE PROCESS: WHO DEFINES THE ISSUES?

Demands upon authorities might come from virtually any person or group under their jurisdiction. Since everyone has desires and preferences, anyone might demand that the government "do something" under the right set of circumstances. Thus, anybody might participate in the process of issue definition. In addition, demands might come from a "foreign" source, as when Hitler demanded the resignation of Austrian Chancellor von Schuschnigg just before the German army marched into Austria. (The strongest kind of "demand," of course, is backed up with force.)

Finally, demands might come from either public or private sources. Presidents, Premiers, or Sheikhs don't just wait for requests from their people; they too have preferences and often use their positions of authority to obtain them. Demands originate from foreign governments and even from foreign nongovernmental groups. Foreign private-investment interests, for example, have been very influential in many capital-poor countries seeking industrial development.

Demands can come from individual persons; individuals can speak, write, and even vote with some political effect. But if they do not act in concert with others their impact usually will be minimal. This reflects the tremendous importance of *organization* for effective political action.

While individuals may gain increased political effectiveness (the ability to demand and be heard) by joining a group, their options may also be limited by group membership. Differences between the personal preferences of members must be muted if the organization is to survive and its goals achieved. When "hawks" and "doves" in the Democratic party were unable to compose their differences in 1968, the stage was set for electoral defeat in the presidential contest of that year. Thus, the very existence of a group means that some degree of demand refinement and issue definition has already taken place; otherwise the individuals would never have formed a group. Group membership requires at least some commonality of goals, interests, or perceptions; some individual demands become group demands, while others are minimized or ignored.

Associational groups

In Western democracies, associational groups representing the interests of labor, business, farmers, ethnic minorities, women, consumers, veterans, lawyers, physicians, dentists, professors, and many others play a large role in the definition of issues—that is, in voicing demands and in proposing policy alternatives. Such groups are often called *interest groups.* Sometimes they are called *lobbies* or *pressure groups,* particularly when they attempt to influence directly the decisions of authorities.

Associational groups are essentially private rather than governmental. Their members are free to join or resign as they choose, and they have more or less explicit objectives. As a result, their leaders know whom they must satisfy (their members), what general objectives to pursue, and to which authorities they must go if their group demands are to be satisfied. Their responsibilities are not primarily to Presidents, members of Congress, or Premiers; indeed, sometimes they seem to go out of their way to show that the interests of their members are paramount. In the fall of 1974, when President Ford called together a cross section of labor leaders to discuss the problems of inflation and unemployment, they told him his "track record" on economic matters "stank!"

Because no two associational groups usually make exactly the same demands, they ordinarily *bargain,* or negotiate, with other groups or with the authorities on policy alternatives. They may have a wide variety of bargaining assets, including status, numbers, wealth, and expertise. Professional groups such as the American Medical Association in the United States have been successful in lobbying activities partly because of the prestige and expertise of physicians. Other groups such as labor unions may depend less on status and more on their ability to promise votes and financial support in elections (labor union membership totals about 20 million workers or 22 percent of the total labor force, while there are only about 330,000 physicians in the United States). These differences in resources result in the use of differing bargaining strategies. But although the strategies of associational groups may differ, they all seek to advance group interests by obtaining favorable policy decisions.

Political parties

Though political parties are organized and operate differently from one country to the next, in almost every case their major purpose is to win or maintain control of the government. Thus Democrats in the United States and Conservatives in Great Britain both seek to win control of those offices which will make their leaders the formal elite. The great variety of political parties is largely a consequence of the different ways in which that purpose can best be achieved in very different contexts. If, on the surface, the Republican party in the United States seems quite different from the Communist party of the Soviet Union, it is not because they differ in their primary goal—to control the government. Rather they differ in their modes of operation in seeking that goal. The Republicans must compete for electoral support and therefore organize to win votes for their candidates. The Soviet Communists must maintain careful control of a complex, modern state and consequently organize to maximize disciplined obedience to party leadership.

In democracies, political parties resemble associations in that they have explicit objectives; they have open, voluntary memberships; and they are even surprisingly independent of government controls. They make demands and policy proposals and often have the political clout to see them enacted into law. Even so, they are clearly different in one crucial respect: their purpose is not only to *influence* policymakers but also to gain positions of authority and to *govern.*

Not all parties resemble associational groups. Some have been conspiratorial bands of revolutionaries—the Russian Communist party in its early stages, for example. Others have been the devoted and completely loyal followers of a national hero—the Argentine Peronists, for instance. Still others are the permanent inner group of authorities of an ongoing political system—the Soviet Communist party of today is an example. Their organizational structures may similarly vary, from a loosely knit grouping of individuals, to a highly integrated paramilitary machine. Their memberships may be closed to all but a few selected individuals who dedicate their lives to party work, or it may be open only to those persons whose skin color or family connection is acceptable.

In order to place their members in positions of authority, political parties must obtain support from a broad range of influential groups and interests. In so doing they play an important, if not dominant, role in the transformation of demands into issues. In democratic countries, parties can succeed only by obtaining votes, and they can obtain those votes only if they promise and provide services or programs desired by many of the voters. Hence, they seek out information on public preferences as a basis for formulating the policy positions which will have the most voter appeal. Their hope is to collect and combine demands and preferences into a package that can win elections for them.

Parties, Groups, and Issue Definition

In his classic study of political parties and pressure groups in democracy, V. O. Key provides the central distinction between the part these two agents play in defining issues. Of pressure groups he says:

> These associations may perform a representative function by communicating the wishes of their members to public authorities; or they may bring "pressure" to bear upon the government. . . . Pressure groups may be in alliance with a political party and they often seek to influence the outcome of elections.

Political parties are described differently:

> They amass sufficient support to buttress the authority of governments; or, on the contrary, they attract or organize discontent and dissatisfaction sufficient to oust the government. [V. O. Key, Jr., *Politics, Parties and Pressure Groups,* 5th ed. (New York: Thomas Y. Crowell, 1964), pp. 9, 11.]

Our focus goes beyond democratic parties, but Professor Key's basic distinction still holds. Groups, whether associational or institutional, communicate the "wishes of their members." Parties "amass support." In defining issues, therefore, parties formulate policy proposals which will appeal to as many groups as possible; groups seek to influence parties as a means to promoting their interests.

In other systems, where elections are not the means of selecting the authorities, political parties can also act as important agents in issue definition. In such cases, party leaders deal with administrative departments, with minority views within the government, or with leaders of groups whose support is important to those who govern. Soviet Communist party leaders consult with the military elite, representatives of agriculture, technicians, scientists, and others, as they develop overall policies such as the 5-year plan. In this way they try to meet and to aggregate at least some expressed needs and/or preferences. Thus, though the Communist party in the Soviet Union is very different from political parties in the United States or Britain, it shares with them the task of refining demands and translating them into policy alternatives and positions.

Institutional groups

Most of us have some idea of the roles played by parties and associations in drafting policy alternatives. We are generally less aware, however, that agencies within the bureaucracy also participate in the process. Many people may not know that the Pentagon "lobbies" in Congress for its budget, or that major economic policies typically originate in the Departments of Treasury, Commerce, Labor, and Agriculture. Yet bureaucratic groups such as these play an important role in defining issues in every political system, and in some they are almost the only agents relied upon by the authorities to provide policy alternatives.

Segments of bureaucracies such as the U.S. Department of Defense or the Soviet Ministry of Heavy Industry may conveniently be labeled *institutional groups.* Like associations, or parties, they have or develop interests and preferences which can be served by the enactment of favorable policies. But unlike associations, they are created by and are responsible to the authorities; they lack the autonomy characteristic of associations.

In a self-interested way, bureaucrats want to have their performance and the performance of their administrative unit judged favorably. In furtherance of this goal, they seek lenient performance criteria and abundant resources. If the demands made upon their subordinates are reasonable, and the human and material resources available are more than adequate, bureaucrats can hope to win favorable judgments from above. If excessive demands are made and low levels of resources are provided, their superiors' expectations might not be met, and low morale and resistance from their personnel might also result. Bureaucrats are likely,

Bureaucrats Make Demands Too; Parkinson's Law

According to C. Northcote Parkinson, "work expands to fill the time alloted for its completion," and people in organizations make work for their subordinates so they can hire more (for whom more "make-work" is created). Thus, "Parkinson's law" leads us to expect that bureaucrats will demand ever bigger staffs and budgets regardless of the need for additional services from their organizations.

Of course Parkinson's "law" is partly facetious. Yet we recognize the reality that administrators do tend to request ever-increasing budgets; they do tend to need just one more secretary, and they almost never underspend their budgets or recommend that any of their operations be terminated.

These tendencies suggest that bureaucrats, together with executives in business and other areas, are strongly committed to maintaining (or even enhancing) their organizations. As they pursue this objective, they make demands upon the authorities. These demands are quite as important as others with which the authorities must deal, particularly since the authorities must rely on the bureaucracy to implement policy. One need only consider the disastrous consequences of a strike or "sick-in" (where most employees call in sick each day until their demands are met) by fire fighters or police officers to realize that public employees can make effective demands on the authorities. Though people in less-sensitive public service jobs might not make as many newspaper headlines as these, they too can lobby effectively for the enhancement of their departments and bureaus.

therefore, to have an interest in lobbying for the allocation of money, personnel, and other resources to their administrative units.

Institutional groups may thus seem to be self-serving, self-interested implementers of Parkinson's law. They can, however, provide representation of broader social interests. In fact, their representation can become analogous to that afforded by associational groups. In seeking resources for itself a Ministry of Agriculture may promote programs which will benefit agricultural industries and farm workers. A Department of Commerce may become an advocate of industrial, marketing, and commercial activities, as well as of public programs which favor them. Thus, the interests and demands of institutional groups can be representative of the interests of segments of society. In hammering out governmental budgets, plans, and programs, departments and bureaus generate and voice their demands and formulate policy alternatives. In doing so, they may serve associations and individual citizens.

In some countries, associational groups are closely controlled or even prohibited by law. Because of their independence, they are viewed as threats to the authorities. In such cases elites may rely upon and proliferate institutional groups. Even sports organizations, children's clubs, labor unions, and professional organizations may be part of the public bureaucracy. Even though they are creatures of government, the interests of their members are not likely to be totally ignored, and they may be of great concern to the authorities. The authorities always need public support; and one way to build support is to take the interests of institutional groups which represent their members into account.

Authorities

In the Soviet Union, authorities play a particularly active role in formulating policy alternatives. Because their system is highly structured, and has many institutional-group interests, an elaborate system of controls has been developed to keep all units responsive to central authority. Multiple lines of communication extend to the Kremlin, not only through the operational bureaucracy, but through the secret police and the Communist party as well. Moreover, separate planning, personnel, and finance ministries gather additional data and monitor performance. The purpose of these arrangements is to weaken the ability of agencies to advance and defend self-serving policy proposals. The Soviet authorities try to leave little issue formulation to others.

To take a less extreme case, British authorities use their party organization not only to sound out popular sentiment, but also to generate support for issues which they advocate or endorse. Demands from associations and other groups are allowed to influence the formulation of issues through regular procedures and channels. Once they are known, weighed, and taken into account, the government articulates a program and defends it.

In the United States, authorities at all levels participate in defining the issues as they actively propose and oppose policy measures. The President listens to the recommendations of the bureaucracy and sounds out public opinion. But in the end he shapes his own program of policy proposals and seeks to win support for it. Representatives, senators, governors, and local officials all seek to promote their own views of the common good and the policies they think are in its interest. Clearly none of these various public officials is willing to allow issues to be developed without their active participation. And where an official has sufficient influence, as in the case of the President, that official typically uses it to define the propositions which will be debated as well as to affect the outcome of debate.

As in the case of policy implementation, control of issue definition by authorities cannot be complete. The same resources used by the bureaucracy to maintain some independence as they execute policy, may also be used to voice preferences. No group of authorities is likely to have the human and material resources necessary to fully control expressions of dissatisfaction or desires for change. All authorities must take into account at least some demands which they have not themselves originated, and which may not be entirely acceptable to them.

Foreign groups: an outside source of demands

Foreign governments are obviously another potential source of demands. Typically, however, foreign demands pose quite different problems for decision makers; other governments are neither understood nor controlled as easily as domestic groups or individuals, and procedures for resolving international disputes are often cumbersome and inadequate. As a result authorities are confronted with greater uncertainty and potential dangers in foreign, as opposed to domestic, affairs.

An example of these differences between domestic and foreign problems can be seen in recent events involving petroleum supplies in the United States. A domestic shortage of gasoline in the summer of 1973 prodded the American President to ask motorists to use restraint in their vacation travel plans. Without any apparent sense of urgency, both the Congress and the administration began to study means by which the nation could best deal with fuel shortages projected for the next decade. This orderly process of problem solving was disrupted a few months later by the refusal of Arab oil-producing nations to sell petroleum to the United States. Fuel and such petroleum derivatives as plastics and fertilizers quickly became scarce, prices soared, a new Federal Energy Administration was created, fuels were allocated among the states, and legal speed limits were lowered to 55 miles per hour.

The contrast between demands generated by domestic problems

and those put forward by foreign groups is sharp in this case. The domestic shortage of the summer produced demands which activated routine decision processes. The winter embargo created an emergency. The domestic problem was, in large part, within the jurisdiction and control of American authorities. The Arab embargo was not.

The ability to act independently, to create severe stress for other political systems, helps to explain why foreign policy issues tend to generate crises more often than do domestic issues. Within a state the authorities, administrators, associations, and individuals must take into account their mutual interest in resolving disputes through processes which support common social goals. Foreign governments, on the other hand, may consider other interests more strongly. Thus, if the goals of one nation greatly conflict with those of another, actions to disrupt the economy and politics of the antagonist may seem to be sound policy, especially when the authorities have adequate or superior military and economic resources vis-à-vis the other party.

In the case of the oil embargo, the Arab nations were not constrained by potentially adverse popular reactions of people in North America, Europe, and Japan. Indeed, their stated aim was to induce hardship and dissatisfaction abroad in order to persuade foreign governments to change their policies toward Israel. Since Arab rulers and citizens were not inconvenienced or penalized by their governments' actions, and since anti-Israeli policies were strongly supported by their people, Arab authorities could act in relative disregard of the resentment of the citizens of industrialized states.

It might be inferred from the above that authorities are relatively free to make trouble for other states. But such an inference would be an oversimplification; not all nations are equally able to make demands upon others. Those nations which have the most power are best able to exercise control over demands made upon them by others, and are able in turn to make effective demands on others. Consequently they can protect their citizens from adverse decisions made by foreign states, and can advance their own interests in the international arena. Prudent authorities seek to build economic and/or military strength, and to use their economic and military resources to forge alliances which will further enhance their power.

In the so-called bipolar world of the 1950s the Soviet Union and the United States were each able to exert tremendous influence over their respective allies. It appeared that either superpower could impose its will, without negotiation or substantial modification. This was particularly evident with the Warsaw Pact countries. Industrial production was diverted from "satellite" states to the U.S.S.R., and a Soviet military presence was used to ensure the compliance of local authorities and citizens with Russian demands. In response to expressions of independence, the Russians sent troops into Hungary in 1956, removed the authorities from power, and assumed control of the government.

In a less obvious way, the dominant economic and military position of the United States was used to shape the military policies and strategies of NATO, and to play a major role in the political and economic development of Western Europe after World War II. And, as polarization of spheres of influence progressed, the two superpowers vied with varying degrees of success to gain the allegiance of the "new" nations of the so-called Third World. Both promises of economic and military aid and threats of economic and military sanctions were utilized to that end.

As these cases show, more powerful nations tend to determine what weaker nations can or will do. Nonetheless, lesser powers sometimes make effective demands—for example, by playing one government off against another. When the United States cut off aid to Egypt for the Aswan Dam project because that country proposed to be "nonaligned," Egypt turned to the Soviet Union. And to protect Egypt from undue Russian influence, Colonel Nasser kept the door open to the West. He was able to obtain economic and military aid without sacrificing his independence. In contrast Castro's Cuba was not so successful in this regard. Cuba became dependent upon Soviet economic aid and military assistance for protection from a hostile superpower 90 miles away.

The demands which nations make upon each other may thus be viewed as attempts to use relatively unrestrained power and influence to protect and promote what each considers to be its vital interests. Lacking a common set of authorities or a central enforcement and implementation structure, the authorities for each nation consider the foreign demands made upon them, the support offered by allies, and formulate their foreign policies in light of domestic situations. In the domestic context, authorities seek to make foreign policy choices which will maximize their ability to meet domestic demands and to minimize stress. The demands made upon other nations reflect strategies to manipulate the international environment in a manner which will enhance support from citizens at home.

An example of this process was the United States reaction to the Arab oil embargo. In response to Israeli requests and to domestic sentiments favoring the continued existence of Israel, the American government sent arms shipments to replenish the Israeli supplies exhausted in the war of October 1973. In doing so, support for Israel was expressed in concrete fashion. But as a price for its aid, the United States also demanded that Israel negotiate with Egypt and Syria, and it urged the Israeli government to grant concessions in the negotiations. At the same time, Egypt and Syria prevailed upon the major oil-producing Arab states to embargo the United States and other nations who expressed sympathy with, or supplied aid to, Israel. The Arab demand on the United States was that support of Israel cease, and the leverage was the promise to renew the shipment of petroleum.

The American authorities responded with domestic measures designed to conserve fuel to meet the impending shortage. Domestic support for the government was widespread even though the Nixon administration was in the midst of its Watergate crisis. The inconveniences and expenses of the situation were attributed to foreign sources rather than to faulty domestic policies. American leverage on the Arabs, in turn, consisted of (1) the threat of potential military intervention, (2) continued aid to Israel, and (3) possible economic assistance to Egypt and Syria. In this context, the demands from Israelis and Arabs could be resolved into two policy alternatives: either direct alignment with Israel and the potential threat of direct military intervention on Israel's side, or a major emphasis upon reducing tension between Israel and its Arab neighbors.

The second option, if successfully pursued, promised to produce less stress than the first. Even a successful emphasis upon force would run the risk of American battle casualties, large expenditures of funds, confrontation with the Soviet Union (as patron of the Arabs), and domestic dissatisfaction with yet another indecisive foreign military engagement.

In dealing with foreign demands, then, the authorities must carefully weigh the demands and supports levied upon them from all relevant foreign states and consider the potential impact of any given policy upon them. But most importantly, maneuvers in international politics must be carefully considered so as to minimize stress in domestic politics. Internal demands and supports must be of paramount concern. The vital interests of the state must be so defined that domestic interests are advanced, or at least protected from adverse foreign actions.

SUMMARY AND CONCLUSION

Issues are formulated from demands which are made upon a political system by elements of its domestic society, by its own organization, or by foreign systems. These demands are accepted, compromised, consolidated, and sometimes rejected as specific policy alternatives are formed with the object of refining issues which can then be decided by the authorities and converted into general policy. Demands are thus the raw materials of issues, just as issues form the bases for decisions.

As the bases for decision, issues must be founded upon accurate information. As changes occur in the domestic and foreign environments of a political system, demands upon and support of the system change, and issues must be formulated and redefined to maintain the effectiveness of the authorities. Demands may change gradually, as is usually the case with ongoing programs and policies. Or they may change suddenly and assume crisis proportions, as when a foreign state issues an unexpected ultimatum. Issues usually develop over time. They may result from the consequences of past policies, the actions of foreign states, or areas of social life which have not previously been subject to general policy control.

In Chapter 2 we began our discussion of policy processes with decision making and have now ended with the process by which the issues are defined. However, issue definition could as easily have been the point of departure, since the processes of making and enforcing policy decisions are closely interwoven. Policies are made in response to demands which are partly reactions to the effects of past policies. This circular pattern, in which new decisions are prompted by public reaction to previous ones, is a form of feedback. The authorities are able to adjust their policies and their means of policy implementation in response to new information. As soon as the study of politics and policymaking is begun, the need to understand relationships between administrators, the public, authorities, and foreign powers becomes apparent. These actors cannot be understood in isolation from each other.

As we proceed to the next two chapters, it will become apparent that political processes must be understood in the context of the cultures in which they operate. The attitudes of citizens and rulers and their patterns of communication must be considered if particular social and political systems are to be adequately analyzed. Decision processes, policy implementation, and the development of issues are all deeply affected by political socialization and communication patterns.

SUGGESTED READINGS

Beer, Samuel: *British Politics in a Collectivist Age* (New York: Knopf, 1966). An impressive study of the interplay between British social conditions and their political processes over the last several centuries.

Duverger, Maurice: *Political Parties: Their Organization and Activity in the Modern State* (New York: Wiley, 1961). A comparative, analytical framework for the study of political parties.

Easton, David: *A Systems Analysis of Political Life* (New York: Wiley, 1965). Easton's most comprehensive statement of his input-output model of a political system. The analysis of the development of policy issues is particularly detailed and thoughtful.

Skilling, Gordon, and Franklyn Griffiths (eds.): *Interest Groups in Soviet Politics* (Princeton, N.J.: Princeton, 1971). This is an important study of post-Stalinist policymaking in the Soviet Union. The contributors generally agree that the authorities now are significantly restrained by speakers for a variety of interests as they make policies.

Truman, David: *The Governmental Process: Political Interests and Public Opinion* (New York: Knopf, 1951). A classic statement of the importance of groups in the political process.

CHAPTER FIVE

POLITICAL SOCIALIZATION

OVERVIEW This chapter deals with patterns whereby we develop political awareness from early childhood to adulthood. It also discusses the parts played by groups and organizations as they influence the development of political orientations.

Take care to note the general pattern of development which is outlined: a child develops *feelings* about political matters before developing accurate *information* or the *ability to think critically* about politics. This pattern is described as development from *affective* to *cognitive* and *evaluative* orientations. The developmental pattern is important. It suggests that adult political attitudes and orientations may be largely shaped in childhood. Early experiences lead us to feel more positively or negatively about various aspects of the political system, and in adolescence we acquire varying amounts of information and the ability to think critically about political leaders and their policies.

Three main categories of socializing agent are identified: primary groups, secondary groups, and reference groups. Schools are treated as a combination of primary and secondary groups, and are in a somewhat special category.

Note that the family is of prime importance in the political socialization process, but that other groups are also influential. The characteristics of each type of socializing agent should be carefully noted, as should the particular potentialities of each type of agent for influencing the socialization of individuals.

It is difficult to overemphasize the importance of socialization processes. So many of them are beyond the political control of most governments that rulers must attune themselves to citizen attitudes more than shape them. Political socialization is an important influence in creating unity or fomenting division in society.

Be sure that you understand the following terms:

Cognitive
Affective
Primary group
Secondary group
Reference group

LEARNING OBJECTIVES

After you have studied this chapter, you should be able to:

1. Identify the pattern in which affective, cognitive, and evaluative orientations develop as individuals mature.
2. Explain the role and relative importance of primary groups, secondary groups, and reference groups, and the schools in influencing the political attitudes of citizens.
3. Explain the significance of political socialization for the likely effectiveness or ineffectiveness of public officials.

From the discussion of decision making, policy implementation, and issue development in Chapters 2 to 4 it should be apparent that public officials must operate in clear recognition of the attitudes of the population they attempt to govern. To obtain compliance with their policies, politicians must formulate rules which are acceptable to the people who are expected to obey them. In enforcing rules, politicians must use procedures which are considered fair by the citizenry. And democratic systems must take account of the demands of their citizens and the means they use to bring pressure to bear upon the government. The prevailing attitudes of the general population are one of the chief factors which condition the operations of the government.

The question we approach in this chapter is, "How do people learn the social values and attitudes which affect political life?" We are interested in this question partly because there is a remarkable stability of national culture over time. Descriptions of the American political life-style which were written 150 years ago capture much of the flavor of the contemporary American style. The same is true of England, France, Spain, and most of the other older nations of the globe. Such stability in national life-style helps to explain the persistent characteristics of the national politics of each nation. The United States Constitution, for instance, has retained its basic form for nearly 200 years. The British Constitution has been gradually and peacefully modified as the British form of government has changed, bit by bit, from an almost absolute monarchy to a constitutional democracy. The national politics of France is persistent in another way. It has remained notorious for its propensity to change constitutional arrangements and for broad swings in political temper. And Spain continues to be ruled by a succession of strong men, usually of military background, as for the most part do Spain's former colonies with similar cultures.

This persistence in cultural patterns and political style exists because societies are able to pass their major values and attitudes from one generation to the next in essentially intact form. But this should not surprise us. Every human society devotes large amounts of energy to raising children to take their place in existing adult society. In so doing, children are taught to behave as adults believe they should, which generally proves to be the way which the adults themselves were taught during childhood. If such training is successful, societies reproduce their most important characteristics in each generation of offspring, and the continuity of social and political patterns is made likely.

The study of the persistence of cultural values has both broad social and individual aspects. The broad social aspect is sometimes called "cultural transmission" since it is the process of transmitting major cultural characteristics from generation to generation. When discussing the way in which individual children come to acquire the major characteristics of their culture, however, it is customary to focus on the individual and to speak of the "socialization" of the child. Socialization thus refers to the way in which children, who are born without social attitudes, learn to live in the society in which they are raised. Political socialization is a part of the larger socialization process. It is that part which relates to the political life of the community or to what is sometimes called "political culture."

The thrust of the study of political socialization is thus twofold. First it is concerned with the process of transmission of cultural characteristics from generation to generation. Secondly, in order to understand the transmission process, the study of political socialization attempts to identify the patterns whereby children gain an awareness of politics and also the ways in which adult attitudes are maintained or changed through later life.

DEVELOPMENT OF POLITICAL ATTITUDES

In assessing the potential effectiveness of any government, it is useful to know as much as possible about such things as (1) the amount of support citizens give their officials, (2) their willingness to comply with public policy decisions, and (3) their expectations of, and demands upon, government. In their attempts to understand these things investigators have studied citizens' political attitudes: their hostility or alienation from government, their loyalties or allegiance, and the level of their interest in politics, among others. Such attitudes tell a lot about the amount of support political leaders can expect for their policies and about the amount of social energy which can be mobilized in attempts to implement those policies.

Childhood socialization in America

Studies of the way in which children learn to be citizens indicate that they come to have *feelings* about political matters well before they gain extensive information about the political system or make critical judgments on public matters. Their first awareness of the political order is generally tied to symbols such as the national flag and in the American case to the Statue of Liberty and Uncle Sam. Only as they grow older do young people learn what politicians do, and it is only in adolescence that they typically form judgments about specific politicians and their policies. The young child thus forms early loyalties and only later gains information about politics and forms judgments about government.[1]

---

[1]The following discussion is based largely upon the findings of David Easton and Jack Dennis, *Children in the Political System* (New York: McGraw-Hill, 1969); Robert D. Hess and Judith V. Torney, *The Development of Political Attitudes in Children* (Chicago: Aldine, 1967); and Fred I. Greenstein, *Children and Politics* (New Haven, Conn.: Yale, 1965).

Early attitudes of American schoolchildren tend to be idealistic, positive, and vague. Between the ages of six and nine, American children generally exhibit affectionate loyalty toward the President of their country, perceiving him as a benevolent figure, much like a father. They have little knowledge of the President's duties, and do not identify him as a political partisan. Fred I. Greenstein found, in a pioneering study of New Haven schoolchildren, that in the early grades youngsters could identify the President and their local mayor, and though they had already learned to label themselves as Democrats or Republicans, they did not tie these labels to political leaders. The young New Haven children gave overwhelming approval to the President, 92 percent rating him as "very good" or "good" at a time when the Gallup poll reported that only 58 percent of American adults similarly approved of President Eisenhower.[2]

The Political Awareness of a Six-Year-Old

Informal interview with the six-year-old daughter of one of the authors, March 1970:

Father: Do you know about the flag?
Laura: That's what's in our school yard.
Father: What kind of flag is it?
Laura: American flag.
Father: What does the American flag mean?
Laura: That's the country we live in.
Father: Who is the boss of our country?
Laura: (Pause) Uh, the Vice President?
Father: No, he works for the President. Do you know the President?
Laura: I know President Nixon.
Father: Do you like President Nixon?
Laura: Yes.
Father: Why do you like him?
Laura: I don't know.
Father: Do you know any other bosses like President Nixon?
Laura: (Pause) Uh, Grandpa.
Father: Any more?

---

[2]Fred I. Greenstein, "The Benevolent Leader: Children's Images of Political Authority," *American Political Science Review*, vol. 54, pp. 934–943, 1960.

Laura: You're a boss
Father: Any other bosses?
Laura: Well, teachers and baby-sitters.
Father: Any more?
Laura: Mommy bosses me sometimes.
Father: Do you know any more bosses?
Laura: No.
Father: What else do you know about America?
Laura: I don't know.
Father: Do you know any other Presidents besides President Nixon?
Laura: Well, (pause) I know President Kennedy.
Father: Do you like President Kennedy?
Laura: Yes.
Father: Do you like anyone who is President?
Laura: Of course!
Father: Why?
Laura: I don't know. Maybe because they're Presidents.
Father: Do you know any other Presidents?
Laura: I don't think so.

Like other six-year-old Americans, Laura felt positively about the President, but she had very little information on which to base her feelings. At six, her main world centered at home and in school.

These early perceptions of political authority are clearly more emotional than intellectual. Such orientations are commonly labeled *affective* (from the same root as the word "affection"), and they probably spring less from systematic education or indoctrination than from casual contact with remarks by adults and with the television and radio. Further, it is significant that these early emotional ties to political leaders are on much the same level as reverence for the national flag. The President, like the flag, seems to operate as a *symbol* of the national community in the minds of these children; only later in life is he seen more concretely and critically. Their earliest political perceptions, then, seem to be tied to a developing sense of loyalty and patriotism.

As children mature, their level of political information rises. They come to understand more about the duties of political leaders and to recognize the partisan character of politicians' roles to a greater extent. Thus, in addition to affective orientations, children begin to accumulate a reservoir of facts, or *cognitive* orientations, which shape their evaluations of politics. Older children are more prone to criticize political leaders such as the President on the basis of what they have learned about their performance. They are also more aware of the wider range of public officials such as members of Congress, state legislators, and judges.

Another general pattern of development in young American children is that they become aware of the policy outputs of the government earlier than the processes whereby citizens might influence political decisions. The earliest input device of which children are aware is voting in elections. But at first these partisan contests seem to be roughly similar to sports contests in the minds of young children. Cheering for Democrats or Republicans is apparently not much different for them than cheering for their hometown football team. In a national study of schoolchildren, David Easton and Jack Dennis found that in the fourth grade only 16 percent felt that it was highly possible for citizens to influence the government, while 56 percent did not think it likely that people could. By the eighth grade the percentages were reversed with 56 percent feeling optimistic about the potential for citizen influence on policy and only 17 percent remaining doubtful.[3] Given the relative dependence of children on adults, such a pattern is probably to be expected. Their lives are closely regulated by authority figures, which include their parents as well as police officers and teachers. Only as they approach adolescence do children usually recognize that as they become adults there will be ways for them to influence political authority.

The crucial years in developing more adult political attitudes, at least in the United States, appear to be those between the ages of eleven and thirteen. During this preadolescent period, children come to be more questioning of authority, their knowledge of their community and its politics grows markedly, and they begin to develop political partisanship based upon this new information. We say, then, that the early *affective,* or emotional, orientations of children are modified by their increased *cognitive* abilities—their capacity to assimilate and organize information. The childhood evaluations of political leaders which linked them to patriotic symbols give way to more critical judgments concerning political perfor-

[3]David Easton and Jack Dennis, "The Child's Acquisition of Regime Norms: Political Efficacy," *American Political Science Review,* vol. 61, p. 33. 1967.

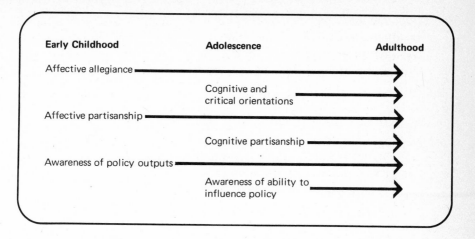

Figure 5-1 General pattern of development of political attitudes in America.

mance. While basic patriotic attachments remain intact, specific politicians are no longer so closely identified with national symbols.

Later adolescent years are mainly a period of further development of the attitudes which children have basically acquired by the age of thirteen. From ages fourteen through eighteen the firmly established tendencies of preadolescence are more fully developed, but no dramatic changes in the types of attitudes held have been observed in research which has been conducted to date. Evidently, major modifications of political awareness must await the entrance of the individual into the arena of active participation in adult society.

Young adults in America have not learned all they will ever know about politics even though their basic dispositions are set. Adult attitudes are susceptible to modifications on the basis of experience gained through working and living in the community, and through perceiving the effects of public policy on personal life. The young adult typically has a basic loyalty to country, ingrained in the earliest childhood years. He or she usually has developed a moderate degree of partisanship, having tentatively decided in favor of the Democrats or the Republicans (though adults under thirty tend to be more politically independent than those who are older). He or she also has a rough notion of how the American system works, and holds public officialdom responsible for war and peace, hard times and prosperity.

Adult attitudes tend to be most changeable on particular issues or political personalities. Their affection for country, gained at an early age, is difficult to challenge or to change. They learn to distinguish somewhat between patriotic support for the nation and qualified support or disapproval of particular policies and leaders.

AGENTS OF SOCIALIZATION

"What is the Younger Generation coming to?"

"How did my boy go wrong?"

"I didn't raise my little girl to be a tramp."

Such complaints about youth, by adults, are common to every historical age and every geographical place. Parents seem always and everywhere to expect that their children will believe as they do, act as they think they should, and live lives similar to those of their elders. There is also a tendency for the older generation to believe that family training is the crucial element in determining the way that children "turn out."

To an extent, these parental feelings have a valid base. The influence of the family is indeed great in determining what children come to believe and how they behave. But there are other influences which shape young attitudes as well. As a child moves out of the narrow world of the family home, new individuals and groups, not necessarily in agreement with his or her parents, come to affect attitudes and behavior. As the child leaves the cozy bosom of the family, there comes an awareness of the broader range of sometimes conflicting expectations which exist in the larger society in which he or she must live.

Major agents—such as the family, friends, schoolmates, teachers, fellow workers, clubs, churches, unions, and ethnic groups—which influence the development of political attitudes may be conveniently divided into three general types: primary groups, secondary groups, and reference groups. *Primary* groups include the family peer groups (friends and personal acquaintances), and local organizations (church groups, social clubs, etc.) wherein people interact on a face-to-face, personal basis. *Secondary* groups are those, such as labor unions, professional associations, national clubs, and others, where large numbers of persons are involved with each other in a common enterprise, but do not usually know each other personally. *Reference* groups are not really groups in one sense; that is, they are not formalized or organized as secondary groups generally are. When an individual is identified as Negro, white, Chicano, working-class, middle-class, Protestant, etc., a reference group is utilized for placement in society. Reference groups are socially defined categories of persons which can shape our attitudes and behavior, and which sometimes have important political consequences.

Primary groups

Of all the agents of political socialization, it would seem to be the family which has the most pronounced and consistent role in molding attitudes. Repeatedly, researchers find that children adopt similar attitudes toward the political community, regime norms, and even toward particular political parties as their parents. This familial transmission of fundamental political values from one generation to another provides an element of stability and continuity in the political life of nations. Since sons and daughters generally tend to agree with mothers and fathers in political matters, it is difficult for societies to make radical breaks with the past. The home, in this sense, is a major conserving force in politics.

Here are a few examples of the observed power of the family in molding political attitudes:

1. Children from most American homes express loyalty and affection for the country and its leaders, but children from homes where parents feel alienated from the American government have a lower opinion of it.[4]
2. American children generally support the same political party as their parents.[5]
3. Children from American families with higher social status, like their parents, feel more able to influence the decisions of public officials and feel more involved in politics.[6]
4. Both Jamaican and American children from homes where no father is present are less interested in politics, and in both countries the economic status of the parents influences political attitudes of the children.[7]

[4]Greenstein, "The Benevolent Leader," op cit.; and Dean Jaros, Herbert Hirsch, and Frederic J. Fleron, Jr., "The Malevolent Leader: Political Socialization in an American Subculture," *American Political Science Review,* vol. 62, pp. 564–575, 1968.

[5]M. Kent Jennings and Richard G. Niemi, "The Transmission of Political Values from Parent to Child," *American Political Science Review,* vol. 62, pp. 169–184, 1968.

[6]David Easton and Jack Dennis, op. cit.; and Joan E. Laurence and Harry M. Scoble, "Ideology and Consensus among Children of the Metropolitan Socioeconomic Elite," *Western Political Quarterly,* vol. 22, pp. 151–162, 1969.

[7]Kenneth P. Langton and David A. Karns, "The Relative Influence of the Family, Peer Group and School in the Development of Political Efficacy," *Western Political Quarterly,* vol. 22, pp. 813–826, 1969.

5. In the newer nations, old tribal attitudes toward authority are still transmitted to children through their parents.[8]

Study after study further refines our knowledge of the influence of family in the socialization process, but it is already quite clear that the attitudes of parents toward things political have great influence on the political development of their children.

The family is a primary group because it involves intimate, continuing face-to-face contact between its members. It is probably the most intimate of human associations, but there are others, particularly peer groups of friends and work associates, which also involve close personal contact. Any primary group will have strong influence on the attitudes, political and otherwise, of its members. Thus, while the family may be seen as the predominant socializing force, other primary groups rank a close second in influence, and the impact of the family on the later socialization of the child and on the adult must be seen against the background of peer-group influence.

As children grow older, they have increasing contact with people outside their homes. As they enter school, they must learn to relate to teachers and to other students. If their teachers and schoolmates have attitudes similar to those evidenced by their parents, entrance into this new situation will very likely strengthen their acceptance of parental values. But where their school contacts are with persons from different backgrounds, children must learn to adjust their attitudes in order to get along in a more complicated world.

Both children and adults can be influenced away from the attitudes learned in the home when their peer groups do not have the same basic orientations as their parents. In investigating the party loyalties of American adults, Herbert McCloskey and Harold Dahlgren found that when families stay in close contact after children are grown, the party preferences of the parents have very strong influences on the party loyalties of the children. Likewise, children stay loyal to the parental party when their life-style remains similar to that of their mothers and fathers. However, when distance increases between parents and adult children, and when children move into new occupations and new life circumstances, the now grown offspring are strongly influenced by their peer groups and more readily switch their support away from the party of their parents.[9]

[8]Robert A. Levine, "The Internalization of Political Values in Stateless Societies," *Human Organization*, vol. 19, pp. 51–58, 1960.

[9]Herbert McClosky and Harold E. Dahlgren, "Primary Group Influence on Party Loyalty," *American Political Science Review*, vol. 53, pp. 757–776, 1959.

Kenneth Langton found that childhood peer groups exert similar influences both in Jamaica and in the United States. In particular, he found that when lower-class children go to school with only those from the same economic background, their lower-class attitudes toward politics become stronger. However, when lower-class children are mixed with middle- and upper-class students, they tend to adopt the views of their high-status schoolmates.[10]

The strong influence of primary groups such as the family and peer groups is typically explained in terms of the deep personal attachments that form in them. When people associate intimately and affectionately, they look to each other for approval and hence for guides to behavior. The expectations of the groups thus come to affect the way individual members express themselves and behave. Through imitating the attitudes and actions of those we respect and like, we come to be more like them.

Secondary groups

Secondary groups are less crucial in determining the attitudes which an individual adopts than are primary groups. Yet the influence of labor unions, professional associations, and other less personal groups should not be underestimated. This is particularly true when the influence of secondary groups on peer groups is considered. Peer groups of pupils, carpenters, or doctors are hardly immune from the influence exerted by the broader association to which they belong. Labor organizations and professional groups take definite stands on political questions and lend their support to specific policies and candidates. And even more crucially, they help to shape the general life-style of their members, encouraging particular patterns of behavior which are influential for the activities of the smaller peer groups which form within their broad, less personal boundaries.

Secondary associations exert their influence on political attitudes in a more indirect fashion than do peer groups and families. Union members may have personal encounters with members of their local, but they seldom are as acutely conscious of, or as attached to, the national organization. Medical doctors, professors, and lawyers typically belong to associations, but seldom encounter them except through the mails or at conventions. The larger organization is thus remote, but local groups of members of the organization tend to know each other on a more daily

[10]Kenneth P. Langton, *Political Socialization* (New York: Oxford University Press, 1969), chap. 5.

basis. And peer groups of workers, doctors, lawyers, and professors tend to be composed of people holding similar kinds of jobs, social status, financial interests, and general life-styles. The secondary group, then, both reflects and potentially influences the attitudes of its members. When the American Federation of Labor takes a stand on political issues, the local unions tend to follow its lead, and groups of friends within the locals tend to carry the union's stand over into other primary group contacts. Likewise, if enough members of an association become dissatisfied with the policies of its leadership, they may split off to form a new secondary group, or they may attempt to get new leadership or introduce resolutions at national meetings, or they may try in any number of ways to bring their association's positions into line with local views.

The very fact that professional meetings of academics such as political scientists, psychologists, sociologists, and historians have recently been marked by grass-roots movements to influence association policy, testifies to the importance which members attach to their secondary associations. Even the staid associations of American medical doctors and lawyers have been divided over political issues in recent years, illustrating the same point. Labor unions are in a class by themselves for

---

Which Associations Are Most Influential?

The general rule is that associations which are formed for nonpolitical purposes tend to be more effective. This has been reconfirmed in a recent study of influential groups in Canada and the United States.

Robert Presthus found that in both countries groups specifically organized to promote a cause or ideology ("altruisitic groups") are less able to affect public policy than are business, professional, and welfare groups whose political aims are not primary. Interestingly, labor organizations, too, were found to be relatively less effective in this study. We can only surmise that perhaps organized labor is more openly political on a broad spectrum of topics, whereas business and professional groups tend to focus more narrowly upon measures which directly affect them. [Robert Presthus, *Elites in the Policy Process* (London: Cambridge, 1974).]

this sort of activity, and have been splintering and rejoining forces for years over both internal organizational policies and national political questions.

Secondary groups thus link the concerns and activities of peer groups to larger interests in society. Plumbers do not join a trade union in order to receive political instruction; but when the union takes a position on a political matter, the stand of the association tends to become the position of the small local groups within it. Through influencing the tenor of discussion in peer groups, a voluntary association can help to mold a more unified outlook among its members. This influence can be found in associations ranging from early childhood membership in youth groups, or in the student body of a school, to adult associations ranging through churches, unions, professional associations, and political action groups.

Schools

Schools occupy a special and complex place in the process of political socialization since they function as *both primary and secondary agents.* Within schools, peer groups are formed which give students cues to socially acceptable attitudes and behavior. These student peer groups are among the earliest and most potent socializing forces outside the parental home. On the other hand, all students in a large school do not come to know each other personally. Loyalty to the alma mater in the broader sense is much like membership in a trade or professional association. Further, student contact with teachers is not as intimate as contact with peer groups or parents, but it is closer than the relationship which students and adults have with authorities such as mayors, councillors, legislators, governors, bureaucrats, or police officers.

Since schools are usually financed by the government, they are particularly susceptible to political influence and are one agent of socialization which can be readily used in attempts to shape attitudes in desired directions. Compared with the schools, families are difficult to control; and though totalitarian governments exert a high degree of control over secondary associations, democratic governments grant their citizens the right of freedom to associate voluntarily. But most governments make school attendance compulsory. Schools, then, are generally the agency of political socialization most susceptible to governmental control or influence, and governments seem to believe they are effective. Even in democratic states the government usually exercises some control over the structure of the school system, establishes guidelines for curricula, and is involved in the hiring and firing of educational personnel.

Contrary to what might be expected, the school curriculum does not seem to be most influential in shaping political attitudes. Studies of American high school students indicate that civics courses do not noticeably affect student interest in politics, their loyalty to the nation, or their feelings of political competence.

What Good Are Civics Courses?

In a nationwide study of high school students in the United States, Kenneth P. Langton and M. Kent Jennings concluded that "there is a lack of evidence that the civics curriculum has a significant effect on the political orientations of the great majority of American high school students."

The exception to this generalization was the case of Negro students. Black students from homes where the parents were less well educated changed their attitudes toward politics so that they became more like white students after taking a civics course. Black students from better-educated families showed a different effect. They tended to have attitudes which were less patriotic and less positive about political participation after taking a civics class than before.

Langton and Jennings had no final explanation for this. They did argue, however, that "because of cultural and social status differences, the Negro students are more likely to encounter new or conflicting perspectives and content. The more usual case for Whites is a further layering of familiar materials which, by and large, repeat the message from other past and contemporary sources." They thus emphasize that for a minority subculture, civics courses may serve as a homogenizer of political attitudes. [Kenneth P. Langton and M. Kent Jennings, "Political Socialization and the High School Civics Curriculum in the United States," *American Political Science Review*, vol. 62, pp. 852–867, 1968.]

Apparently the general pattern of school life, including student peer groups, the manner in which students are encouraged to achieve, and the type of campus political activity, has more effect than does the content of specific courses. Urie Bronfenbrenner, in an insightful study of Russian and American schools, explains how the schools of each of these two countries help to develop adults who can relate to the social and political system. In Russia, schools are structured in such a way as to teach young people to work as members of groups. Students compete for the teacher's favor as members of the classroom row in which they sit, and individual failures are criticized for their effect on the standing of the group. Peer groups in Russian schools discipline themselves in order to encourage each member of the team to do his or her best for the common good. Teachers enforce discipline through student courts, which they advise. At every turn, the Russian student is encouraged to submit to the social peer-group pressure as directed by adult authorities. Russian educational experience is thus designed to make students cooperative members of a centrally directed socialist state. The good of the group becomes the child's (and subsequently the adult's) guide to proper attitudes and behavior.

Bronfenbrenner finds that American schools, in contrast, train students to compete with each other on an individual basis for personal rather than group rewards. Individuals, not rows or classrooms, are graded and disciplined, and the teacher enforces the rules. American children are thus taught to compete with each other for the favors of the educational system. They come to see their own performance as something divorced from the group, and to view the teacher as a semifriendly authority with whom they must deal cleverly in order to gain personal satisfaction. The American classroom is thus the laboratory of a larger society in which people must compete for personal rewards and must deal with the political system in such a fashion as to maximize their personal fortunes.[11]

In addition to structured classroom activities, schools influence the learning of social and political attitudes through bringing students into contact with each other on the playground and in social activities. The school is generally the first place where a child gains experience with peer groups outside of the family. Where peer-group activity is closely controlled, as in the Soviet Union, the authorities gain powerful leverage over child development. In more unstructured systems, student peer groups may function to sensitize the child to the attitudes of other social classes, religions, and ethnic groups. We have already noted the effect which mixing students from different economic backgrounds can have in imparting middle- and upper-class values to lower-class students. It is

[11]Urie Bronfenbrenner, *Two Worlds of Childhood: U.S. and U.S.S.R.* (New York: Russell Sage, 1970).

reasonable to assume that where students of many different backgrounds meet in school, they come to develop lasting patterns of reaction to the diverse groups which make up their society.

To summarize, schools are generally the most convenient agency for governments to use in any attempt to influence the socialization process. School curricula are not, however, as influential as other aspects of school life. The way in which a student learns to gain approval and to relate to peers will probably have more to do with the kind of citizen the student becomes than will courses in national history and politics. Further, the informal peer groups which students form have the potential of either reinforcing or modifying the attitudes which the child learns at home. Schools are training grounds for future citizens, less for the bookish teachings they impart than for the way of living which is learned there.

Various studies have found that the amount of formal schooling people receive is closely related to their level of political awareness and participation. Gabriel Almond and Sidney Verba, for instance, concluded that their systematic study of five nations showed "education to be the most important determinant of political attitudes."[12] And in a study of six of the newer nations, Alex Inkeles found that "formal education is clearly the most consistently powerful influence" in producing active citizenship.[13] On the basis of such findings, it would be easy to conclude that the level of citizen participation could be raised significantly if every man, woman, and child were given a college education. There are, however, other considerations which cast doubt upon this proposition.

For one thing, it has been found—in the United States, at least—that students from higher-income families and those with higher intelligence quotients are likely both to receive more schooling and to display more interest in and knowledge of politics.[14] This raises the distinct possibility that it is not education so much as family background and native intelligence that produce active citizens. The same factors that keep students in school may also, independently, make them politically concerned. Thus, while education may have a major impact on citizen development, it is not clear that all classes of people respond to schooling in the same

[12]Gabriel A. Almond and Sidney Verba, *The Civic Culture* (New York: Little, Brown, 1965), p. 370.

[13]Alex Inkeles, "Participant Citizenship in Six Developing Countries," *American Political Science Review,* vol. 63, p. 1132, 1969.

[14]Cf. S. K. Harvey and T. G. Harvey, "Adolescent Political Outlooks: The Effects of Intelligence as an Independent Variable," *Midwest Journal of Political Science,* vol. 14, pp. 565–595, 1970; Langton and Jennings, op. cit.

ways, nor is it at all certain to what degree formal education, rather than intelligence and family background, is decisive in the determination of political attitudes.

Reference groups

Reference groups are social categories which people use to define themselves and their neighbors. They are not necessarily organized, and can rest on a wide variety of distinctions between classes of individuals. For instance, women's liberation is based upon a reference-group distinction grounded in sexual differences perceived to be important. For the ardent feminist, human beings are divided into two major groups—male and female—which have great meaning for her social attitudes and actions. Reference groups may be based upon race, as in the distinction between black and white Americans. They may be based upon ethnicity as in the case of immigrant groups and their offspring in the United States, or European Gypsies or African tribal divisions. Or, as with American Jews, a combination of ethnicity, race, and religion may serve as a basis for definition of a reference group.

Reference groups may serve as a basis for either dividing or unifying people. Epithets like "nigger," "kike," "wop," "spick," or "redneck" arise from stereotyping whole groups of people on the basis of socially defined reference groups and making them objects of derision and discrimination. On the other hand, members of these groups may take great pride in their socially defined status, and the reference group may serve to unite them with their "brothers" and "sisters" to whom they are not related by blood. Beyond this, national political parties may be seen as one form of broad, unifying reference group, since mass parties such as the American Democrats and Republicans do not have exhaustive formal membership rolls. Individuals need only consider themselves to be aligned with such a party in order to utilize it as a reference for their own definition of themselves and of national politics. Even the concept of national loyalty, which is a unifying force underlying the cohesion of modern states, can be seen as a form of reference group. In defining ourselves as American or English, Lebanese or Egyptian, Japanese or Filipino, we find a meaningful basis for distinguishing members of our own national community from other peoples of the world.

Individuals generally become aware of reference-group categories through interactions with various social groups outside the home. Consequently, reference-group identification tends to develop during and after the years when a child is in school. There are exceptions, of course. We have seen that basic national loyalties can be implanted in the home. And some groups make concerted efforts to teach young children that they are different from the rest of society by virtue of race, religion, or national origin. When preschool Negro children are taught the principles of "black pride" in special schools, when Jewish children are taught to separate themselves from Gentiles, when Mexican-American youths are indoctrinated concerning the horrors of the "Anglo-world," reference-group consciousness comes very early in life. Generally, however, individuals become conscious of reference-group identification as they learn, from experience, that people in society are given different treatment according to rather subtly defined characteristics.

Intense reference-group consciousness can have major social consequences and can produce a broad range of political responses. The news of the assassination of Martin Luther King triggered riots and racial disturbances in major American cities and fostered an outpouring of grief from blacks who knew him only as a symbol of their socially referenced status. Jews who identify with the trials of the State of Israel may have no firsthand knowledge of the people living there, but they identify with a broadly defined group of people in which they include themselves. These intense reference-group identifications are based upon symbolic identification with people who are seen to be brothers, even though they may be personally unknown to the individual, and even though there may be no objective economic or political grounds upon which the reference group might base its unity.

Most reference-group orientations are not so intense as those used in the illustrations above. In this country, at least, people do not generally feel strongly about their economic class; who, until the "silent majority" appeared, went for "Middle America"? Most people are not unduly influenced by their self-identification as "Easterners," or "Midwesterners," or even "Southerners"—though there is a special pride there. Though people in the United States have recently divided sharply along reference-group lines, the general proposition nevertheless holds true for most times and places; reference groups do not generally provide specific orientations for individuals; they do not shape the attitudes which condition the normal give-and-take of politics to the extent that primary and secondary groups do.

Currently, American politics are greatly affected by secondary groups based upon reference-group identifications such as race and sex. Normally, however, reference groups serve mainly to reinforce or at least to complement the secondary-group identifications of citizens. In Britain, this may be seen in the striking chain of orientations characteristic of the typical Labour party member who is also a manual laborer. David Butler and Donald Stokes have shown that 73 percent of union members identify themselves with the Labour party, and 78 percent of unskilled and 72 percent of skilled manual laborers voted for Labour in 1964.[15] For such persons, their primary-group relationship with other manual laborers is reinforced by their secondary association with the union, which is in turn reinforced by identification of the Labour party with policies which are supposedly of benefit to the laboring class. Reference-group identification is here a part of the total social and political identification of the individual. As a laborer, the individual can identify with the laboring class peer group, represented in the political system as a whole by the larger association of the Labour party. This general self-image as a laborer leads the individual to find satisfaction in political support of intermediate organizations and reference groups which are also identified with laboring interest.

In the United States, the Democratic party has commanded substantial labor support for much the same reasons; but even more strikingly, that party has since 1960 drawn nearly unanimous (over 90 percent) support from black voters in presidential elections. From primary groups in black neighborhoods, through secondary groups concerned with Negro rights, through the Democratic party, black Americans have seemed, for a time, to find a consistent channel of identification with one of the major forces shaping government policy. In this case, as in the case of laborers in Britain, reference-group identifications have worked to reinforce secondary and primary groups so as to produce a firmer sense of the part which the individual plays in the larger political process.

Most individuals have a number of reference groups with which they identify, but only some of them have political meaning for them and not all reference groups are so obviously relevant to the political process as the above examples might indicate. In the United States, Protestants tend to be more heavily Republican in partisan leanings than Catholics or Jews. There is no clear indication, however, that this reference-group identification is crucial to voters in defining their sense of where their interests lie in the political process. Rather, it would seem that the Republicanism of Protestants stems more from their generally higher class status and from the historical development of the nation, that Protestant regions of the country grew to support the Republican party

[15]David Butler and Donald Stokes, *Political Change in Britain: Forces Shaping Electoral Choice* (New York: St. Martin's, 1969), pp. 155–157.

for reasons other than religion. Likewise, women tend to be more Republican than men, but the Republican party seems to attract slightly more women, less because it promotes feminist causes than because its more conservative stands appeal more strongly to women.

SUMMARY AND CONCLUSION

Viewed from the perspective of the individual citizen, political socialization is the process whereby affective, cognitive, and evaluative orientations toward politics are developed. From the broader social view, it is the process whereby the values of one generation are passed on to the next.

Children develop affective ties to their community and nation by their sixth year, and become cognitively aware and evaluatively critical as they grow into early adolescence. Political experiences and altered social situations can change the attitudes of adults, but most people retain the orientations learned in childhood without major modifications. This is particularly true of deep loyalties to the community, though commitments to political parties and other secondary groups also tend to persist. Attitudes toward individual public officials and particular policies are more easily changed.

Primary groups—family and peers—are most decisive in the formation of political attitudes. An individual whose friends and associates are of the same basic social background is likely to adopt and to hold his family's attitudes without much change. When the views of parents and peers conflict, or when different peer groups have diverse orientations, a person may adopt views counter to those learned at home. For example, mixing school children from upper-, middle-, and lower-class homes is considered to be a potential means to alter the political attitudes of the lower classes.

For most people, their affiliations with secondary groups complement the views of their primary groups. They reinforce each other, providing a coherent perspective whereby small groups of citizens can focus upon broader aspects of political life. Secondary groups are usually formed upon the basis of commonly held, concrete interests of their memberships, such as their occupations or professions. They are, therefore, different from reference groups which are more usually defined along class, racial, religious, or ethnic lines. Both secondary groups and reference groups are potentially divisive. The practical basis of secondary groups, however, tends to make disputes between them more susceptible to compromise. Reference-group conflict, on the other hand, is potentially more explosive, as ghetto riots in the United States or Muslim uprisings in India will attest. When secondary groups are institutional, as against associational, they are clearly more susceptible to political control than are reference groups.

Through political socialization the values of parents, peer groups, and reference groups are transmitted to children. Continuity between generations of citizens and authorities is thereby promoted. Where social relations are tranquil, continuance of tranquility is promoted. Where conflict between groups exists, resocialization of conflicting attitudes perpetuates the basis of the conflict. Cultural transmission through socialization thus perpetuates both unifying and divisive characteristics of society.

The early development of emotional ties to one's country, government, religion, race, or ethnic group is of especially great consequence for society. These early emotional ties generally persist into adulthood. They therefore largely define the loyalties of citizens. If strong loyalties to nation are widely shared, the task of gaining compliance to national policies is made easier. If, on the other hand, loyalties to regions or other subnational divisions are stronger, national authorities may have difficulty implementing policy. Rivalries between groups can make even the basic task of maintaining order difficult, as racial, religious, and cultural conflicts within contemporary nations will attest.

Public officials build their authority on the loyalties of citizens. Socialization processes, which are usually beyond governmental control, condition those loyalties. Those who would govern must generally, therefore, call upon existing loyalties, rather than attempt to create new ones.

SUGGESTED READINGS

Dawson, Richard E., and Kenneth Prewitt: *Political Socialization* (New York: Little, Brown, 1969). A readable and well-organized treatment of the topic for the general political science student.

Hyman, Herbert H.: *Political Socialization* (New York: Free Press, 1959). The seminal volume in the contemporary upsurge of scholarly interest in political socialization, this is an argument for a focus on political learning in order to relate the insights of psychology to political science.

Jaros, Dean: *Socialization to Politics* (New York: Praeger, 1973). A sound introduction to the subject with emphasis upon social issues as well as contemporary research.

Langton, Kenneth P., *Political Socialization* (Toronto: Oxford University Press, 1969). An authoritative treatment of the functions of socializing agents based in large part upon the author's own research.

From the classics

In addition to Plato's *Republic* which deals at length with the proper means of socializing citizens in the ideal state, *Emile,* by Jean-Jacques Rousseau, combined with his *Social Contract,* foreshadows the intensive concern for citizen education typical of contemporary states.

CHAPTER SIX

POLITICAL COMMUNICA-TION

OVERVIEW **T**his chapter focuses on the importance of symbols and messages in politics. As you read the material, keep in mind that communication, including political communication, is greatly affected by the subjective perceptions of the persons involved. You should therefore be particularly sensitive to those sections of the chapter which deal with the subjective frames of reference of individual persons. Also take careful note of the ways in which political leaders seek to overcome differences in frames of reference. Discussion of these points will center on the encoding and decoding of messages, on channels of communication, on specialized communications roles, on distortion, and on the concept of national ideology (shared frames of reference).

Be sure that you understand the following terms:

Senders	Selective perception
Receivers	Selective retention
Channels	Reinforcement
Feedback	Frame of reference
Selective attention	Encoding

Decoding
Perceptual screening
Opinion leaders
Two-step flow of communications

Gatekeepers
Distortion
Channel capacity
National ideology

LEARNING OBJECTIVES

After you have studied this chapter, you should be able to:

1. Diagram the simple model of the communications process as presented in the text.
2. Explain the effects of selective perception, attention, and retention on the communication process.
3. Understand the impact of groups and opinion leaders on political communications.
4. Explain the impact of perceptual screening upon the decoding and encoding of messages.
5. Define channel capacity and explain how it affects the ability of the authorities to reach appropriate decisions and to communicate those decisions to individuals in society.
6. Define the term "gatekeeper."
7. Define "distortion" in political communication and identify its sources.
8. Explain the relationship between shared frames of reference and the ability of the authorities to gain compliance with their decisions.

Some scholars have argued that all political life should be understood in terms of communication processes.[1] There are strong arguments in support of this stand, and it cannot be passed over lightly. Human social life, including politics, is based upon the ability of people to exchange messages with each other—messages which convey love, hate, fear, and respect and which are used to command, persuade, argue, and protest.

The functional aspects of politics which we previously discussed are dependent upon communications. *Decisions* must be based upon adequate information, which can be provided only if communications relay the needed facts, opinions, and attitudes to those in authority. *Policy implementation* can be effective only if the rules and their interpretation

---

[1]Cf. H. Mark Roelofs, *The Language of Modern Politics: An Introduction to the Study of Government* (Homewood, Ill.: Dorsey, 1967).

are communicated to those whom they are intended to affect. Citizens rely on communication with appropriate officials to make their *demands* known and to provide *feedback* on policy to the political system. And *political socialization,* like all learning, can be viewed as a process of exchanging messages between parents and children, teachers and students, and members of peer groups and secondary associations, not to mention communications from the mass media to society at large.

Communication, then, pervades every aspect of political and social activity. Virtually any operation of a political system can be described in terms of the communications which take place between political actors. The politically relevant activities of citizens consist mainly of messages exchanged among them or transmitted to public officials. Patterns of political interaction can be traced largely through describing communications flow and message content.

In this chapter we will deal with four major topics. Firstly, a *simple model* of communication will be discussed in order to identify the major elements which all communications processes have in common. Secondly, we will examine the *attitudinal context* of political communication, since the meaning which individuals assign to messages depends upon their attitudes and the past learning through which they have learned to decipher communications from others. Thirdly, the *implications* of various *patterns* of political communications for the functioning of political systems will be explored. Finally, the relationship of communications patterns to political *authority* will be examined in order to gain a better understanding of why political systems vary in their ability to elicit support and participation from their environments.

SIMPLE MODEL OF COMMUNICATION

Figure 6-1 is a diagram of a simple communications model which can be used to illustrate a wide variety of communications situations. In the diagram the major elements of the communication process are identified as (1) senders, (2) receivers, (3) channels which link senders and receivers, (4) transmitted messages, and (5) the feedback process. The model and its major elements may appear to be simplistic at first glance. But these simple concepts are quite useful in the analysis of complex communications processes.

Senders or *sources* are the persons to whom receivers attribute origination of a communication. In practice, of course, not every apparent sender is the true source of the message transmitted. Walter Cronkite

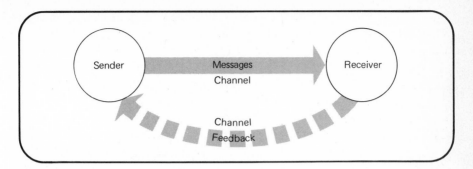

Figure 6-1 A simple model of the communications process.

does not write all the news copy he reads on the nightly news. Political candidates do not always draft the speeches they deliver. Books are often "ghostwritten" so that the "author" is not the "writer." Nevertheless, it is useful to consider the person whose name is identified with a message to be its sender or source in most cases. Newscasters, politicians, and authors with ghostwriters take public credit and responsibility for the messages which they speak or publish, thus becoming the social disseminators of the messages in question.

Receivers are those toward whom messages are directed, or who may inadvertently intercept a message intended for someone else. In personal conversation, receivers are simply those who are listening to others speak at a given moment. When mass media are used as channels of communication, the receivers of a given message are more difficult to identify. But it may be assumed that the senders of messages through television, radio, newspapers, and magazines are generally trying to reach as many potential viewers, listeners, or readers as possible. The position of receivers in the model is crucial since individual listeners, readers, or observers interpret what they see and hear, and their interpretation of messages largely determines the outcome of any information exchange.

In the broadest sense, *messages* carry information. But information must be understood to include any possible content, including not only factual material but emotional states, opinions, arguments, appeals, and virtually anything else which one human being may wish to know or tell. The content of messages is jointly determined by sender and receiver. Any given message may mean quite different things to the person sending it and the person or persons receiving it. In other words, message content is always subject to interpretation.

Channels of communication are the means whereby messages are transmitted between senders and receivers. A channel may be as simple as the sound waves which carry words a short distance between two people engaged in face-to-face conversation, or they may be as complex as the contemporary mass media of radio and television, where elaborate mechanical devices and hundreds of supporting workers are used to carry messages from one source to millions of receivers. The character and the capacity of available communications channels have important implications for effective political action. Governmental officials must communicate large volumes of messages among themselves and from their offices to their constituents. Thus a modern government needs many channels of communications in order to coordinate governmental policymaking and enforcement activities, and in order to relate to the opinions and behavior of the populace.

Communications *feedback* occurs when an original sender becomes a receiver—when, in a sense, the positions of sender and receiver are reversed and the original sender receives information concerning audience reaction to information transmitted. In face-to-face conversation, feedback is achieved very simply since a listener may indicate reactions quite directly, either through words or by facial expressions or physical gestures. In mass communications, however, the process is much more complicated. "Letters to the Editor" still serve a very useful purpose, but publishers and broadcasters must use sophisticated, indirect means to attempt to estimate the size, character, and reactions of their audiences. Depth interviews of thousands of viewers, listeners, or readers might be necessary in order to get feedback which even approximated the quality so easily gained in face-to-face situations. Such elaborate studies are not always practical, and much contemporary communication is carried on without benefit of entirely effective feedback. The implication is that in the age of mass communications, senders operate half blindly, sending out millions of messages without receiving clear and direct indications of their effectiveness with the audience.

These major elements of communications—senders, receivers, messages, channels, and feedback—are common to all communications situations. Whether two lovers exchange vows of love, whether a head of state addresses a nation, or whether two bureaucrats exchange memoranda, we can at least tentatively identify who is saying what to whom, by what means, and with what effect in each case, thus breaking the process of communication into discrete elements. The significance of the elements, however, can only become clear through looking at specific situations, and to illustrate this, we now turn to an example of political communications.

THE MODEL APPLIED: 1960 CAMPAIGN DEBATES

On September 26, 1960, John F. Kennedy and Richard M. Nixon, the Democratic and Republican candidates for the American Presidency, faced each other in the first of four scheduled face-to-face debates which were broadcast over national radio and television. After each candidate had made a brief opening statement, a panel of news reporters directed questions to the two men for about 45 minutes. At the close of the hour-long debate, first Nixon and then Kennedy made brief closing remarks. This first debate, and the three which followed, attracted the largest television audience of any programs which had been broadcast to that date, providing a unique event for the study of mass communications in political campaigns. Over 80 percent of the American electorate watched at least one of the face-to-face encounters between the candidates.

Though news reporters participated in these broadcasts, there is no doubt that Nixon and Kennedy were the *senders* of the important messages. Prior to the debates, Nixon had earned a reputation as a skilled, tough debater during his 1946 bid for a seat in Congress and through his famous "kitchen debate" with Soviet Premier Nikita Khrushchev. Kennedy's debating skills were largely unknown, and it was expected that he would have difficulty in performing well against his opponent. Kennedy's Democratic supporters were therefore prepared, before the first debate took place, to discount its importance and to argue that debating skill was not a prerequisite for high political office.

As it turned out, the *messages* transmitted by the candidates in the first debate proved to be crucial. These messages included not only the words which were spoken but also the facial expressions, gestures, tone of voice, and general appearance of the two men. Of particular importance was the appearance of candidate Nixon; he appeared to be gaunt, tired, and poorly shaved, and commentators felt that his responses to questions lacked toughness. After the event, Nixon's staff attributed his poor visual appearance to improperly applied makeup and unfavorable studio lighting. Indeed, some writers have come close to blaming Nixon's 1960 electoral defeat on his apparent "five o'clock shadow" on that fateful evening. In contrast to Richard Nixon, John Kennedy projected a youthful, confident, hard-hitting image in the first debate. Since he was running as the youngest candidate ever to seek the American Presidency, his apparent coolness under fire as well as his command of the issues was an important message to transmit to the voters in order to win their confidence. Thus, the way the candidates looked and spoke, as well as their spoken words, constituted a powerful set of messages which had great potential for influencing voter decisions.

Without the availability of television as a *channel* of communication, it is quite possible that the audience might have reacted differently to the first debate. Some observers who heard the radio broadcast of the debate before viewing the televised version felt that, on the basis of their verbal exchange, the candidates came off nearly even. It is likely, then, that Mr. Nixon's *televised* image swung the outcome of the debate in favor of Senator Kennedy. Television, with its capacity to send pictures as well as sound, transmits a more complex set of messages than radio (or the printed page). And the video portion of television messages seem to influence the way in which the audience reacts to the *words* in them.

An understanding of the audience or *receivers* of the messages transmitted by the 1960 television debates is also crucial. It is quite likely that the debates aroused interest in the political campaign on the part of people who do not normally bother to vote. Substantially more Americans voted in November of 1960 than had gone to the polls in any previous election in the United States. Many of these voters were not strong partisans of either the Democrats or the Republicans. If the debates both aroused their interest and influenced their vote, the effect of the debates may well have been particularly strong for them. Further, we know that communications generally have the effect of reinforcing opinions and attitudes which people already hold. And since the American people were much more heavily Democratic than Republican in their loyalties, Kennedy stood a good chance of increasing the enthusiasm of voters who could normally be expected to favor a Democrat if he made a favorable impression in the debates, regardless of how poorly or well Nixon performed.

The entire communications situation, then, leads to the question of what *effect* the debates, given their character and context, had on the audience, and also to the question of what *feedback* the candidates received about their performances. Before the first television debate, the Gallup poll showed Nixon leading Kennedy by 47 to 46 percent in voter preferences. After that debate, the lead switched to favor Kennedy by 49 to 46 percent. Further, when asked which man did the better job in the debate, those who had seen the program named Kennedy by 43 to 23 percent. Other surveys similarly showed Kennedy making gains as a result of his performance in the first television debate. As a result of feedback information, Kennedy began to request that the debates be continued right up to election eve. Nixon, on the other hand, refused to agree to any more than four debates. As the second and succeeding debates proceeded, his staff paid close attention to the candidate's makeup and the studio lighting, and Nixon became more argumentative and assertive in his debating style. Both men were thus influenced in their campaign behavior by feedback information from the audience and from "expert" observers such as news commentators. The feedback which they received helped to shape their future communications so as better to promote their attempts to use campaign messages to assist them to win the election.

Through this example, the simple communications model which we have been using can be seen to be applicable to a complex communications event involving over a hundred million people. But there are other considerations to be taken into account. Not every viewer thought Kennedy won the first television debate, and about 35 percent of the viewers said that they did not think either candidate clearly did a better job. Since all viewers presumably watched the same program, we must ask why, in our model, the same messages are interpreted differently by different receivers. This brings us to the role which *attitudes* play in the communications process.

PERCEPTIONS AND POLITICAL COMMUNICATION

Since political life most directly involves adults who already have an extensive history of political socialization behind them, their past learning has great impact upon the way they interpret political reality and the political messages which they receive. The senders and receivers involved in communication situations act in accordance with their acquired cognitive, affective, and evaluative orientations. Every individual, then, has an existing *frame of reference,* which is used to determine whether received information is reliable and relevant to personal concerns, whether one feels positively or negatively about the message, and what sort of evaluation is appropriate. In much the same way, frames of reference determine the kinds of messages which are sent, since senders make estimates of audience interest and reactions based upon their own past learning and experience.

Public reaction to the first Kennedy-Nixon debate reflected the operation of voters' frames of reference, as is illustrated in Table 6-1. Those who were predisposed to favor Nixon thought that he won the debate by a margin of 52 to 14 percent, while 34 percent of Nixon's supporters picked neither man as the winner. Kennedy supporters thought their man beat Nixon by a 70 to 4 percent margin, with only 26 percent perceiving no winner in the debate. Thus, while all the viewers saw the same pictures and heard the same words, their own tendencies to favor one man or the other strongly influenced the way they judged the relative performances of the two candidates.

Notice that we are forced to conclude that the viewers' frames of reference *influenced* their opinion as to who won the debate. We cannot say that their opinions were *determined* by prior attitudes, for that would fail to explain why 14 percent of Nixon's supporters thought Kennedy won and why 4 percent of Kennedy's backers chose Nixon's performance over their own man's. Further, there is a pattern in Table 6-1 which suggests that, overall, the viewers concluded that Kennedy won. Why else did Nixon convince a noticeably smaller proportion (54 to 70 percent) of his followers than did Kennedy? And why did Kennedy manage to convey the impression that he won to more of Nixon's supporters than Nixon did to his (14 to 4 percent)? And why were more Nixon supporters unable to make a choice between the two men (34 to 26 percent)? It would seem that the *general* impact of the messages transmitted in the first debate was more favorable to Kennedy, regardless of the previous inclinations of the viewers. The response to the first Kennedy-Nixon debate, then, was conditioned both by the messages transmitted and by the preexisting attitudes in members of the audience.

Table 6-1 Who "won" the first Kennedy-Nixon Television debate, according to viewers?

Of voters who were	Percent saying Nixon won	Percent saying Kennedy won	Percent not picking a winner
Pro-Nixon	52	14	34
Pro-Kennedy	4	70	26

Source: Adapted from E. Katz and J. J. Feldman, "The Kennedy-Nixon Debates: A Survey of Surveys," *Studies in Public Communication*, no. 4, p. 145. Autumn 1962. Figures are averaged from those presented for the Gallup, Kraft, and Opinion Research Corporation national public opinion polls.

Selective perception, attention, and retention

Such differential responses to communications result from *selective perception.* Selective perception operates so that we essentially see and hear what we want, or are prepared, to see and hear. Most of us are aware of "tuning out" certain kinds of messages, as when a smoker avoids accepting evidence that cigarettes and cancer are linked, or when a loving wife "ignores" her husband's bad behavior even to the point of not believing it exists. Studies of public opinion and laboratory experiments have repeatedly confirmed that individuals select the facts they wish to perceive, and, even further, that people can completely reverse the meaning of a message so that it accords with their own opinion. For instance, in a classic study of propaganda and prejudice it was found that strongly anti-Semitic persons would convert a prejudiced buffoon in satirical cartoons into a hero figure.

Not only do we selectively perceive those portions of messages which we actually receive, we also prescreen the messages to which we will expose ourselves. Thus, we pay *selective attention* to communications. We read newspapers and magazines which print material which accords with our interests and very often select publications with an eye to their editorial policy. We tend to choose friends whose opinions are similar to, or conform with, our own. In many ways, then, we seek to avoid communications which would conflict with our frame of reference, and at the same time seek to expose ourselves to messages which will reinforce what we already hold to be true.

Selective attention and perception are buttressed by *selective retention*—we remember best those things which most closely fit within our preexisting frames of reference. This phenomenon is similar to remembering pleasant experiences and forgetting painful ones. Most people cannot recall painful experiences as vividly as pleasurable ones. Conflict and contradiction are painful. We are more comfortable if our opinions tend to fit neatly together, without apparent contradiction. Consequently, it is easier to remember information which reinforces our beliefs than information which contradicts them.

The principles of selective attention, perception, and retention are so widely documented and accepted that little research is currently conducted to verify them further. It should be noted, however, that our communications behavior is not always selective. We noted that in the public response to the first Kennedy-Nixon debate there were large number of partisans who did not think that their own man won, and still more individuals did not think either candidate carried the day over his opponent. Still, people react selectively, much of the time, to the multi-tude of messages which are available to them. And political communica-tions would be imperfectly understood if this were not taken into account.

The net effect of selective behavior is to *reinforce* preexisting atti-tudes. Understanding this, we can appreciate that it is difficult to convert people from one partisan position to another, unless they do not feel strongly about it in the first place. In this light, the power of political socialization which was discussed in Chapter 5 can be even more strongly appreciated. For once an individual has grown to adulthood, he or she has formed a strong frame of reference composed of cognitive, affective, and evaluative orientations. The messages which he receives will be filtered through this frame of reference so as to hold it as constant as possible. Early learning, then, makes most adults resistant to changes in attitude, even though they may have ample opportunity to be exposed to information which contradicts what they have learned to believe.

Group influence

When the behavior of large numbers of individuals is analyzed, it becomes apparent that they do not react to social situations either as an undifferentiated mass or as isolated individuals. Rather, in any large social phenomenon, such as a national election, or reactions to mass communications, members of the public behave differently according to the primary and secondary groups with which they associate or identify. It is, for instance, widely recognized that voters behave as groups (or "blocs"). This recognition is evident in the common use of such terms as the "labor vote," "farm vote," "black vote," "city vote," and many others. It is perhaps less well understood that such group voting patterns are not spontaneous; that is, any particular farmer will not necessarily vote on a given issue the same way a majority of the farm bloc will. There are varying strengths of group cohesiveness, and some individuals are more swayed by the groups with which they associate or identify than are others.

Part of the strong influence of groups on activities such as voting stems from their role in the communications process. We have already noted that primary, secondary, and reference groups play important parts in the process of political socialization. It should now be made clear that by shaping the affective, cognitive, and evaluative orientations of individ-uals, groups influence the frames of reference which will be used to selectively attend to, perceive, and retain communications content. Beyond that, however, the *interaction* of group members plays an ongoing part in helping members form common perceptions of the social world. This can be illustrated by considering some alternative theories of how the content of mass communications is interpreted by the general public.

The first model illustrated in Figure 6-2 is a simpleminded view of how the mass media reach the public. It assumes that every individual is reached, if reached at all, in isolation from others. In this view, a television program goes directly from the transmitter to individual television sets and is received individually by each person watching. If the model were taken literally, there would be no need to understand the comments which family members might make to each other about the program in order to understand the impact on individual family members. If we understood the frames of reference of the individuals who watched the program, and knew something of the program's content, we should be able to determine pretty well how the viewers would react. Obviously, this model is too simple, for even with entertainment communication, the comments of friends and relatives can shape our tastes and perceptions. In the case of a political program such as the 1960 television debates, it would be folly to ignore the fact that these broadcasts were probably the most widely discussed campaign communications in American history. Over three-fourths of the American public reported informally discussing them at home, at work, or with friends.

The second model illustrates what has long been called the "two-step" flow of communications. The theory of a two-step mass-communications process was developed as a result of the discovery that (1) some individuals are more avid consumers of mass-media political communications and (2) these persons influence others through informal discussion. In its strictest form, the two-step flow model posits that mass-media messages are primarily consumed by opinion leaders who interpret the messages through their own frames of reference, and pass on their interpretations and judgments to the individuals with whom they associate through group activity, both formal and informal.

The two-step model takes into account the obvious fact that our individual opinions are not formed simply on the basis of isolated reception of mass-media messages, but are shaped by discussion of the content of those messages with others. On the other hand, an event such as the Kennedy-Nixon debates was not seen by a relatively few opinion leaders and then passed to the general public. We must assume that discussion of the debates took place among people who had seen at least part of them firsthand. Whether there were opinion leaders or not in such discussions, the mass media reached both the individual who was less

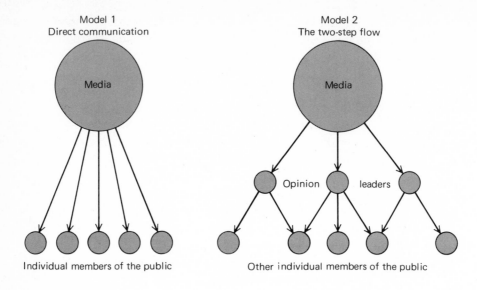

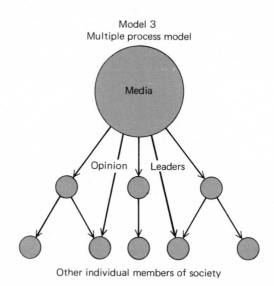

Figure 6-2 Models of the mass-communications process.

well informed generally and had less influence with associates, and the better-informed and more influential "opinion leader."

This leads us to posit a third model (number 3 in Figure 6-2) in which mass communications reaches the public as individual receivers as well as opinion leaders. Once messages have been received, they may or may not be discussed in group situations. When they do elicit further discussion, the role of opinion leaders comes into play, and the interaction of their perception of the communication with those of their associates can serve to create a group opinion—the individuals in the group will perceive and evaluate the communication in a more common light than if they had not had group discussion. If individuals do not discuss the communications further, their own individual frames of reference will be crucial in interpreting the messages received.

Note, then, that the key factor in determining the degree of influence that groups will have on interpreting communications content is the extent to which an individual is involved with the group. This need not always, as the model suggests, involve direct discussion of a message; but it can be shown that persons who engage in active discussion tend to share the group viewpoint more intensely than do those who identify with the group, but do not participate regularly in group activities. Both identification with the group and regular participation are important, but group solidarity is increased when group members regularly interact with each other.

These points can be illustrated by an examination of the influence of religious affiliation on American voters, with particular reference to the 1960 election, in which John F. Kennedy became the first Catholic to be elected to the American Presidency. Table 6-2 illustrates the pattern of Protestant and Catholic identification with the Democratic party and vote for the Democratic presidential nominee between 1956 and 1968. In each of these four elections, Catholics were proportionately more Democratic than Protestants and they cast a higher proportion of their vote for the Democratic candidate. Over the four elections, an average of 45.5 percent of Protestants as compared with 57 percent of Catholics considered themselves to be Democrats. An average of 43 percent of Protestants compared with 67 percent of Catholics cast their votes for the Democratic candidate for President. Clearly Americans who identified themselves as Catholics tended also to identify themselves with the Democratic party, and to vote for it, more frequently than did Americans who identified themselves as Protestants.

Such observations do not establish the influence of regular group interaction on political attitudes and behavior. They only describe general patterns among persons who *identify* with a particular group. But as we turn to the effect of regular association with other group identifiers, we find that, generally, the more frequently a person has contact with the group, the more his attitudes and behavior conform to the group pattern.

Table 6-2 Religious identification, party identification, and presidential vote: 1956–1968

Religious identification	Party identification (% Democratic)	Presidential vote (% Democratic)
Protestant		
1956	43	36
1960	43	34
1964	51	63
1968	45	39
Catholic		
1956	52	46
1960	64	82
1964	58	79
1968	54	60

Source: Adapted from Everret Carl Ladd, Jr.,'s use of Survey Research Center data in *American Political Parties: Social Change and Political Response* (New York: Norton, 1970), p. 294.

This can be seen in Table 6-3, which shows that while Catholics generally voted more heavily for John Kennedy than they would normally be expected to, regular church attenders swung to Kennedy much more heavily than those who attended church seldom or never. Regular contact with other Catholics in a situation where religion was the important common element of association *seemingly* (the fact that church attendance and a vote for Kennedy are *associated* with each other does not

Table 6-3 Effect of regular church attendance by American Catholics on their vote for John F. Kennedy in 1960

	Catholics who attended church	
	Regularly	Seldom or never
Percentage increase of vote for John F. Kennedy over "normal" vote of Catholics for Democratic candidates	+16%	+10%

Source: Adapted from Philip E. Converse, "Religion and Politics: the 1960 Election," in Angus Campbell et al., *Elections and the Political Order* (New York: Wiley, 1966), p. 108.

prove that one *caused* the other) had a large influence in reinforcing the political tendencies which Catholics shared as a group.

Decoding, encoding, and distortion

When individual frames of reference and group interactions are taken into account it is obvious that the simple model of communication with which we began must be modified. Between the sender of a message and the receivers, individual psychological characteristics and social group interaction act as "screening" devices. Such screenings are commonly called *decoding* processes because through them messages achieve their meaning for individuals, and thus their eventual social and political significance. In addition, it is important to note that senders are not unaware of the peculiarities of their audiences, and hence attempt to frame their messages in terms which will enable them to penetrate social screens which might cause their messages either to be ignored or to be interpreted in ways other than those intended. We recognize here that communications are tailored for the audiences toward which they are directed. A shorthand way of describing this behavior of senders is to speak of the *encoding* of messages.

Our simple model of communication (Figure 6-1) should therefore be expanded to show that messages are encoded before they enter the channels of communications and are decoded before they are assimilated by receivers. When expanded in this fashion, the model takes into account the possibility of misinterpretation and distortion in communications: the encoding and decoding may be faulty. That is, the effect of senders' messages depends upon their ability to encode the message so that their receivers will attend to them, and will decode it in the way they desire. With our model thus expanded, we may proceed to talk about the larger implications of the process of political communication for the operation of political systems.

COMMUNICATION AND POLITICAL SYSTEMS

The ability of a political leadership to maintain close communications with its society largely determines the degree to which it can be effective in gaining cooperation from citizens in order to direct, or steer, them toward common goals. In this sense, the communications capability of a political unit is analogous to the nervous system of a human body, the automatic pilot of an aircraft, or the operating system of a computer. In each case, a steering function is performed through gathering information (inputs) necessary for a successful attempt to attain goals or reach destinations. In the political case, information is processed through human centers of decision making; in the case of mechanical guidance, computational machinery makes the decisions. Finally decisions are transmitted to units which execute commands designed to direct the units—social or mechanical—to the desired destination. When the effects of a command are observed through the feedback of new inputs, further decisions and commands may be necessary to adjust the direction which is being taken. While political processes are much more complex than mechanical guidance systems, the principle of self-correction through information processes is the same.

Communications capability has been compared to the "nerves" of government by Karl Deutsch,[2] and it has been suggested that the state of political development in the newer nations can be measured effectively through assessing communications patterns in a state. If the importance of communications to governmental effectiveness is accepted, there are a number of indicators of communications capacity which can be used by the student of politics. First, it is possible to measure *channel capacity* in terms of the mechanical channels available to a society (i.e., telephones, roads, electronic broadcasting). Second, the existence of *specialized communications roles* and the availability of trained communications personnel can be determined. Third, the degree to which elites and their followers share a *common frame of reference* is related to the amount of distortion which might be expected in the process of encoding and decoding messages.

Together, knowledge of these elements will facilitate an assessment of the ability of public officials to coordinate and guide a society, and to adjust social directions to meet changing internal and external conditions, for only as officials are aware of the opinions and reactions of citizens can they frame public policy which will be most effective.

Channel capacity

In every social or mechanical system there is a limit to the number of messages which can be transmitted through available channels. This is obvious when the VHF band for television broadcasting, with its maximum of twelve channels, is considered. Once a given area is served by

---

[2]Karl Deutsch, *The Nerves of Government* (New York: Free Press, 1963).

stations using VHF channels 2 through 13, there is no way that additional stations, transmitting more information, can be established without shutting down an existing transmitter. Even if UHF television capability is added, there are a finite number of stations which can serve a given broadcasting region. The sum total of electronic (including telephone), printed, and transportation media channels which exist in a society can give a raw estimate of its total communications channel capacity. While that capacity might appear to be almost infinite in a country such as the United States, it is nonetheless finite, as anyone who has had to wait for several minutes to get an open telephone line in a large city during peak business hours will testify.

In technologically underdeveloped countries, the lack of channel capacity can pose serious political problems. There are areas of Kenya, for example, where messages can be carried overland much of the way only on foot. After the 1968 Olympic Games, Kip Kano, a Kenyan long-distance runner, carried the news of his victory to his village 10 days after the event was over. While his compatriots in the capital city of Nairobi received the news almost instantaneously over radio and television, the lack of any channel but primitive trails made it necessary for him to bring the word home in person. Such rural isolation hampers the technological ability of the Kenyan government to gather information about remote parts of its society, and makes the transmission and enforcement of national policy decisions extremely difficult.

In technologically more advanced countries, too, channel capacity limitations at crucial junctures can impose restrictions on information flow to and from the centers of decision making. While virtually everyone in the United States has access to a telephone which can be used to call any other set in the world, a single telephone line in the Office of the President can handle only so many calls. Even considering every communications channel into the President's office, not all of the messages which people in the country might desire to transmit to the Chief Executive can be accommodated. In the case of mass-communications media, only a limited number of persons can speak over radio or television at a given time, due both to the limited number of channels and to limitations in the ability of any one individual to receive more than one message at a time. There are thus points at which messages converge in a political system as they are directed toward a policymaking center, and points where channels must branch so that messages can go from one sender to many receivers.

A graphic portrayal of channel capacity in a political system is displayed in Figure 6-3. As information flows from multiple sources

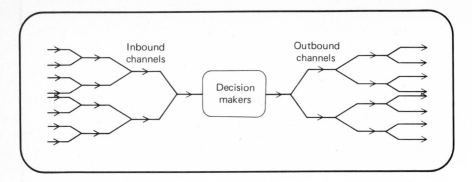

Figure 6-3 Channel capacity, messages and decision makers.

toward those responsible for making decisions, it is necessary to reduce the volume of messages to suit the limited channel capacity near the decision-making area. Some messages are blocked out, others are combined, and a relatively few may flow on directly. Thus, a senator or a President cannot read all of his mail, but he may be told that it is running 2 to 1 against the military draft and that he is receiving 600 letters a day on the subject. Many messages would thereby be consolidated into one. He might also be told that the county leader of his party favors the draft, but not even get the message sent by Mrs. Jones of Hickory Junction protesting the fluoridation of her water supply.

Branching outward from the congresswoman's office occurs when she calls a press conference to announce that she opposes the draft and her message is carried by newspapers, radio, television, and word of mouth to thousands of her constituents. Each junction of channels in the diagram thus represents a constriction or expansion of channel capacity as messages either flow toward a decision-making center or flow away from it. Since the capacity of a single decision maker to assimilate messages is severely limited, it is to be expected that the total capacity of channels leading directly to or away from the decision maker will be much more limited than the capacity of channels which are further removed. The communications problem in a country like Kenya, then, is that even the farther-removed channels are, at present, severely restricted.

Specialized communications roles

Because of limitations in channel capacity leading to decision-making centers, complex organizations must develop means for regulating information flow so that decision makers can operate with maximum efficiency. It is of crucial importance to the effectiveness of public officials that they receive as much of the important information which flows toward them as it is possible to assimilate and to act upon. It is also vital that they have available the best possible system for utilizing available outward channels so that their policies will be distributed widely once they have made up their mind. If a head of state is not told that millions of people are dissatisfied with the tax policies, he or she cannot cope with an important source of social unrest. Even if the people are clogging communications channels with complaints, the head of state will not get their messages if the incoming channels are saturated with good news. If, on the other hand, he or she changes the tax policy and announces the change, it will be of little avail if outbound channels do not carry the message to the people, but are used rather to tell them what their leader had for breakfast.

In attempting to ensure efficiency, specialized tasks relating to communications flow are assigned to qualified persons in complex organizations. Such persons may be seen as operating as "gatekeepers" at various junctions in inbound and outbound communications channels. They regulate the flow of messages much as a traffic police officer directs traffic in the attempt to ensure that as many cars as possible traverse the streets safely. Gatekeepers block, combine, interpret, and pass along messages that flow in from numerous channels and send the reduced number of messages toward the decision-making center. They also determine which outbound messages will be most widely distributed over the available outbound channels. An administrative assistant, for instance, may use his or her staff to monitor hundreds of letters and calls, reducing them to a single memorandum for the eyes of the boss. On the outbound side, a newscaster selects a limited number of communications from the government to broadcast over radio or television, giving broad dissemination to some messages and restricting the distribution of others. As societies become more complex, the number of specialized roles which develop to regulate communications flow increases, so that in contrast to a rural village where virtually everyone is his or her own gatekeeper, particular individuals in key roles come to have great influence on the communications process.

A gatekeeper in communications can be as simple as a secretary who allows only certain telephone calls to be received by the boss, or gatekeeping can be performed by a worldwide organization of news reporters who report to a newspaper or broadcasting network which selects and edits thousands of reports a day in an attempt to condense world events to manageable proportions for its audience. But it would be a mistake to view the editorial staff of the *New York Times* or the National Broadcasting Company as the only type of true communications specialists in modern society. Complex communications networks require thousands of highly organized specialists to maintain the channels of communication which are used. Communications satellites, for instance, depend upon thousands of engineers and technicians for their installation and maintenance. (So does the more down-to-earth network of overland telephone communications.) And the efforts of rocket and electronic technicians would be futile if there were no large organizations to decide how to schedule the use of satellites and to devote great energy and skill to the formatting of messages to be transmitted over them. Earlier complex societies such as Imperial China or the Incan Empire used nonmechanical transmission technology for communications, but they, too, were dependent upon complex communications in the form of thousands of scribes and messengers for effective government.

Communications thus will reflect the complexity of social organization generally, as well as the available technology. A single village blacksmith could, a century ago, keep wagons repaired and horses shod. But the blacksmith has been replaced by large corporations which manufacture trucks and automobiles and by automobile repair shops and service stations, manned by individuals with special skills, who today perform similar maintenance functions. Similarly, runners, horseback riders, and jungle drummers could once handle communications traffic between villages and towns. But radio, television, telephone, and postal service have given rise to hundreds of specialized roles which must be highly organized and filled by persons with specialized skills. Where once there were only a few communications roles which required special skills, there are now many. And where the maintenance and use of communications channels required little organization in the past, vast bureaucracies are currently needed.

The implications of complex communications for political effectiveness should be clear. A society which does not have enough communications specialists cannot maintain a high level of communications activity, and without that activity, the coordination of individual efforts is impaired. Leaders of modern states with large territories and populations cannot effectively compete in today's world arena if their people cannot be coordinated toward achieving common goals, and the standard of living made possible by industrial technology cannot be realized without the organizational competence to make use of modern communications technology. In simpler times, a nation could take months to prepare for an attack from another power. Now missile technology provides for only minutes of lead time. When a single small village could produce most of the necessities of life, there was little need for intensive interaction with outside communities. But when the goods consumed by a family are produced all over the globe, communications must be highly organized and supported by highly trained specialists at every point. Specialized communications roles are thus vital to the ability of modern societies to meet their daily needs and to function effectively in a technologically sophisticated world.

Distortion

The most sophisticated of transmission capabilities can be of little use to public officials if gross distortion in the interpretation of messages occurs in encoding and decoding processes. There are many potential sources of such distortion, ranging from subtle differences between the frames of reference of officials and their public to linguistic barriers to communication. Distortion due to encoding and decoding problems can be particularly acute in countries with diverse languages and cultures, since a message intended for all of the people will almost inevitably be interpreted in different ways by the diverse cultural groups which receive it. Gene Overstreet cites a poignant example from India where instructions for a village fair in India asked that the fair include "a show of healthy babies up to the age of three," but the village mothers interpreted it to mean, "There will be a wrestling match of three-year-old children."[3] Such a misunderstanding might, in itself, have little impact upon Indian politics, but linguistic differences in that country have, on occasion, made it very difficult for the Delhi government to direct and coordinate an effective community development program to raise the rural standard of living.

Even where linguistic differences are not as severe as in India, there are likely to be important barriers to communication which are rooted in deep cleavages in attitudes between various groups in a society. Relatively minor differences, such as basic loyalties to Republican or Democratic candidates in the United States, do not pose insuperable barriers to communications since there are overriding commitments to a common view of the nation which are shared by most Americans. But severe disagreements between basic frames of reference can cause a single message to be interpreted quite differently by different groups. A news report of the 1971 suppression of Bengalis by the Punjabi government in

[3]Gene D. Overstreet, "India," in James B. Christoph (ed.), *Cases in Comparative Politics* (Boston: Little, Brown, 1965), p. 463.

Pakistan, for instance, might be interpreted by a Punjabi as a triumph for Pakistani national unity. But a Bengali would be likely to understand the report as a description of events which were rending the national fabric asunder. News that the British government was sending troops to keep peace in Northern Ireland could be seen by Protestants as an expression of British support for law and order, and by Catholics as evidence of coming political repression. In these cases, the frames of reference of the contending groups are so different that they react as if they were not really part of the same political community.

It is hardly to be hoped that millions of people would ever share exactly the same cognitive, affective, and evaluative orientations. Differences between frames of reference are inevitable since life situations and socializing processes inevitably vary to some degree between segments of large and complex societies. But communication, coordination, and political control are made difficult when there are severe differences in perceptions and evaluations in a nominally unified society. And the ability of a political system to guide society effectively is partially dependent upon its ability to communicate with the diverse groups it governs through a common frame of reference which encompasses at least general principles of social action and national direction.

Such a common frame of reference is sometimes called a *national ideology,* or ideological framework. Harold Lasswell and Satish Arora have maintained that a national ideological framework serves to assist in communications by providing a set of common political expectations which bind elites and nonelites together in a frame of reference within which the "goals and objectives of public policy can be clarified."[4] In their analysis, national crises and difficulties are endured by a society through a shared dedication to values and goals which are understood and accepted through a frame of reference which overrides narrower divisions between classes and groups. It is crucial to social cooperation that communications among segments of society and between various groups and the elite take place within a context which minimizes the distortion of messages.

While there is no convenient method whereby the degree of commonality between frames of reference in society can be measured, the key principle is clear. Effective political communication depends upon the existence of shared frames of reference among the important groups involved in political interaction. These groups need not agree on every

---

[4]Harold D. Lasswell and Satish K. Arora, *Political Communication: The Public Language of Political Elites in India and the United States* (New York: Holt, 1969), especially p. 7.

point, but they must be able to communicate with each other within a shared context of meaning which enables them to interact constructively in the process of defining goals and courses of action for the society.

Within a nation, national ideologies serve to facilitate communications, but between nations, they can provide a basis for conflict. Amercians and Chinese were called to arms against each other in Korea on the basis of conflicting national perceptions of that war. On the basis of their national ideology, Americans could be called to action to defend "freedom" and to fight against "Communist aggression." Chinese citizens, on the other hand, were mobilized in opposition to the United States through communications which described the war as one of "Imperialist aggression." Each of the two countries was reasonably united internally on the matter of the war, with each government and its citizens accepting a common interpretation of it. Differences between the national ideologies of China and the United States, however, led them to quite different conclusions about Korea, and contributed to a bloody confrontation.

POLITICAL COMMUNICATION AND LEGITIMACY

The framework of shared attitudes between citizens provides a key basis for *legitimizing* the acts of public officials. It is neither a quaint curiosity nor an accident of fate that politicians lace their speeches with appeals to their listeners' patriotism and references to the national interest, and references to their listeners as "fellow countrymen." (American Presidents are especially fond of beginning their addresses with the words, "Good evening, my fellow Americans.") These symbols provide a potential means to bridge differences in interests and values between subgroups of the population. For instance, if in spite of their differences, workers and business executives can be persuaded that it is necessary to sacrifice higher wages and profits for the sake of national welfare, a freeze on wages and prices is likely to be more effective and better received. In order to be accepted as authoritative, policies must be presented in terms which appeal to the tenets of national ideology, and accepted symbols are useful communications tools which public officials use in persuading citizens to accept their policies. The details of a bill to expand welfare programs may be beyond the interests or capacity of the average citizen to understand. But if its sponsors can convince him or her that the bill will promote shared goals of alleviating human suffering and strengthening the nation, the average citizen is more likely to accept the additional tax burden the reform bill will impose.

Public officials and political candidates are not the only ones who must pay their respects to the national ideology. Private groups wishing to promote public policies which serve their interests are forced to present them in the language of the nationally shared frame of reference in order to gain support from other groups and from public officials. A large corporation cannot advocate tax subsidies or governmental loans simply in order to boost its own profits. But if it can convince governmental officials and the public that the welfare of the corporation is tied to national defense or the general economic welfare, it is more likely to get public assistance. This strategy of appealing to the common welfare is open and obvious in such places as the United States or Great Britain, where groups compete publicly for policies which will favor their members' interests. While it is less obvious in a country such as the Soviet Union, it nonetheless takes place as various industries compete for priority positions in plans for future development within the framework of Communist party politics.

In politics, then, unifying ideological symbols are used to facilitate communications between divergent groups. Even in the absence of sharp cultural cleavages, all societies contain groups with specialized interests and particular frames of reference. The existence of shared attitudes concerning the nation gives them a vehicle for translating their particular needs and interests from the narrower frame of reference of the group to the more encompassing national ideology. Disputes over particular policies can thus take place in a communications arena where at least some elements of common perception exist, and where arguments can be lifted somewhat above the level of selfish competition even though elements of selfishness are inevitably present in debate concerning the character of the greater good.

SUMMARY AND CONCLUSION

Like political socialization, political communication can be viewed as an *integrating* function. When citizens are socialized so that their attitudes are supportive of the regime under which they live, and when communications function to foster cooperation and coordination toward common goals, the ability of a society to organize and direct its collective efforts is enhanced. When, on the other hand, there are discontinuities in the socialization or communications processes, the task of political leadership is made much more difficult, and drastic changes in the operation of a political system may result. A crucial element of each of these integrating functions is the pattern of attitudes held by segments of a population. Where political attitudes are reasonably uniform within society, socialization can act to preserve the status quo, with modest changes occurring over time. Likewise, agreement on at least the broad tenets of a national ideology is necessary if communications are not to be unduly distorted in the process of encoding and decoding messages. It is in regard to the role of attitudes that groups come to play an important part in determining the efficiency with which socialization and communication can be performed. Group interaction, particularly within primary groups, is largely beyond control of public officials. Yet within groups, individuals acquire cognitive, affective, and evaluative orientations which strongly influence their perceptions, evaluations, and behavior with respect to public affairs. Even in an age of mass communication, groups function continuously to reinforce or alter existing attitudes held by the individuals belonging to them, and discussion of communications can serve to bring about closer agreement among group members than might occur if each individual formed opinions independently.

Political communication, like political socialization, serves as a link between the political system and its environment. Through communications processes public officials gather information from society and dispense policy statements and explanations to the population. It is communications which provides the potential for effective self-steering of political systems and the societies they govern. Deficiencies in communication capability may arise from a lack of sufficient channels for transmitting messages, from a lack of trained communications personnel, or from distortions in the sending and receiving processes. The availability of channels and specialized personnel is largely a technical problem, though overloading of necessarily limited channels leading to and from the centers of decision making may result from a variety of causes. Distortion in encoding and decoding is based upon differences in frames of reference between a sender and receivers, or between various groups of receivers who require different types of encoding in order for messages to reach all of them effectively.

SUGGESTED READINGS

Lucian W. Pye, ed., *Communications and Political Development* (Princeton, N.J.: Princeton, 1963). Essays on political communication and social, economic, and political development.

Karl W. Deutsch, *The Nerves of Government* (New York: Free Press, 1963). Sophisticated treatment of the importance of communications to politics.

Murray Edelman, *The Symbolic Uses of Politics* (Urbana: University of Illinois Press, 1964). A definitive exposition of the role of symbols in politics.

Elihu Katz and Paul F. Lazersfeld, *Personal Influence* (New York: Free Press, 1955). Opinion leaders in the communication process.

Walter A. Rosenbaum, *Political Culture* (New York: Praeger, 1975). An introduction to political culture as it relates to political integration.

CHAPTER SEVEN

CONCILIATION AND COMMAND
Models of Policy Processes

OVERVIEW

This chapter explores two models of policy processes: conciliation and command. Neither model actually operates in pure form in the real world. Actual governments do not operate strictly by controlling society or by allowing competing demands to be compromised without state intervention. Each model is thus an abstraction of reality. But each helps us focus more clearly on those aspects of reality we are really interested in—one function of any good model.

In our earlier descriptions of decision making, policy implementation, and issue definition, the authorities were seen to play a part in each of them. The key to understanding the models in this chapter is to imagine two extreme roles for the authorities. At one extreme they control all decision making, policy implementation, and issue definition. At the other, they passively endorse bargains and compromises struck between competing parties. Further, under extreme command, socialization and communication would be centrally controlled; under conciliation, they would not be.

Keep clearly in mind that real societies are governed by various mixtures of conciliation and command. The degree to which each type of functioning is found depends largely upon the four social factors identified in the chapter. Note that none of these factors is new to you; all have been previously discussed in different contexts. *Elites* were specifically part of our study of who decides or "who governs," where the ideas of formal elites, influentials, and authorities were introduced. *Groups* were emphasized as important agents in issue definition, political socialization, and political communication. Citizen *participation* was an implicit part of the refining of wants and demands into issues. *Ideals* and ideologies are central to the communication process, where the importance of frames of reference to clear understanding between citizens and rulers was seen.

If you clearly understand the elements of the models you will be able to make comparisons of political systems which will bring their similarities and differences into sharper focus.

Take care to note and to understand the following terms:

Model	Citizen Participation
Command	Voluntary
Conciliation	Controlled
Elites	Ideals
Competing	Diversity
Dominant	Exclusivist
Social Groups	
Associational	
Institutional	

Note that in each pair under elites, social groups, citizen participation, and ideals, the first term is associated with conciliation; the second, with control.

LEARNING OBJECTIVES

After you have studied this chapter, you should be able to:

1. Describe the conciliation model of politics in terms of the characteristics of elites, groups, participation, and ideals which encourage its processes.
2. Describe the command model of politics in terms of the characteris-

tics of elites, groups, participation, and ideals which encourage its processes.

3. Explain how competing elites, associational groups, voluntary participation, and diverse ideals promote conciliation.
4. Contrast these with dominant elites, institutional groups, controlled participation, and ideological orthodoxy. Explain how the latter characteristics facilitate control.
5. Identify examples of conciliation and command processes and the social features which support them.
6. Explain why parochial groups are not easily governed through either conciliation or command.

There is a deceptive similarity in the expressed ideals of contemporary states and leaders. Most contemporary political leaders claim they believe in "democracy." The rhetoric of presidents and premiers from all parts of the world stresses such values as "popular welfare," "freedom," and "equality." Sukarno of Indonesia called his own particular brand of rule "guided democracy," and Eastern European leaders call their governments "people's democracies." Even when military leaders oust popularly elected governments as they have recently in Greece (1967) or Chile (1974), they usually justify their actions as being necessary to save "the people."

Such praises of democracy are, it seems, an essential part of political rhetoric in all parts of the globe. But we all know that political systems do clearly differ from each other. Some are more easily disrupted by popular dissatisfaction than others. Leaders come to office through competitive elections in some, while in others leadership is gained by intrigue, or by force. And in some states, policy decisions are greatly conditioned by public debate, while in others, secretive discussion in small groups is more influential.

In the preceding six chapters we have stressed political processes which are typical of all large states. Like democratic rhetoric, these processes are found wherever there is effective government. Also like democratic rhetoric, the manifestations of these processes can be seen to take various forms. It is to the differences between the forms which policy processes take that we now turn our attention.

In the following discussion we will develop two distinctive and very different general models of political processes, and will examine the social and political conditions which support them. Like all models, they are simplifications of reality. But like all useful models, they are based on certain important aspects of reality—in this case on real political systems—and they provide useful points of reference against which different political systems can be compared and analyzed.

CONCILIATION AND COMMAND

The two models presented below can appropriately be labeled the *conciliation* and the *command* models. Each focuses on contrasting processes by which political systems reach decisions and pursue goals. All actual political systems employ combinations of both processes, which will vary with the particular situation and with the purposes of the authorities. But some systems regularly employ one process more heavily than the other and may, as a result, be largely thought of and characterized as conciliation or command systems. In the conciliation model decisions and support are developed through the *accommodation of competing positions.* In command, they result from the *exercise of social control.*

A military unit engaged in battle is a simply understood, concrete example of the command model. Such a unit's objectives can be accomplished only when every soldier in it unquestioningly obeys the orders of superiors. Those who fail to obey must be harshly disciplined or even shot; the individual is merely an instrument of the larger group and must subordinate personal opinions, interests, and desires to the imperatives of command. Further, the objectives of the individual's unit are defined by an even higher headquarters. As part of an army, the unit must not define its own mission. Though information about the enemy's strength, the number of casualties, and the needs for supplies are sent up through channels, the battle plan belongs to the generals, not the privates, or even the captains.

Contrast a battle situation with a marketplace encounter. A buyer finds an antique he or she would like to purchase, but only at a certain price. The dealer wants to sell, of course, but only for a profit. Both parties have an interest in making a deal, but each wants somewhat different terms. Neither person can force the other to reach an agreement; the only tangible "punishment" either can administer is to break off negotiations. In this situation, each party can only persuade or entice the other toward a compromise. A price is finally agreed upon and the deal is made. It probably is acceptable, but not ideal, for both parties.

The individuals involved in each example above complied with decisions. The soldiers obeyed orders; the buyer paid the price that was agreed upon when he or she and the seller decided to proceed with the transaction, and the seller delivered the merchandise. But in the com-

The Dictionary on Conciliation and Command

We do not use the words "conciliation" and "command" precisely according to any one dictionary definition. Rather, the full meaning of the terms must be gleaned from the text discussion. Nevertheless, the following dictionary definitions approximate the meanings of the words as they apply to the conciliation and command models of politics:

Conciliate: to make compatible; reconcile; to overcome distrust or hostility; win over; to bring together.

Command: to have or exercise control over; to be master of, have at one's bidding or disposal; to exercise controlling authority. [*The Random House Dictionary of the English Language* (New York: Random House, 1967).]

mand model, those who obeyed did not participate in making the rules. In both cases, people worked toward objectives—soldiers to hold or to take ground, hagglers to make a deal. But the bargainers set their own goals; the soldiers did not. And whereas military superiors could coerce compliance, neither buyer nor seller could coerce the other; a mutually acceptable agreement had to be hammered out.

These are, of course, simple examples of the command and conciliation processes. Even countries with small populations are much more complex organizations than an army unit or two people negotiating at the marketplace. Governments also tend to last longer than the duration of a battle or a bargaining session in an antique store. Nevertheless, political leaders sometimes do issue orders much as if they were leading troops into battle, and when they do, they often gain compliance. In other cases, political leaders bargain—with each other, and with their constituents—in ways that call marketplace negotiations to mind.

Command model

If a nation were to be governed *purely* by command, all the policy processes discussed in the previous chapters would be controlled by the authorities. Decisions would be made and implemented without need to consider the demands of groups or political parties, or the contending resources of a resistant bureaucracy. The development of issues would be controlled through manipulation of group activities by the elite. There would be no means whereby bureaucrats could develop obstructive loyalties to each other or to their clients. Even the voicing of demands would thus be determined by central command.

Political socialization processes would necessarily be commanded as well. Citizens would be schooled in unquestioning compliance with the directives of the government. In order to control political learning, family and peers as well as schools and secondary groups would work the will of the authorities. No aspect of social life would escape political manipulation.

Finally, all communications would either originate with the ruling elite or respond to their directives. Since the attitudes of citizens would be engineered through control of socialization, distortion could be eliminated. Selective attention, perception, and retention would respond everywhere to orchestration from the top. Not only would citizens act in accordance with command, but they would speak and hear as they were told.

Conciliation model

In a society governed *purely* by conciliation, no single person or group would control another. All policy processes would be characterized by mutual accommodation and compromise. Issues would develop from competing opinions and interests and would be resolved through resolution of differences, with no interest ignored or made subordinate to others. Decisions would thus result from consensus built by discovering the common ground between competing positions. Policy would be implemented by consent, without need for coercive enforcement. Since all would agree on policy, none would find it expedient to deviate from the rules of society.

Such conciliation processes would be based upon decentralized political socialization processes. No central control of family, peer groups, schools, or secondary groups would exist. Many diverse cultures might be produced or maintained. And it would be assumed that, in spite of differences which might thus arise, an overriding interest in reaching agreement would make conflict manageable through compromise.

Similarly, communications might originate anywhere in society. There would be no central control, either of sending capability or of message content. Since divergent attitudes and values would exist, selective attention, perception, and retention would introduce continuous distortion. The process of compromise would thus depend upon constructive two-way communication. All parties would need to listen to each other as they attempted to understand their differences and search for common understandings.

The pure conciliation model may seem naive in its vision of politics by negotiation and agreement, but government by absolute control is also unrealistic. People are never entirely commanded or conciliated. These starkly simplified models can nevertheless assist our understanding of politics. Rather than characterize governments with such prejudicial terms as "dictatorial" or "democratic," we can search for the peculiar mixture of conciliation and command which is typical of each. And when we do, we will find that all actual governments are combinations of both models.

Models as Metaphors

Some readers may not be familiar with the way the term "model" is used in the social sciences. Abraham Kaplan describes models in this way:

> Models have been defined as "scientific metaphors". A metaphor, like an aphorism, condenses in a phrase a significant similarity. When the poet writes, "the morn in russet mantle clad, walks o'er the dew of yon high eastern hill", he evokes awareness of a real resemblance, and such awarenesses may be made to serve the purposes of science. When they do serve in this way we are likely to conceptualize the situation as involving the use of *analogy*. The scientist recognizes similarities that have previously escaped us, and systematizes them. Electricity exhibits a "flow"; there is a "current" exerting a certain pressure (the voltage), having a certain volume (the amperage), and so on. [Abraham Kaplan, *The Conduct of Inquiry: Methodology for Behavioral Science* (San Francisco: Chandler, 1964), p. 265.]

The essential characteristics of the command and conciliation models should now be clear. In the case of conciliation: (1) all persons have some resources which can be used in making binding decisions; (2) decisions are made through negotiation and compromise; (3) decisions are implemented through voluntary compliance based on general acceptance of their fairness; and (4) the system is sustained because the persons involved want it to persist.

On the other hand, the command model postulates: (1) a monopoly of resources is in the hands of only some of the participants; (2) decisions are made by those with a monopoly of resources and for reasons which they alone think are sufficient; (3) decisions are implemented by strict control of a bureaucracy; and (4) the system is sustained by use of the resources the elite possesses.

SOCIAL AND POLITICAL BASES OF CONCILIATION AND COMMAND

There are situations and times when command is the obviously appropriate means to achieve commonly held goals. Bureaucracies and military organizations are organized on the principle of command because they are designed to achieve goals set by others, and to achieve them efficiently. Conciliation would be destructive of the ability of a fighting army to do battle, and it is disruptive of any goal-seeking activity where success requires every participant's conformity to a central plan or policy. Alternatively, conciliation is probably the best way to reach decisions in some other situations. Under command, individuals are considered as instruments or *means* to be used to achieve the common end. In conciliation, individuals become ends in themselves; the common end cannot be defined without taking the views and interests of the participants into account. There are few who would think it appropriate for either the United Auto Workers or General Motors to command each other or to subdue each other with force—they are expected to compromise. Similarly, there are powerful interests in every society (even those which resist conciliation) which must be consulted and heeded before decisions are reached concerning them.

Our concern here is to identify the underlying conditions or foundations which support or sustain the political processes of command and conciliation. Four distinguishable social and political characteristics of societies will be examined and related to the models: (1) the interrelationships of elites; (2) the dominant features of groups and their patterns of interaction; (3) the nature of citizen participation; and (4) the dominant values or patterns of ideals of the society.

In general terms, the foundations of *conciliation* include (1) the sharing of power by competing elites; (2) the presence of many voluntary

Which Is Best, Conciliation or Command?

In our discussion of the conciliation and command models, we do not indicate that one is "better" than the other. This is not because we would just as soon be governed by one as by the other, or because we are insensitive to the need to make moral judgments about government. We, like other Americans, prefer the politics of conciliation to predominate in the society in which we live. On the other hand, we recognize that conciliation is not always possible, in the United States or elsewhere. And in much of the world, effective government can only be sustained through command—through tight social control. It would serve no useful purpose to fail to recognize that reality.

It is for these reasons that we try to identify the social conditions which are supportive of each type of policy process, rather than to discuss the morality of either. As we proceed to examine specific governments, we trust that it will become clear that these models are more useful in understanding various societies and their politics than in judging their morality.

associations and/or the opportunity to organize such groups; (3) the opportunity for significant and varied participation by most citizens in political processes; and (4) social values which stress toleration and accommodation of differences of opinion.

Table 7-1 Summary of the Conciliation and Command Models

	Conciliation	Command
Elites	Competing	One dominant
Social groups	Associational	Institutional
Participation	Voluntary	Controlled
Ideals	Diversity	Exclusivist
Policy made through:	Compromise	Control

In contrast, *command* is based upon (1) the ability of one individual or elite group to control all others; (2) the institutionalization of groups; (3) carefully regulated citizen participation in the political process; and (4) an exclusivist set of values or ideals which justifies and legitimizes the dominant position of the political elite.

Elites

Even in less-complex contemporary nations, there is more than one elite—for example, leaders of military, economic, social, and religious organizations. Since each elite is expected to serve the interests of the group it heads, and since each perceives issues from a different vantage point, disagreement between them is almost inevitable. Corporation executives want to maximize profits, while labor leaders want higher wages at the expense of profits. Military leaders seek resources for defense; others want those resources to be used for other purposes. The presence of conflicts among elites is common to all political systems. Differences between systems lie in the ways such conflicts are resolved.

Where conciliation is operative, conflict between elites is resolved by negotiation and compromise. Though in part this may be the case because social norms support compromise, the root cause of conciliation is the absence of an alternative. In the United States business executives might or might not wish to grant their workers high wages. Regardless of what they prefer, however, they know that labor leaders have enough political and economic clout to make it unwise to ignore their demands. Union leaders can deliver votes in important elections, and they also have the capacity to force work stoppages. Often, business executives must compromise for lack of a better alternative—which can also be said of representatives of organized labor. Similarly Democrats in Congress might or might not want to cooperate with Republicans. However they feel, they must work together if anything is to be accomplished, for a small number of the members of Congress can stall the legislative process.

Where command operates, the dominant political elite requires the obedience and support of all others. Military and managerial leaders, for example, must follow the battle or economic plan as directed. Open challenges or opposition to the political elite is treated as subversion, or at least as improper.

Dominant elites have sometimes gone to sharp extremes to ensure the preservation of their positions. Systems of informers and secret police with their own independent reporting lines to the top leaders have been established. In Stalinist Russia, for example, the secret police, as well as the Communist party itself, penetrated all parts of society, and both police agents and party members were responsible first to their own organizations. Thus, intelligence was gathered through special agencies, as well as through the normal bureaucratic or military channels. These special agencies were also authorized to punish those who deviated from the correct policies or otherwise failed to act as directed. Because of these elaborate measures, leaders in industry, in academia, and on the farms were made extremely vulnerable and put in a state of constant fear. When Stalin said, "Jump!" they had no choice but to reply, "How far?"

Stalinist Russia and Nazi Germany are unusually clear-cut examples of states organized along the lines of the command model. But "dictatorships" are not the only political systems which rely upon command to bring about desired outcomes. Even political leaders in such "democratic" nations as the United States have used coercion and control mechanisms to dominate other elites. In wartime, particularly, political authorities here have generally dominated social and economic life. The railroads were nationalized in World War I and dissenting opinions were suppressed. During World War II, the political parties submerged their differences and entered into a bipartisan coalition. Business and labor leaders were brought into government to advise and implement policies made at the highest levels. Support of the government was expected on all matters—wage levels, distribution of resources, and even the relocation of segments of the population.

To put the point differently, all states have the ability to coerce their citizens, at least some of the time. As much as political leaders might wish to reconcile differences between contending groups, they periodically find they must compel some to act contrary to their own preferences. When compulsion is introduced, the political elite assumes the dominant position and follows the dictates of the command model.

Social groups

In contemporary societies, the relationships between social groups and the authorities differ considerably from case to case. Some groups determine their own membership policies, activities, and purposes with little or no interference or intrusions by the political elite. In other cases, groups are creatures of the authorities, and their activities are intended to fulfill the needs of the governing elite.

These differences have many implications for the performance of a political system since, as we noted in Chapters 4 to 6, groups are vital links between individuals and government. It will be recalled that groups are central to the process of issue definition, that they play a crucial role in the transmission of political values from one generation to the next, and that they condition the reception of communications by citizens. If groups are closely regulated and supervised by the authorities, the formulation of policy proposals, the socialization of citizens, and the process of communications can be controlled. On the other hand, to the extent groups are independent, political socialization, issue definition, and communications may be correspondingly beyond the reach of the authorities.

It is easy to see why a dominant elite which utilizes command techniques prefers to rely upon controlled or institutional groups. The command model, then, postulates that the authorities will control membership policy, purposes, and the internal relationships of the groups within their society. It is also easy to see why authorities who cannot or will not dominate other groups must accept or support an independent or associational group structure. The conciliation model postulates that group membership policies, group purposes, and group autonomy will not be subject to pervasive centralized controls. The ways in which controlled groups can promote the ends of a dominant elite, and the contribution independent groups can make to the political processes of conciliation, will be developed below.

Associational groups   Associational groups are an important agency in the refinement of political demands into issues. They also serve as a vital link between individual citizens and the political system, even if their ends are not avowedly political. The linkages they provide promote bargaining—and conciliation. Let us see why.

Associational groups tend to proliferate, assuming they are free to do so. Should workers organize and achieve some of their objectives, business executives will tend to organize to "protect" themselves against the new "threat." If religious forces organize to obtain aid for parochial schools, others might well attempt to counter their efforts with a group of their own. Thus, the stage is set for competition among many groups, rather than domination by one or a few.

Proliferation and competition are not by themselves sufficient to ensure conciliation processes. Competition can result in confrontation and deadlock as well as conciliation and compromise. British coal miners who paralyzed national industry in the winter of 1974, forcing the country to adopt a 3-day workweek, placed their wage-increase demands above the pleas of the government to compromise. When demands become "nonnegotiable"—when the group's interests are paramount over all others—conciliation is difficult. Competition between such intransigent demands can result in capitulation of one group or another, or in the use of force to end the deadlock. In either case, one group will dominate others (recalling command processes); compromise and accommodation of various interests will not occur as conciliation processes require.

If, however, groups are unable to dominate each other, or to win their demands regardless of the cost to other groups or to society as a whole, conciliation is likely to result. The interests of many influential groups will be taken into account as policies are made and implemented. In this respect, the proliferation of associational groups helps to promote conciliation—where many groups share influence, no single group is likely to dominate the others.

Conciliation will be further promoted if associational groups develop *overlapping memberships* as they proliferate. This is so for two reasons. First, persons who belong to several groups have divided allegiances. They cannot support one totally at the expense of the other. As a result, if they are asked by their leaders to make a greater commitment than they are willing to do, they are likely to refuse, or even rebel. Group leaders must consequently make moderate demands upon their members and pursue moderate goals. If they do not, they risk the alienation of their rank and file, and a weakening of the group's resources.

Second, overlapping memberships also promote moderation and conciliation because members of diverse groups are thus brought together in a common bond. When an employer belongs to a church and is a fellow deacon with a union steward, he is likely to be more understanding of labor's political positions than if his only contact with unions was at the bargaining table. In fact, the two deacons might even use their contacts at church to discuss their differences from time to time. Thus, informal communication channels opened by overlapping membership may sometimes serve to resolve conflicts, as when black and white business leaders who belong to a common chamber of commerce work to calm tempers after a racial confrontation in their city.

Associations, then, support conciliation because their internal relationships as well as their ties to each other and to the political elite are based on a kind of reciprocity. As between leaders and their members, the latter must be satisfied at least to the point that their support of the organization will be continued. As between associations, and in their dealings with the authorities, there is a sharing of resources; each has some, but not a monopoly of, influence. And, since these interactions take place formally and informally, and at several levels, the bargaining opportunities are many and varied.

Institutional groups   The establishment and use of controlled or institutional groups is a logical strategy for any dominant elite. By their very nature, they can be used to organize and coordinate the activities of many individuals and thus provide the means for central control. If such institutions are pervasive and effectively integrated, entire societies can be made subject to the commands of the authorities. On the other hand, if institutional groups coexist with associations or other groups, the ability of the political elite to control the political process will be correspondingly diminished.

Institutional groups are an effective means for implementing commands because authorities can control virtually all aspects of their activities, and in fact, even their reason for existence. The authorities determine their objectives, their membership policies, the resources they will have to achieve their goals, the criteria by which group performance will be measured, and the sanctions or rewards their performance will receive. Ideally, no independent authority need be delegated to the group or its leaders, though in practice few groups are so entirely without autonomy. Whether one considers them in the abstract or looks at concrete cases, however, institutional groups are distinctive and fundamentally different from associations.

Political elites fully committed to the command principle have shown considerable skill in developing networks of institutional groups and in denying other bodies the opportunity to organize or maintain an independent existence. In the Soviet Union, for example, virtually every citizen must belong to, or is subject to, the controls of one government agency or another. Farm workers must belong to collective farms or must work on state farms. Workers are subject to the controls of unions whose goals are set by the state. Writers and artists must belong to organizations run by the state if their works are to be published or exhibited. Even children's groups like the Young. Pioneers and sport organizations are creations of the authorities and serve their ends. In addition, of course, citizens are subject to legal and administrative regulation and organizations.

Given the logic of the command principle, dominant elites who act by it discourage or even prohibit the formation of voluntary organizations; or failing that, they seek to bring them under institutionalized control. Voluntary associations in such cases are as inappropriate as voluntary participation in the military activities of an army. Just as such an army would be difficult to control, voluntary organizations are not always easily mobilized for the purposes of a dictator.

Though we have identified institutional groups as the agencies of command-oriented authorities, it must be emphasized that they are not peculiar to states ruled by dictators. They occur wherever organized compulsion is used and general policy is imposed on some persons by others. One example from our own past did not even directly involve government officials. Prior to the development of labor unions as voluntary associations in the United States, mining and manufacturing companies sometimes succeeded in structuring the group life of their workers in order to control them. Company towns with company stores limited the contact of workers with the outside world. Companies were able to control both the economic and the recreational activities of the employees. Company-dominated unions, company spies, and informers were used to thwart attempts to form voluntary associations. Control of the working force, and even of the family, was thus made virtually complete.

But it should not be concluded that institutional groups are necessarily oppressive. Members of controlled organizations, like members of voluntary associations, may find that group memberships can provide personal satisfaction and a way to relate to the system. A soldier may take pride in and develop close friendships within the combat unit. Institutional group memberships can provide a sense of social place even though group goals are determined externally rather than by intragroup action.

Citizen participation

All authorities need the active support of their citizens; the ambitious programs of modern governments require that citizens devote time and resources to make them successful. In this sense, citizen "participation" is essential to the effective performance of all political systems.

Nevertheless, participation may take significantly different forms. Chinese citizens who are gathered together each morning to read from the works of Chairman Mao "participate" in a way quite different from Japanese who work to elect fellow party members to the Diet, or legislature. And Germans who massed to hear Adolph Hitler in a torchlight meeting in Nuremberg were not participating politically in the same way as the Germans who 30 years later voted for the election of Willy Brandt as Chancellor.

Participation in conciliation processes Where conciliation processes prevail, citizen participation may take many forms, including demonstrations of patriotism and general compliance with the law. But in addition to such supportive acts, participation will sometimes result from the beliefs of individuals who think they can and should influence the making of public policy. When, on the other hand, individuals accept and obey the laws and relate *only* to the established bureaucratic and law-enforcement machinery, they may properly be viewed as *controlled.*

Citizens who believe they can influence public policy ordinarily justify their belief by pointing to specific mechanisms through which they can be heard. One, of course, might be the process by which the authorities are chosen. If the citizenry at large has a role in such processes, directly and indirectly—as in periodic, competitive elections—the candidates competing for votes will be forced to adopt popular policy positions or suffer the electoral consequences. And once in office, authorities must be responsive or risk defeat in the next election. This is especially so when voters feel free to change camps. President Johnson, for example, found out how quickly voters could move from support to opposition to his policies.

In addition to participation in competitive elections, citizens may exert influence through membership in associational groups. Unemployed union members, for example, may apply pressures for governmental assistance through the professional lobbyists their organizations employ; in extreme cases, they may even call a general strike.

It is not necessary for citizens to take action for conciliation to be fostered. It is sufficient that the potential for participation be real; that is, the threat of action is often enough to foster conciliation. When that is the case, elites are likely to be attentive. Where elites are in competition with each other, they must look to their constituents—whose welfare must be advanced if they are to continue to provide support. To support policies which might produce widespread resentment, resistance or loss of support runs counter to the interests of any competing elite.

Conciliation, then, will be fostered when citizens believe they have mechanisms to influence policies—one mechanism being the freedom to choose between competing elites and associational groups—and when they actually act upon those beliefs at least some of the time.

Controlled participation When a dominant elite governs by command, individual participation is controlled. Much of the time this will be accomplished by placing citizens into one or several institutional groups, as when soldiers participate by following the command to do battle. But controlled participation might result in other ways as well. Newspapers might be directly used to arouse support for a policy or opposition to an "enemy" of "the people." And controls might be indirect, as when a government withholds information which might lead to loss of public support, or creates a climate of intimidation in which a newspaper or broadcasting station fears to criticize a governmental policy or support an idea that is opposed by the government.

It is easy, of course, to identify controlled participation in so-called totalitarian states like the Soviet Union or China. Parades, noncompetetive elections, concerted expressions of support for the authorities and their public policies are commonplace events there.

But controlled participation occurs elsewhere as well. President Johnson obtained congressional support for his "Tonkin Gulf Resolution" by controlling information about the conditions leading to the incident. President Nixon's staff paid for telegrams sent to the White House in support of the President's policies, and even organized and paid for delegations to go to Washington to demonstrate for the President. And who has not seen school children and public officials standing at parades honoring important political officials when they ordinarily would be in school or on the job?

Ideals: orthodoxy and diversity

The importance of shared attitudes or a national ideology was emphasized in Chapter 6. It was seen that communication between officials and citizens requires their frames of reference to have at least some elements in common. If citizens are to understand, much less to obey, they must perceive facts, and value goals, in ways which support their public officials' interpretations of social reality. For this reason, political leaders seek a degree of consistency and conformity among the ideals of individual followers.

When elites make and enforce policies by command, they tend to demand ideological *orthodoxy* from their citizens. The state ideology supersedes any competing religion, view of history, or loyalty. Extreme contemporary examples are the Soviet Union and the People's Republic of China, where dissent from the authorities' interpretations of Marxism is severely punished.

Less-extreme examples are found everywhere, including the United States. When American leaders feel it is necessary to mobilize the nation, as in wartime, they call for unity of purpose, for dedication to common goals. During World Wars I and II supposedly "dangerous" dissenters were imprisoned in the United States. During the more recent Vietnam conflict, where dissent was more widespread and vocal, denunciation of dissent by politicians was supplemented by "America, Love it or Leave it" bumperstickers in response to youthful protest.

Whether the content of the political orthodoxy is mainly nationalistic, religious, a social doctrine, or some combination of these, it will be promoted and enforced as unity of purpose is sought. As a state moves closer to the command model, the dedication of citizens to the purposes of the elite is increasingly demanded, and dissent is more strongly suppressed.

In contrast, conciliation is fostered by the tolerance of diverse ideals, and by a willingness to compromise narrower interests for a larger social good. Members of society agree to disagree. On the Great Seal of the United States the words *E Pluribus Unum* are inscribed. Roughly translated, these words mean "diversity within unity." Generally, the words express the sentiment that society ought to be built upon a consensus which does not necessarily extend to specific social and political policies or doctrines. While unity is sought, diverse opinions within the larger whole are recognized as legitimate. To the extent that this kind of ideational base actually exists, conciliatory functioning becomes possible.

COMMAND AND CONCILIATION: IMPORTANCE OF SOCIAL EXPECTATIONS

We have now described the social bases of two simple models of the political process. Where command processes predominate, one elite dominates. The elite uses controlled groups and organizes the citizenry according to its purposes. Its supremacy is rationalized by an orthodox set of values and ideals with which the people may not properly disagree. Where conciliation processes predominate, elites interact and compete, groups are formed and act apart from government direction and control, citizens play a variety of political roles, and a diversity of ideals is generally accepted.

A second major theme has also been stressed: existing political systems combine elements of both conciliation and command. For example, institutional groups such as military forces, bureaucracies, and public schools are found in all nation-states. In all states, as well, some persons outside the elite structure make demands upon the political leaders in the fashion we would expect in a conciliation situation. But we have not yet considered why it is that these seemingly inconsistent models can be meshed within a stable political entity, and why both command and conciliation processes are viable alternatives for political systems.

The crucial factor for the preservation of any political system is the existence of a reasonable balance between the general expectations of a people and their perceptions of political reality. When we think it is appropriate to be ordered around, and in fact expect to be commanded to "march!" or stand at "parade rest!" we probably will comply when the order is given. But if those same orders were to be issued to us in different and inappropriate circumstances (say, in a classroom), we would probably react with laughter, hostility, or both; compliance would certainly be less than automatic.

Expectations vary from one nation to the next. In some, policies are ordinarily expected to result from discussion and compromises. In others, the authorities are presumed to have the right to decide pretty much as they want. In still others, expectations about which process is appropriate—conciliation or command—might depend upon the specific issue. In the first case, compliance with policy decisions would be maximized when they were derived from conciliation processes. In the second, the command model would meet with general approval. And in the third, either or both might be appropriate. But whichever the case, frustrated expectations would reduce the ability of the authorities to govern.

Public officials, of course, sometimes try to alter expectations so as to further their objectives. Franklin Roosevelt sought to "educate" the American people to the needs of breaking with an isolationist past. Stalin expended great efforts and resources to create a new Soviet mentality. And leaders in the third world have similarly voiced hopes of changing public attitudes. Most of the time, however, public officials have not been able to fully control the processes of socialization. Consequently, they have been forced in the short run to deal with public attitudes they can do little to change. For example, attempts to legislate racial equality in the United States have not been notably successful; large numbers of Americans do not want to comply with open-housing laws or fair-employment regulations. Similarly, Soviet leaders have been unable to implement a policy of planned migration from the rural to the urban areas of the U.S.S.R.; peasants have all too often decided on their own that life in the city is what they must have.

Over longer periods of time, perhaps two or three generations, authorities undoubtedly can have a significant impact on public attitudes and expectations. The use of educational institutions, the control over secondary groups, and even the regulation of family activities and relationships are all options available to the authorities, particularly if they are used prudently.

Where citizen ideals are reasonably homogeneous and the national culture is stable, governments typically employ mixtures of conciliation and command to suit the expectations of the people. Officials usually know where the sensibilities of the people will not allow political control; when they do not, their actions may trigger a widespread public outcry— as in the "firestorm" of public protest when President Nixon fired Special Prosecutor Archibald Cox—or evasion and defiance—as in the case of deserters and draft evaders during the Vietnam war. Even in societies governed more by command than by conciliation processes, officials must know what their citizens can be expected to "put up with." Russian peasants, long used to the command process, nevertheless offered massive resistance to Stalin's policy of the collectivization of agriculture in the 1930s. (Stalin was able to overcome this resistance only by using the most extreme possible measures: he killed thousands of peasants.) They are aware of influential groups and elites which must be placated. And they can appeal to a national ideology to rally support, resolve differences, and exercise command. When, however, the national ideology does not provide a set of expectations concerning a given policy, when (as in the case of some of the newer "emerging" nations composed of several different cultural or tribal groups) there is no national ideology, or when subcultures regularly resist authority, then severe problems can emerge. Most large states have these difficulties to some degree but they are more obvious in the newer nations.

Problems of parochialism

With the decline of European colonial domination since World War II, independent nations have been established in Asia and Africa. These nations typically are composed of people who do not share a common cultural background, and who are "nations" in name, but not in strong feelings of popular unity. Having united to oppose rule by European foreigners, they have found upon achieving independence that it is difficult to coordinate the efforts of their culturally diverse populations. The bitter civil war in Nigeria, earlier thought to be one of the more stable of the new nations, underlined the problems of achieving national unity in the developing states. The war was fostered by long-standing conflicts between the cultures and the people of Ibo, Hausa, and Yoruba tribal groups—conflicts of a type by no means peculiar to Nigeria.

The first generation of leaders of many new states were typically men who had been trained in Western schools, having there acquired Western skills related to law and administration. They were, thus, subject to socialization processes quite different from those which still shaped the attitudes of the ordinary tribesmen and villagers over whom they attempted to govern. For these leaders, nationhood was seen as a means to achieve greater economic prosperity and a more important role in world affairs. For tribal peoples, on the other hand, the national government was distant from everyday concerns, and its programs were thought to undermine treasured ways of life in much the same way that the European colonialists did. This state of affairs—based on the unfavorable attitudes toward the national government—we may call *parochialism.*

Such parochialism was, of course, once characteristic of the Western "colonialistic" nations. In their infancy, nation-states such as France, Great Britain, and Germany were parochial in the extreme; their first kings were ambitious leaders of smaller political units (which were often distinct cultural groups) who unified—often by force—two or more smaller units into a single "nation-state." And, like the leaders of modern societies which are still "parochial," they sought to establish and strengthen their society's nationhood partly in order to achieve greater economic prosperity and a more important role in world affairs. It took generations—even centuries—for the European nation-states to reduce parochialism to manageable proportions, and even today Western nations are not free of the problem. French Canadians resist the English-speaking majority, Basques resent the governments of Spain and France, and Welsh and Scottish separatists seek to separate from Britain.

In any case, parochialism is an obstacle to modernization by the political leaders of new states precisely because the parochial citizen thinks his own values are superior to those of other portions of the population and to the programs of the central government. Thus we can speak of the "problem" of parochialism from the perspective of national leaders who have difficulty in gaining sufficient support for their policies from the subcultures contained within their national boundaries. In practical terms, such leaders must try to alter popular attitudes sufficiently to unify their states, without alienating major groups of people in the process.

The problem of parochialism is thus severe for leaders whenever it is a dominant element in the attitudes of a people. It comes down to the proposition that parochial attitudes are not suited to the ambitions of national governments. Both conciliation and command require a degree of citizen involvement which can only be obtained from citizens who will work toward common national goals, holding their allegiance to less-inclusive cultural values as secondary to their ties to the national state.

SUMMARY AND CONCLUSION

Both conciliation and command processes demand that the persons involved have common interests—that there be a mutually perceived stake in the outcome. It is difficult to command groups which define authority by their own cultural values rather than by those of the dominant political culture or by the values of the central elite. Such groups conceivably could be "conciliated" if the term were used to mean mollified or placated. As we are using the term, however, conciliation processes require participation in defining the common goals and policies of an organization or a state.

Thus, groups which perceive their fate and aspirations as independent of the policies of others are unlikely to be involved in conciliation processes. In the community of nations, American isolationism was surrendered only when Americans came to perceive that their national fate was related to the actions of European and Asian powers. Tribal government has not been surrendered by the American Indians in spite of Washington's attempts both to command them and to involve them in political participation. Tribal culture and tribal authority is still viewed as more legitimate than the White Man's.

The mix of conciliation and command which will develop in any given state will depend upon its political culture and upon the ideology of the political elite. In any case, the authorities must appeal to cultural values to legitimate their actions and enhance their ability to govern. Where ideology is imposed by the elite, coercion through force and repression is usually necessary. This can be as true of the republicanism imposed on the defeated Confederated States after the American Civil War as of the imposition of Leninist ideology on the countries of Eastern Europe after World War II. In both of these examples, massive armed force was needed to impose an ideology. It should also be noted that in both cases the mixture of conciliation and command processes in the subjugated states remains different from the mixture in the subjugating power to the current day. Southern politics is distinctively different from politics in the rest of the United States; and the politics of the non-Russian communist states varies from country to country under the influence of culture transmitted from the past.

We will now turn to five examples of contemporary nation-states and examine the varying patterns of conciliation and command which have emerged in them. In each case it will be seen that current patterns of elite interaction, group activity, citizen participation, and political ideals rest upon values transmitted form the political culture of the past. History and traditions strongly influence political practices.

SUGGESTED READINGS

Gabriel A. Almond and Sidney Verba, *The Civic Culture* (Boston: Little, Brown, 1965). The classic survey research study which attempts to relate political culture to governmental performance.

William Kornhauser, *The Politics of Mass Society* (New York: Free Press, 1959). A provocative analysis of the role of groups in mediating between individuals and government, and their importance to governmental stability.

Gabriel A. Almond and G. Bingham Powell, Jr., *Comparative Politics: An Analytic Study* (Boston: Little, Brown, 1966). Good introduction to comparative political systems and the functional approach to the study of politics.

David E. Apter, *The Politics of Modernization* (Chicago: University of Chicago Press, 1966). Sophisticated treatment of models as tools for analyzing social and political development.

CHAPTER EIGHT

AMERICAN SOCIETY AND POLITICS

OVERVIEW   This is the first of five chapters which will compare the politics of five nations with each other and with our models of conciliation and command. None of these chapters will present a comprehensive introduction to the nation in question. Rather, a summary of major features of each will be presented, and aspects of command and conciliation politics will be discussed as they apply to each country.

It is important to note that the *formal* institutions of a nation do not fully describe its politics. In the American case, the formal definition of elites and provisions for free citizen participation serve as a strong basis for conciliation politics. However, the formal provisions are both supported and subverted by social elements which are not formally defined.

This chapter is organized to help you to compare the United States with the other countries in a systematic way. It moves from (1) the formal elites (constitutional framework) and a brief discussion of actual relationships between the formal elites (presidential ascendance), to (2)

184   ☆

elites which are not formally defined, but which are influential (parties and groups), to (3) citizen participation, and finally to (4) the cultural and political ideals of Americans.

This chapter thus covers the four basic elements of the conciliation and command models: (1) elites, (2) groups, (3) participation, and (4) ideals. These four topics will be treated for each of the four other countries as well.

You may find that selective review of Chapters 2 through 5 is helpful as you read Chapter 8.

Be sure that you understand the following terms:

Constitution of 1787
Separation of powers
   Legislative
   Executive
   Judicial
Checks and balances
Federalism
Representative government
Constitutionalism
Congress
   House of Representatives

Senate
President
Supreme Court
   Judicial review
Bicameral
Unicameral
Two-party system
   Republican party
   Democratic party

LEARNING OBJECTIVES

After you have studied this chapter, you should be able to:

1. List the *formal* elites of American politics as defined by the Constitution of the United States.
2. Describe the formal features of American government which promote conciliation in politics.
3. Explain how constituencies combine with the formal features of American politics to promote conciliation.
4. Identify the major political parties in the United States and the major similarities and differences between them.
5. Explain why associational group differences in the United States do not generally lead to violent confrontations.
6. Identify two major social groups which experience American politics as a command system.

If the government of the United States operated solely according to the formal provisions of its Constitution, it would be relatively simple to describe and to understand. The important and complex influences from such bodies as political parties, interest groups, and the press could be ignored. Only occupants of formally defined roles such as representatives, senators, Supreme Court justices, and the President would shape public policy. Elections and public debate would be the most important means of citizen participation.

However, American politics, like politics everywhere, is only partly defined by the formal rules of the political game. Also involved are other important social and political customs and practices which operate without formal definition. It is therefore important to understand both the formal and the informal features of politics in the United States.

The major characteristics of the American system can be summarized as follows: The Constitution of 1787 establishes a *presidential* executive system, and divides governmental responsibility between the President, a *bicameral legislature,* and an *independent judiciary.* Its *federal* system divides authority between the national government and the states. This formal, constitutional provision for roles and powers is supplemented by a *two-party system* and by numerous competing and influential associations or *interest groups.* Political parties and interest groups are not accorded formally defined powers and roles by the Constitution, but they are crucial in the development and resolution of issues in American politics as actually practiced.

FORMAL RULES: THE CONSTITUTIONAL FRAMEWORK

The basic structure of American politics is defined by the Constitution of 1787, which provides for competing elites and representative government. It further places limits on the authority of the governing elites, as, for example, the power of impeachment, which enables the Congress to remove "the President, Vice President, and all civil officers" from office (Article II, Section 4), or the prohibition against governmental interference with the rights of citizens to speak or to assemble and criticize officials and their policies (First Amendment). The formal, legal framework of American politics, then, has a strong bias toward conciliation, as against command; elites are placed in competition, and broad popular rights to participate in policy formulation are "guaranteed." Command functions in the United States because of (1) the need to enforce policies, (2) deviation from the legal framework of government, and (3) social factors which exclude some citizens from participation.

Separation of powers

The American Constitution vests largely independent powers in three coordinate branches of government—the President, the Congress, and the Supreme Court. It assigns *executive* powers to the President, *legislative* powers to the Congress, and *judicial* powers to the courts. This division of responsibility has traditionally been known as *separation of powers.* In the framework of the earlier chapters of this text, a strict adherence to separation of powers would mean that Congress would bear primary responsibility for evaluating issues and making policy decisions, the President for implementing them, and the courts for resolving disputes under the Constitution and laws.

The drafters of the Constitution of 1787 institutionalized this separation of powers both out of philosophical conviction and on the basis of their experience with British rule. They generally agreed with the reasoning of the French philosopher Montesquieu who had defined tyranny as the concentration of legislative, executive, and judicial powers in the hands of one person or group. He prescribed the separation of these powers as a means to preserve the liberty of citizens. The Founding Fathers had also experienced the rule of British governors who attempted, as they saw it, to render their colonial legislatures ineffective. Consequently any executive, including the President, was seen as a potential king, and Presidential influence on policy decisions was therefore to be kept within bounds. The Congress and the courts were to serve as independent checks upon Presidential power, hence the formal separation of decision making, policy implementation, and adjudication.

Checks and balances

In practice, of course, the separation of powers is far from absolute. Even the Constitution provides that the President should propose policy measures to Congress, and approve its legislative acts, thus involving the "executive" in "legislation." Likewise, the Senate must review Presidential appointments to administrative agencies, and both houses of Congress act as watchdogs over the implementation of laws by the President and his subordinates. These overlappings of function within the separation of powers contribute to a system of *checks and balances* between the constitutionally designated centers of power. The President, Congress, and the courts are able to influence and restrain each other.

The system of checks and balances is further enhanced by a formal division of the Congress into two houses—the Senate and the House of Representatives. When a legislature is divided in this fashion it is called *bicameral,* denoting that there are two chambers, as opposed to a *unica-*

meral legislature, which is composed of only one body. In the United States, both the Senate and the House must concur upon legislation before it is forwarded to the President for approval or disapproval. Because of this requirement, differences in policy must be reconciled, usually through compromise and negotiation.

Bicameralism in the United States promotes bargaining and compromise both formally and operationally. Representatives and senators are jealous of the prestige and influence of their respective houses. Neither senators nor representatives take lightly any indication that their own house is less than equal to the other in prestige, power, or responsibility. This sense of identification on their parts helps to ensure that neither house of Congress will dominate or dictate to the other. (See Figure 8-1.)

A unique practice in the United States has further enhanced the system of checks and balances. Though not explicitly authorized by the Constitution to do so, the courts have assumed the right to declare actions of the Congress or the President null and void when they violate provisions of the Constitution. This is called *judicial review.* Through this practice the courts have effectively developed the ability to veto policy decisions. Many observers have cited the doctrine of judicial review in maintaining that American courts actually *make* law (or at least unmake it), rather than confining themselves to the *interpretation* of it. In any case, courts in the United States play a more active role in policy processes than their counterparts do in other nations; their prestige and authority are formidable.

Judicial Review

The doctrine and practice of judicial review was introduced to American government by Chief Justice John Marshall in the now-famous case of *Marbury v. Madison* in 1803. Marshall ruled that the court could not enforce an unconstitutional law. In so doing, he effectively set aside an act of Congress and the President. Marshall held that congressional acts had to conform to the Constitution, and implied that the Constitution meant what the Supreme Court said it did.

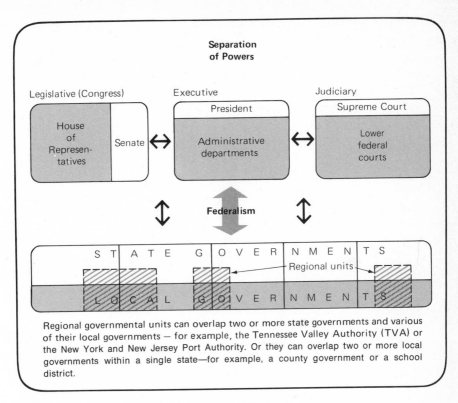

Figure 8-1. Separation of powers in the United States.

Federalism

In addition to separating powers at the national level, the Constitution establishes a further division of authority, usually called *federalism.* While the central, or "federal" government is supreme in its area of competency, states are nevertheless guaranteed substantial autonomy. This arrangement resulted because the original thirteen states existed prior to the federal government. While they accepted a balance of powers between the federal and state levels, they were not willing to surrender broad areas of their own authority.

Federalism is an important feature of the American system. The various state governments operate somewhat differently from each other, mainly because of historical differences; their basic patterns were established long ago, when their jurisdictions were virtually autonomous and when there were real regional differences in the ways of life of their citizens. But even today, of course, there is a distinctive flavor to both politics and social life in South Carolina as compared with New Hampshire, or in Texas as compared with Oregon. Moreover, none of the states is able to impose its will on the others. Each state has its own set of political institutions. While the federal government may act as a referee in disputes which arise between states, it is not supposed to act as a central directing agency. That is, American state governments expect to make—and do make—many independent decisions. They do not simply carry out orders from the central system, or from each other.

Supremacy of the Federal Government

From 1798 to 1865 there were periodically heated debates as to the extent of federal powers over the several states of the United States. In response to the Alien and Sedition Acts of the Adams administration the Jeffersonians formulated the argument that since the states created the Union, they were empowered to interpret the Constitution for themselves. If a state should find a law to be unconstitutional, it could declare it null, void, and unenforceable within its boundaries. As friction developed between the Northern and Southern states, the South further developed this doctrine of "nullification" and finally claimed the right of any state to withdraw or "secede" from the Union.

The point is still debated, but for practical purposes it was settled by the Civil War, or as it is known in the South, the War Between the States.

Representative government

It will be recalled from Chapter 7 that competition between elites is one of the main conditions which supports conciliation. Separation of powers, checks and balances, and federalism provide a formal framework which could logically be expected to produce competition between elites in American government. The President and his department heads, the House of Representatives, the Senate, the Supreme Court, and governors of states might reasonably be expected to have differing perspectives and policy opinions. Each of these potentially competing elites has constitutional standing, and has a legally sanctioned role in decision making and implementation. Thus the formal structure of government which establishes several independent political elites in the United States should promote conciliation in politics.

But the establishment of several interdependent but powerful elites would have little effect if they did not hold competing positions on issues. If the Congress, the President, the Courts, and the state governments were always in agreement, or if one of them in practice (as opposed to theory) controlled the others, decisions by compromise and conciliation would not be likely to occur.

Representative government serves to make the *formal* provisions for competition between elites *actual.* High public officials in the United States are either chosen in competitive elections by the citizenry or else hold office at the pleasure of those who are so elected. (Even Supreme Court justices, who are appointed for life, can be impeached and removed from office by Congress.) While selecting officeholders by popular election does not guarantee that every wish of every voter will be translated into government action, it does assure that officials will have a degree of sensitivity to the desires of those who can give or take away their jobs.

This sensitivity is particularly important to conciliation when different elites are elected by different constituencies, as in the United States. Because the Founding Fathers took care to see that the Constitution stipulated that officials be elected by different constituencies, the officials tend to have different policy preferences and priorities. The President is elected by a national constituency; candidates for that office seek votes from the entire voting-age population. Senators, on the other hand, are elected by the voters of their respective states. Representatives are chosen by districts which are usually smaller than a state. We should expect then that Presidents would be sensitive to demands of a national public, senators to the dominant sentiments in their states, and members of the House to the voters of their local districts. Each of these leaders or groups of leaders thus tends to have a different perspective on policy, for each will be sensitive to the wishes of different sets of voters. In addition, each group serves terms in office of different length (the President, 4 years; representatives, 2 years; and senators, 6 years—one-third standing for election each 2 years), so that as public debate changes over time, their responses will be to different issues at election time.

The number of constituencies voicing particular demands is greatly increased by the federal character of the political system. Each state has its own government and independently conducts elections to fill state political offices. State governments consequently differ widely in interests and orientations. State officials vie with each other for funds from Washington and represent the interests of their constituents to each other and to the federal government.

Representative government promotes conciliation in local politics as it does at the federal and state levels. The American states are subdivided into almost countless overlapping local political units—counties, cities, townships, school districts, and many others. In fact, there are over 100,000 separate units of local government in the United States, virtually all of which are headed by elected officials. Each has a separate constituency. This situation has been described as chaotic, but it is obvious that such a vast number of local governments ensures that a good deal of interchange between local officials will take place. Since none of these political actors can dominate the others, these officials are forced to accommodate one another's interests if they are to achieve desired ends at all.

The formal provisions of the basic law of the United States thus provide clearly for two of the reinforcing and basic conditions which foster conciliation in politics: (1) competition between elites and (2) citizen participation. No single elite is authorized to control issue development, or policy decisions and implementation under the separation of powers and federalism. Elections provide a vehicle for citizen participation and promote competition between elites as they respond to differing constituencies. There is a clear basis in the law, then, to expect American policy processes to reflect conciliation rather than command.

Presidential ascendance: bending the formal framework

The constitutional framework of American government leads to the expectation that Congress, the President, and the courts will have essentially equal influence on policymaking. In practice, however, the President has become considerably more powerful than the legislative and judicial branches. There are a number of reasons for this development, including the organizational effectiveness of the executive, its wealth of resources, the increasing importance of foreign affairs, and the great prestige of the Presidential office.

Congress is granted "all legislative power" by the Constitution. This could be interpreted to mean that as congressional constituents make demands, representatives and senators work to develop and decide issues, sending their policy decisions to the President in the form of laws. If this were the case, the House and the Senate would speak for the people, and the President and his administration would execute the people's will.

In practice, the Congress is usually unable to formulate clear programs of public policy. It generally reacts to the President's proposals, rather than formulating its own, and in fact has passed laws requiring the President to submit his programs for congressional action. This is a consequence of the fact that neither house of Congress, much less both of them together, is sufficiently unified to formulate a full legislative program of its own. The leaders in Congress cannot command a consistent majority of votes; rather, they patch together temporary coalitions on the various matters which come before them.

The difficulty of building a solid congressional majority reflects the American two-party system. Both parties are loose coalitions of diverse interests. While one party (usually the Democrats in recent years) may have sufficient votes to elect the leaders of the House of Representatives and the Senate, its members will agree unanimously on little else. Northern and Southern Democrats divide on many issues, as do Eastern and Western Republicans. Each party has its more "conservative" and its more "liberal" members, and on some issues conservative Republicans find their ranks swelled by Democrats of similar persuasion, while liberal Republicans desert to the Democratic side. Members of Congress thus must work continuously to compromise their differences and build coalitions on specific legislative proposals. Their leaders are rarely able to build a comprehensive program and pass it.

In contrast to the Congress, the President can speak with one voice. He is the only elected officer in American government with a national constituency. Further, he heads the vast resources of the federal bureaucracy, which is a command structure designed to respond to Presidential direction. While the bureaucracy does not always respond automatically to his direction, its departments are headed by Presidential appointees who usually will not openly oppose his orders.

The President and the bureaucracy are also better able to develop issues than are representatives and senators because administrators have specialized expertise and information about policy problems, which is not readily available to the Congress. They deal directly with the people who are affected by policy decisions and can note the effects of existing policy. Their knowledge and skill serves as the basis for recommendations to the President, who in turn formulates them into his own policy programs for submission to Congress. Congress is thus placed in the position of reacting to clearly and expertly drafted proposals. Representatives and senators must deal with the broad range of policy matters put before them. Their staffs cannot duplicate the specialized focus and skills of the bureaucracy. Without staff resources to watch the executive branch, Congress is clearly at a disadvantage in formulating the issues which become the basis of policy.

Another factor which has promoted executive power is the increasing importance of foreign affairs. It is to the clear advantage of any nation to present a unified front in international affairs. If many conflicting voices are heard, its position is obscure and its interests are likely to suffer. Since the President has primary responsibility for foreign affairs, the Congress has tended to support him fully so that foreign governments will not be able to exploit internal differences. As a result, while the Senate must ratify treaties, and only Congress can legally declare war, the President nevertheless has come to have virtually unchecked power to make foreign policy.

Foreign affairs have become increasingly crucial for the United States since the nation emerged as a world power at the end of the nineteenth century. As America grew in wealth and power, it was no longer possible to maintain an aloof neutrality in international affairs. Twice in this century the United States played a major part in world wars. And since 1945, the American government has had an active interest in developments everywhere on the globe.

Foreign matters have consequently consumed increasing amounts of time, attention, and money, and have enhanced the authority and discretion of the Chief Executive at the expense of Congress. As Commanders-in-chief of the military, recent Presidents have ordered troops onto foreign soil as emergency measures to protect what they believed were America's global interests. In Korea and Vietnam, lengthy wars were conducted without formal congressional declarations of war as required by the Constitution. Once American troops were engaged, it was almost impossible for Congress to refuse to support them. When the President acted with speed and decisiveness, Congress had little choice but to support him.

The ascendance of the President is further buttressed because he is the ceremonial *chief of state* as well as the chief executive officer of the government. As such, the President is a living symbol of the nation. The occupant of the White House is accorded patriotic deference and is sometimes regarded with almost mystic awe. Even the scandals uncovered in the Nixon administration did not do serious damage to the *office,* though the President himself was forced to resign.

Thus, in spite of the formal powers granted to the legislature and the courts to check the Executive, the President and the bureaucracy he heads have become "more equal than others" in policymaking processes. Though Congress still must enact laws, levy taxes, and appropriate funds before a President's program can be put into effect, and high administrative appointments require the advice and consent of the Senate, congressional power to obstruct is more real than its ability to originate policies to meet the changing conditions of American social life.

INFORMAL REALITIES: PARTIES AND GROUPS

Political parties

The drafters of the American Constitution made no formal provision for political parties. The delegates to the Constitutional Convention feared partisan divisiveness and selfishness as much as they feared "the tyranny of the majority," and they hoped that by giving them no place in the Constitution, they would not come into being. Nevertheless, politicians in the young American republic soon found that in order to win public office, they had to build political organizations. As Thomas Jefferson, James Madison, and Aaron Burr sought to oppose the policies of George Washington, John Adams, and Alexander Hamilton, they developed the first popularly based political party in a modern nation. The Democratic party has its origins in this infant opposition movement.

The constitutional provisions for representative government might well not have had the same effect if political parties had not developed. Parties began as practical expedients to serve the interests of office seekers, and they continue to serve that function. But as a corollary, they provide the vehicle whereby American voters can take part in the selection of the competing elites their Constitution defines. The party affiliation of candidates helps voters to choose meaningfully among them. Without political parties, elections would be considerably more chaotic, and popular participation might well be less than it currently is.

In recent years, about three out of four adult Americans have considered themselves to be either Democrats or Republicans. Of those who call themselves "independents," most will, when pressed, express a leaning toward one or the other of the major parties; typically, less than 10 percent refuse to express any party preference at all. A very small percentage of voters typically cast ballots for other parties.

This division of most Americans into two political camps could suggest a serious cleavage in society. However, partisan differences do not usually undermine American national unity, for the division between

Democrats and Republicans does not generally reflect deep personal or ideological animosities. In their five-nation survey, Almond and Verba found that Americans did not attribute significantly more negative characteristics to members of the opposite party than to their own. Only about 4 percent of each party's supporters said they would be displeased if their sons or daughters married someone from the opposite party.[1]

Further, other studies have shown that party cleavage on day-to-day political issues is not intense. It has been found that though the *leadership* of the Republican and Democratic parties differs significantly on such matters, the *average voter* in each party tends to have views similar to counterpart voters in the other party.[2] Political parties in the United States thus seem to serve basically as points of reference for choosing between candidates for office. They do not, as a rule, divide Americans deeply on matters of intense personal or social concern.

Thus, in spite of the fears of the Founding Fathers, parties have become important, and even indispensable to the American political process. Without them it would be difficult or impossible to organize effective opposition to incumbent government officials and policies. It would be much easier for a sitting President or member of Congress to name his or her successor, and more difficult for newcomers to enter public life. And without effective opposition, it is more likely that a dominant elite could stifle its competition and govern by command. While partisan politics sometimes appears to be base and demeaning, the absence of political parties would probably make politics less relevant and acceptable to most Americans.

Associational groups

Like political parties, groups representing various interests play an important role in American politics, despite the lack of constitutional provisions for them to do so. When the American republic was founded, it was widely assumed that differences between interests were geographically distributed. The major differences in economic interests seemed to be between agriculture and commerce. Rural states and districts would, it was thought, elect representatives to promote and protect their interests, and city people would do likewise. Elections would thus produce ade-

---

[1]Gabriel A. Almond and Sydney Verba, *The Civic Culture* (Boston: Little, Brown, 1965), pp. 64–65.

[2]Herbert McClosky, "Issue Conflict and Consensus among Leaders and Followers," *American Political Science Review,* vol. 54, pp. 406–427, 1960.

quate representation of interests, and differences could be reconciled in the Congress and state legislatures. But whether or not various interests are in fact adequately represented through the electoral process, they have not left it to government to interpret their needs without further pressure and assistance. Associations in the United States seek to influence public policy by spending money on propaganda ("presenting their point of view") and campaign contributions, by lobbying in the Congress and state legislature; and through working closely with administrative offices responsible for implementing policies which affect them. The popular image of these groups and their attempts to influence government is one of questionable activities: of smoke-filled rooms, bribery, and big campaign contributions in exchange for favorable governmental treatment. Thus, while partisan politics may sometimes seem distasteful, interest-group politics is often felt to be immoral. While parties only seek to win positions of authority, groups appear to distort the will of the people—to redirect it to favor narrower interests.

This popular American view is understandable, given the recurrent scandals which have surrounded interest-group activities. From the filching of the Revolutionary Army treasury by Philadelphia merchants, to the machinations of Teapot Dome and Watergate, private interests have used the American government for selfish ends. Still, we have seen that groups are important to the policy process in that they articulate and support the demands of segments of society which the authorities must satisfy. In the American case, what should be at issue is not so much the legitimacy of associational groups as the apparent ability of some groups to advance their interests unfairly, at the expense of others.

That is, while voluntary associations are necessary to conciliation processes, they almost inevitably develop varying abilities to influence policy decisions. Hence, instead of "perfect" competition between varying interests, some gain near monopolies of influence and can then command the policies they desire. The result is a dilemma: the conciliation of competing interests could not take place if interest groups did not assert themselves in the public arena. But as they participate in bargaining processes, stronger groups tend to use any means available in order to achieve their ends. Since organization is the key to their success, the interests of the isolated or unorganized tend to be ignored.

Thus, in some ways, interest groups clearly promote conciliation in American politics. The competing demands of organizational representatives help to shape the actions of legislators and bureaucrats. To the extent that the interests of citizens are strongly represented by such groups, their ability to participate in decision making is enhanced. But on

Milk Fund: Taking Unfair Advantage

The disclosures of illegal campaign activities connected with the Nixon administration included a series of revelations concerning the Associated Milk Producers, Inc. (AMPI), a large association of dairy product producers. The AMPI regularly collected and disbursed large amounts of money to support friendly political candidates—both Republicans and Democrats. The gifts were illegal since corporations are not allowed to donate to political campaigns, but several devices were used to conceal the source of the money.

The "milk fund" was designed to influence elected public officials to give the dairy industry favorable treatment. But the disclosure that the Nixon administration raised price supports in 1971 in exchange for a pledge of $2 million in campaign contributions led to the end of a "good thing." The officers of AMPI were tried and convicted, and its past activities made public.

Lobbying and influence peddling are far from new. They contribute to the bad public image of politics. But the abuses of associational groups should not obscure the useful role they play in bringing the concerns of their members to the attention of public officials.

the other hand, to the extent that citizens are not represented by associations, they tend to experience American government more as a *command* system. They are required to conform to policies shaped by others. Interest groups thus work to promote conciliation for some, and impose command on other citizens.

CITIZEN PARTICIPATION

Political parties and interest groups provide ways for American citizens to participate in politics, and to the extent that their voluntary participation in these organizations influences policy decisions, conciliation processes are promoted. An implicit implication of the discussion to this point is that some Americans, particularly those who are active in party politics and belong to influential groups, are more clearly involved in conciliation activities than are those who merely vote. Further, if there are Americans who obey the law without having opportunities to shape it, they are commanded.

Americans who wish to contest government policies have various means available. The most obvious is the ballot; incumbent officials can be voted out and new faces voted in. Beyond that, a group can be organized in order to pressure legislators and bureaucrats for policy changes. Further, appeals to the courts may achieve changes in interpretations of the law, or a member of Congress or a state legislator may be importuned to introduce or to amend laws. There are a variety of means available, then, for Americans to try to influence the rules and decisions they are expected to obey. To the extent that citizens are aware of such opportunities and use them, they participate in conciliation processes.

Though only a minority of citizens are highly active politically, many more feel they could influence the government if they chose to do so. Americans seem fond of the idea that they can "vote the rascals out," write to their representatives in government, or take a case to court. Almond and Verba found in their survey that nearly two-thirds of all Americans felt they could do something about an unjust law on the local or national level. This was a higher percentage of persons with such attitudes than the authors found in the other four Western nations they studied (Britain, West Germany, Italy, and Mexico).[3] These attitudes encourage the authorities to exercise restraint, for even marginally attentive citizens could react strongly against real or imagined slights from those in office.

In spite of the wide variety of channels available for citizen participation, only a small minority of Americans actually use them fully. In presidential elections, less than two-thirds of those old enough to vote typically cast ballots. In nonpresidential years, less than half the voting-age population votes for congressional candidates. Far fewer citizens vote in local elections, work actively for political candidates, participate in interest group activities, or otherwise try to influence policy issues in which they might have an interest.

To a degree, then, political participation in the United States is the province of the interested as well as of the influential few. Those who have the inclination and the resources to attempt to influence public

---

[3]Almond and Verba, op. cit., pp. 171–174.

policy have a disproportionately large effect upon the authorities. This applies to influential consumer advocates and environmentalists as well as to corporation officials and labor leaders.

Low participation and command politics

It is sometimes maintained that political participation in nations with representative government is directly related to the size of the middle class, and to the extent that citizens are involved in voluntary associations. The United States has a relatively high rate of citizen involvement in voluntary associations. It also has a large middle class. Both of these factors may help to explain why so many American citizens feel they can influence government if they choose. At the same time, however, they raise questions about the participation of lower-class citizens in processes of bargaining and conciliation. For those who do not belong to associational groups, and for the economically deprived, American middle-class democracy sometimes appears hypocritical. It preaches equality of opportunity and the value of political participation without really making either of these things readily available to the lower economic and social strata of society.

Thus, any description of the United States as a conciliating political system might be accurate for about two-thirds of the population at best. For the rest, full involvement in the political process is inhibited by their social position. The poor, the black, and various other unassimilated subcultures are essentially excluded from influence in politics because participation demands time, money, and attitudes which only middle- and upper-class citizens acquire readily. Other citizens also have great difficulty in obtaining the resources and learning the behaviors necessary for political effectiveness.

For example, it is much easier for middle-class people to be successful in American economic and political life than it is for lower-class children. Middle-class children learn from parents and peers to value educational and business achievement. Their early socialization equips them to succeed in white, middle-class schools, businesses, and politics. Lower-class children are not equally well prepared by their early socialization. The behaviors and attitudes valued by their middle-class teachers are often different from those valued at home. The lower-class child is thus tempted to believe that the "opportunity" proffered at school is really an invitation to reject the familiar values of parents and peers for those of an alien middle class. Adjustment to that society is difficult, if it is possible at all. And, if the lower-class child is black or brown or yellow, even an adjustment to middle-class ideals may not be enough. Such a child wears the badge of skin color no matter what his or her educational or professional achievements may be; color alone is sufficient to bar some Americans from full societal acceptance, and equal participation.

On Becoming a Chicano

An American graduate student painfully recalls how he discovered he had discarded his Mexican-American heritage.

Today I am only technically the person I once felt myself to be—a Mexican-American, a Chicano. Partly because I had no way of comprehending my racial identity except in this technical sense, I gave up long ago the cultural consequences of being a Chicano.

The change came gradually but early. When I was beginning grade school, I noted to myself the fact that the classroom environment was so different in its styles and assumptions from my own family environment that survival would essentially entail a choice between both worlds. When I became a student, I was literally "remade"; neither I nor my teachers considered anything I had known before as relevant. I had to forget most of what my culture had provided, because to remember it was a disadvantage. The past and its cultural values became detachable, like a piece of clothing grown heavy on a warm day and finally put away.

Strangely, the discovery that I have been inattentive to my cultural past has arisen because others—student colleagues and faculty members—have started to assume that I am a Chicano. The ease with which the assumption is made forces me to suspect that the label is not meant to suggest cultural, but racial, identity. . . .

Education seemed to mean not only a gradual dissolving of familial and class ties but also a change of racial identity. The new language I spoke was only the most obvious reason for my associating the classroom with "gringo" society. . . .

When I could not imitate Spanish pronunciations or the dialect of the barrio, when I was plainly uninterested in wearing ethnic costumes and could not master a special handshake that minority students often used with one another, they knew I was different. And I was. I was assimilated into the culture of a graduate department of English. As a result, I watched how in less than five years nearly every minority graduate student I knew dropped out of school, largely for cultural reasons. Often they didn't understand the value of analyzing literature in professional jargon, which others around them readily adopted. Nor did they move as readily to lofty heights of abstraction. They became easily depressed by the seeming uselessness of the talk they heard around them. "It's not for real," I still hear a minority student murmur to herself and perhaps to me, shaking her head slowly, as we sat together in a class listening to a discussion on punctuation in a Renaissance epic. [Richard Rodriguez, *The Saturday Review*, pp. 46–47, Feb. 8, 1975.]

There are, of course, exceptions to the general pattern. Poor and black persons do enter middle-class society and attain high positions. Recent years have seen Negroes in the President's Cabinet and on the Supreme Court bench, as well as in Congress and in other areas of government. This demonstrates the existence of at least some opportunity for mobility. Yet such instances suggest only that when performance as measured by middle-class standards has been clearly superior, a few of the excluded have overcome the handicap of being born the wrong color or on the wrong side of the tracks.

The criteria used to judge high performance are often alien, however, for they are the standards of the dominant classes of society. While street fighting may be a means of winning recognition among adolescents in the lower-class community, it is antisocial behavior to the middle classes. Modes of dress and speech which are required in middle-class society may be considered ridiculous and affected in the ghetto or barrio. Thus, lower-class persons who aspire to rise in status must set aside behavior which aids in surviving the dangers of lower-class life. They must put on the mantle of middle-class gentility in order to gain the education, the jobs, and the status of the dominant society.

Since anti-lower-class attitudes dominate American political and economic life and lower-class values clash with middle-class morality, the vast majority of the politically and socially excluded find that meaningful social mobility and political participation are not possible. They and their values are outside the dominant pattern. They are subject to laws passed by representatives of the more affluent elements of American society. Since they have little opportunity to participate in making those laws, they are basically *commanded* by the political system. They must obey decisions without real opportunity to exercise influence on the authorities.

It is true that the right to vote is nominally possessed by all Americans and that in elections all classes may legally participate in the leadership selection process. The social condition of lower-class people, however, minimizes both their participation in elections and their propensity to join voluntary associations. As a consequence, the links with policymakers which associational groups provide to middle- and upper-class citizens are not as available to the poor. Conciliation politics is not, therefore, a reality for the poor, the black, and other excluded groups. In their social world, laws are commands from a government which is essentially alien—a tool of another culture.

AMERICAN IDEALS

Tolerance for different opinions and a willingness to compromise to promote the general good is a necessary basis of conciliation. In contrast, willingness to obey supports command. Both types of ideals are found in the United States. The Constitution formally protects freedom of speech, assembly, and the press, thus recognizing the legitimacy of differences of opinion. The society is held together by strong bonds of national patriotism which are necessary to promote compromise. Nevertheless, intolerance of unpopular opinions and groups, and pockets of separation, are also present.

The American Constitution Provides for the Expression of Diversity of Ideals

Congress shall make no law respecting an establishment of religion, or prohibiting the free exercise thereof; or abridging the freedom of speech, or of the press; or the right of the people peaceably to assemble, and to petition the Government for a redress of grievances. [Amendment I. The Constitution of the United States of America.]

The day-to-day workings of government demonstrate the ability of American institutions to compromise diverse viewpoints and to make and enforce policies which are generally accepted and obeyed. Such compromises would not be possible without the tolerance and good will of the major elements of society.

Further evidence of diverse opinions can be seen in the mass media. Public officials are regularly criticized. Virtually every shade of ideology finds expression in publications distributed openly, and using the public mails. Pamphlets, magazines, books, and newspapers advocate everything from anarchy to dictatorship, from fascism to communism, from theocracy to secular socialism.

Within a framework of social unity, then, there is a wide diversity of cultural values and opinions in American society. In part this results because Americans come from diverse ethnic and national backgrounds. Almost all citizens either are immigrants themselves, or are descended from someone who emigrated to the Western hemisphere in the last 300 years. As wave upon wave of immigrants arrived, each with a unique culture, American society had to find the means to assimilate new elements of cultural diversity. The new residents had to learn allegiance to the national regime and its symbols. As a result, the United States has a markedly mixed cultural heritage.

Perhaps in part as a consequence of this mixed heritage, Americans are notably self-conscious of national symbols. The Constitution and the national flag, for instance, are invoked reverentially as symbolic manifestations of the political community. Patriotic and historical holidays such as Independence Day, Flag Day, Memorial Day, Veterans Day, and Thanksgiving are officially designated and observed. In both public and private education, American history and politics are stressed from primary grades through the university. All in all, substantial social effort is expended to instill a deep commitment to national symbols which will unite a nation of immigrants. (See Table 8-1.)

Commitment to flag and country does not ensure agreement upon how the country should be run, nor does it guarantee tolerance for dissenting opinions. When young men refused to serve in Vietnam because they said it was an immoral war, they were jailed or went into exile. The American government has continually spied upon, infiltrated, and manipulated groups which it has defined as "subversive" since the 1940s. Anticommunist sentiment in the 1950s was so intense that Marxists were afraid to speak—or even reveal their political sympathies—lest they lose their jobs.

Such examples of public and private intolerance of unpopular views

Table 8-1 Pride in country: how Americans compare with people of other nations

Percentage who say they are proud of:	United States	United Kingdom	Germany	Italy	Mexico
Governmental, political institutions	85	46	7	3	30
Social legislation	13	18	6	1	2
Position in international affairs	5	11	5	2	3
Economic system	23	10	5	2	3
Characteristics of people	7	18	36	11	15
Spiritual virtues and religion	3	1	3	6	8
Contributions to the arts	1	6	11	16	9
Contributions to science	3	7	12	3	1
Physical attributes of country	5	10	17	25	22

Source: Adapted from Gabriel A. Almond and Sydney Verba, *The Civic Culture* (Boston: Little, Brown, 1965), p. 64.

are recurrent in American history. From the Alien and Sedition Acts of the administration of John Adams to the current activities of the CIA the government has been prone to violate the formal guarantees of its charter in the name of national security. Similarly, private groups which would stifle freedom of opinion in the name of "loyalty" or "Americanism" have a history extending from radicals in the Revolutionary War to the Ku Klux Klan.

A further important element of American political culture is pockets of unassimilated, basically separatist ideals. The most marked of these belong to the various surviving tribes of American Indians. The tribes are treated as subjugated, dependent foreign nations and are administered by a government bureau (the Bureau of Indian Affairs). While Indians have served in the American armed services and while many individual Indians have adopted the ways of the white man, others continue to resist the dominant culture and to preserve the old ways. For them, American politics is imposed. Government policies are commands which they play little part in formulating.

The stated American creed supports the ideals which are the basis of conciliation. In practice, we find that some Americans are continually chiding others for intolerance, suppression of opinion, and repression of political participation. The struggle for equal rights for black Americans is perhaps the most dramatic example. In the struggle to win the right to vote, to organize interest groups, and to influence national, state, and local governments, blacks used the provisions of the Constitution and the expressed ideals of tolerance, freedom, and equality. They used the words of their antagonists against them. Ideals of toleration in America, then, are not universally held or manifested in practice. Partly in consequence, both conciliation and command are practiced in politics or society. The formal commitment to toleration of dissent is, however, a strong weapon which those holding unpopular views can use to gain a hearing.

SUMMARY AND CONCLUSION

As in any complex society, Americans are governed through both conciliation and command. Much depends upon the social station of an individual, and upon the particular situation in question. Almost any American can experience conciliation politics in a social group or club where officers are elected and votes taken. Conversely, nearly anyone can experience the extreme command situation of being arrested and detained by the police, even if on mistaken charges.

More importantly, the degree to which public policy takes the opinion of citizens into account depends largely upon which citizens one considers. In general, citizens with higher incomes and social status have more opportunity to exert influence on issue definition and decision than do those less fortunate. But even this generalization does not hold up entirely. Those who are represented by powerful associational groups may find that their interests are considered in spite of lower socioeconomic status.

The United States is neither an ideal democracy nor a repressive dictatorship of the haves over the have-nots. It is a society with political institutions which have proven repeatedly that new groups and new ideas can be absorbed. American political parties are not closed clubs. They are vulnerable to dissenting factions and ideologies, and historically they have found the means to absorb potential splinter groups. The power of group pressure and associations is real, and is particularly effective when backed by ballots and/or dollars. On the other hand, even after 200 years of independence in the name of liberty, there remain excluded and repressed subpopulations in the United States. There are still a great many Americans who think their lives and opinions do not count for much with the politicians.

SUGGESTED READINGS

James M. Burns and J. W. Peltason with Thomas E. Cronin, *Government by the People,* 9th ed. (Englewood Cliffs, N.J.: Prentice-Hall, 1975). One of numerous good general introductions to American government.

V. O. Key, Jr., *Parties and Pressure Groups,* 5th ed. (New York: Thomas Y. Crowell, 1964). Still a standard work in the role of groups and parties in American politics.

Clinton Rossiter, *The American Presidency,* 2d ed. (New York: Harcourt, Brace & World, 1960). A readable introduction to the powers and problems of the American chief executive.

E. E. Schattschneider, *The Semi-Sovereign People* (New York: Holt, 1960). An authoritative analysis of gaps between the promise and performance of the American system.

David J. Vogler, *The Politics of Congress* (Boston: Allyn and Bacon, 1974). A concise, contemporary, and critical introduction to the American legislative branch.

CHAPTER NINE

THE BRITISH POLITICAL SYSTEM

OVERVIEW **T**his chapter contrasts patterns of conciliation and command politics in Great Britain and the United States. While there is a great deal of conciliation in politics in both Britain and the United States, British and American political and social institutions can be contrasted. This is conciliation with a difference.

Note that the formal structure of British politics provides the direct contrast of unitary as opposed to federal, and of parliamentary as opposed to presidential, institutions. Separation of powers is absent, and though Parliament is bicameral, one house clearly dominates. These formal arrangements are important in that they serve to concentrate great authority in the Prime Minister and his Cabinet.

Given this particular concentration of authority, it is important to note the way in which Cabinet power is limited so that conciliation takes place.

British political parties and groups are similar in some important ways to their American counterparts, but there are also important differences between the two countries. In particular, note the important role which the social elite plays in the area of associations, parties, and civil service.

Be sure that you understand the following terms:

Unitary government
Parliamentary system
Vote of confidence
Parliament
  House of Commons
  House of Lords
Cabinet government

Prime Minister
Responsible parties
Conservative party
Labour party
Liberal party
The Establishment
Tory Democracy

LEARNING OBJECTIVES

After you have studied this chapter, you should be able to:

1. Identify the formal institutions of British government.
2. Compare and contrast parliamentary and presidential political institutions.
3. Explain how conciliation processes work in Britain in spite of the strong concentration of authority in the Cabinet.
4. Explain the significance of responsible political parties for British politics.
5. Compare and contrast the ways in which associations influence policy in the United States and Britain.
6. Explain the significance of the British aristocratic tradition for contemporary British politics.
7. Compare and contrast the United States and Britain with respect to the four basic conditions promoting conciliation or command: elites, groups, participation, and ideals.

The last several decades have been a difficult time for Great Britain. Its once great empire has been dismantled; its economy has been beset by one crisis after another, and bombings by Irish separatists have shattered its domestic tranquility. In the fall and winter of 1974, a lengthy coal strike nearly halted its commercial and manufacturing activity. Its economic deterioration caused Middle Eastern oil-producing countries to announce that British currency would no longer be accepted in payment for petroleum fuels. In response to that announcement, the British pound fell to an all-time low on the international money markets.

By early 1975, some observers had seriously begun to wonder if Britain's social and political order would survive in the face of the nation's many problems. But the British political order possesses a resiliency which can strongly assist Britain's leaders as they try to reduce the stress their political system is presently experiencing. That political system has shown an extraordinary capacity to manage stress in the past.

Is Britain Dying?

The London street where I live and work was built up in the Edwardian heyday—a church and churchyard on one side, on the other a row of low apartment houses, their red-brick facades elaborated with domes and pediments, bays and balconies, mullioned windows and ornamental ironwork. It seems at first glance the very picture of a prosperous, well-ordered community. But look a little closer. Alarming piles of garbage lie heaped along the curb; soggy debris clogs the gutter; the sidewalk wobbles with loose, broken paving blocks. Wherever the eye rests, past solidity collides with present disorder.

So it is with Britain. Yesterday's glories and today's troubles mingle in perplexing confrontation. We all know that Britain is awash in a sea of adversity—that year after year it spends more than it earns, that its industrial plant is obsolescent and its labor force unproductive, that it totters on the brink of runaway inflation, that it has dropped within living memory from being the richest of Europe's nations to a position where it will soon be running neck and neck with Italy for tenth place in the continent's pecking order. These unpleasant truths make up the uncollected garbage on the curb, but they seem so utterly discordant with what we know of British history, so out of tune with British tradition, that we avert our eyes and focus instead on the imposing edifice behind—on the mother of Parliaments, the cradle of industrial technology, the land of poets and philosophers and explorers and scientists—whistling to ourselves all the while that there'll always be an England.

> But the garbage continues to accumulate. . . . If we expect to find the "spirit of Dunkirk" or other echoes of Britain's finest hours animating the body politic today, we are in for disappointment.
>
> Those finest hours are in fact part of the problem. The trauma of "winning" a war and losing an empire still afflicts the British psyche. That empire and its comforting mythos served to obscure crucial weaknesses in the pre-war social and economic fabric. When empire and myth suddenly evaporated in the hard days of austerity and withdrawal following World War II, the fabric ripped apart and Britain's present difficulties began to surface. [Roland Gelatt, "Is Britain Dying?" *Saturday Review*, pp. 12–13, Feb. 8, 1975.]

The outstanding quality of the British political system is its capacity for combining permanence with flexibility. The institutions of the Crown and Parliament, for example, have existed almost continuously since the Middle Ages. On the other hand, their functions within the political system have changed drastically over time. The Monarch, once the supreme decision maker, is now mainly of symbolic importance; the King or Queen is a head of state without effective political influence. The Parliament has been equally changed; its powers have expanded as the Crown's have been reduced.

This combination of stability and adaptability has permitted the political system to deal effectively with social pressures for change. Whether one looks at the demands by nobles in the thirteenth century for checks on the prerogatives of the Crown, or at more contemporary pressures by workers for a broadening of political participation, forces for change have mainly operated within the system's "rules of the game." And often, those forces have been successful.

BRITISH POLITICAL INSTITUTIONS: THE FORMAL STRUCTURE

British and American political institutions are markedly different in their formal structures. For example, the operations and functions of the United States Congress contrast sharply with the British Parliament; the powers and responsibilities of the British Prime Minister contrast with those of the American President; and the relationships between the central and local governments are defined differently. When the actual performance of the two systems is examined, however, a number of essential similarities may be discerned.

The British government is, like the American, a *representative government.* That is, the authorities are chosen in free, competitive, and frequent elections in which a large proportion of adult citizens participate. As a result, political leaders respond to their voting constituencies, and are held responsible or accountable for their actions while in power.

But British political institutions, unlike their American counterparts, are organized on the *unitary* rather than on the *federal* principle. That is, most of the political authority and responsibility resides with the central government. This is not to say that regional or local governmental units are always and necessarily without important powers or areas or competence. Northern Ireland has had its own legislature; and it, like Scotland, has had its own system of local government. Nevertheless, such provisions for local rule are made by the central government, and the same authority can also make changes as it sees fit.

Further, the British political system is properly described as *parliamentary* rather than *presidential.* Parliament has ultimate political authority. It, or more specifically the House of Commons, installs, supports, or removes the Chief Executive and his Cabinet officers by a mere *vote of confidence* or *no confidence.* Parliament's laws may not be overturned by any other governmental body; they are not subject to judicial review as is the case with laws in the United States. And there are no legal or constitutional restrictions upon its power to make policy. Parliament could pass a law making redheadedness a crime, if in its collective wisdom it felt such action was appropriate and enforceable. (Of course, Parliament would not pass such a law since it would be viewed by everyone as both foolish and barbaric. Though Parliament can *legally* act as it sees fit, it must not ignore public expectations so capriciously.) As a result, unlike the United States, no formal equality among separate "branches" of government exists in Britain. Rather, Parliament formally stands above executive and judicial agencies alike.

We have just noted that it is not all of Parliament but more specifically the House of Commons which has the right to extend confidence to (or withhold it from) the British executive. To many, the distinction seems trivial; for them, the House of Commons *is* Parliament. Strictly speaking, however, Parliament, like Congress, is *bicameral;* it includes an upper chamber, the *House of Lords.* The Lords, however, have only slight authority. They merely review the acts of the House of Commons. The House of Lords can *delay* passage of money bills for up to 30 days, and other legislation for up to 1 year. It may also offer modifications or amendments to programs, and in practice these are often accepted by Commons and incorporated into the final provisions of the law. Nevertheless, since the passage of the 1911 Parliament Act, which reduced the Lords' power from the right to veto to the right to delay, the House of Lords has been accorded more honor than authority.

Cabinet government

Given the commanding authority of the House of Commons, it might seem strange that the British are often said to have a *Cabinet* system. But although Parliament retains ultimate authority in all matters, it has delegated awesome responsibilities and powers to the Prime Minister and his Cabinet, including the following:

a. The final determination of policy to be submitted to Parliament.
b. The supreme control of the national executive in accordance with the policy endorsed by Parliament; and,
c. The continuous coordination and delimitation of the activities of the several Departments of State.[1]

Taken together, these powers give the Cabinet the opportunity to initiate policy, to see it through the Parliament, and to administer it once it becomes law.

The Cabinet is thus delegated broad powers, but any given group of Cabinet members may exercise them only so long as they collectively retain the confidence of the House of Commons. The Cabinet, in other words, has great authority; the individuals who occupy Cabinet posts, however, find their actions under the continuous review of the Parliament. The formal structure of British government is diagrammed in Figure 9-1.

In practice, the British Cabinet ordinarily has the confidence of Parliament, a condition not always present in the parliamentary systems of other nations. The chief reasons for this are two: First, Britain has only two major political parties, and second, they are disciplined or "responsible." That is, members of the British Parliament who belong to the same political party will ordinarily vote as a solid bloc. Only when "the whips are off"—meaning that individuals are not required by the leadership to vote the party position—are party members free to vote as they please with no threat of retaliation from their leaders. This contrasts sharply with

---

[1] Quoted in Sir Ivor Jennings, *Cabinet Government* (Cambridge: Cambridge, 1961), p. 232.

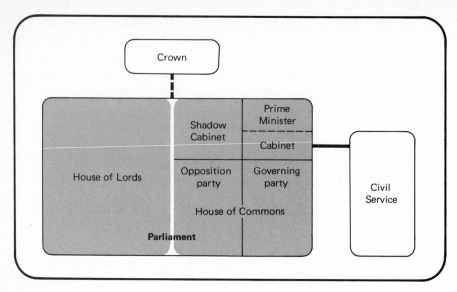

Figure 9-1 Structure of British political institutions.

the American Congress, where members vote according to their conscience or what they deem to be the needs of their constituencies at least as often as they respond to the party leadership.

The implications of a disciplined party system for Cabinet government may not be obvious. But under this system if a single party holds a clear majority in the House of Commons (as it usually will in a two-party system), it can control both the Parliament and its Cabinet. By voting as a bloc, the majority party can install a Cabinet made up of Ministers of its choice, and can then support that Cabinet in Parliament with assured majorities on all "divisions" (votes). Historically, a single party has in fact usually held a majority of seats in the House of Commons, with substantially the above results. Only when an emergency has dictated the establishment of a coalition, or when a third party has held sufficient seats in Commons to deny either of the two major parties a majority, has the "normal" single-party control disappeared.

Formal relationships between elites

The formal relationships between Britain's important political institutions are simple and involve essentially vertical delegations of authority and transmissions of commands. British citizens delegate great authority to the House of Commons, which in turn delegates virtually all of it to the

The "Government" in Britain and the United States

When Americans refer to "the government," they might be speaking of almost any and every public official or administrative agency. Even school teachers in the United States work for "the government."

The British, on the other hand, refer specifically to their Prime Minister and his Cabinet when they speak of "the Government." Thus, Prime Minister Harold Wilson "formed a new Government" following the 1974 elections. Or the "Chamberlain Government" resigned when its policies toward Hitler had obviously failed. Other public bodies in Britain are typically called such things as Royal Commissions or Ministries, not "the government."

This difference in word usage is more than a curiosity. It points up a significant difference between the two political systems. In the United States authority is dispersed through the executive and legislative branches of government, and between federal, state, and local levels of government. In Britain, authority is concentrated in the Cabinet. Hence the different usages of the term "government" indicate a difference in the degree to which authority both is, and is perceived to be, concentrated or dispersed.

Cabinet. These delegations are made on the condition that those to whom authority is granted must retain the confidence of those from whom it came. The Cabinet must hold the confidence of the House of Commons, and Commons of the electorate. With its authority, the Cabinet initiates policy proposals which are almost always approved in Parliament. They are then implemented by the Ministries, and compliance by citizens typically prevails; the British reputation for respecting the law is renowned.

This formal structure might suggest that the British system is organized to support command in decision making and implementation. Though no individual or group in Britain holds power unconditionally, Cabinet government concentrates tremendous power in the hands of the few persons who are simultaneously party leaders and Cabinet officials. It is difficult to see how competition and compromise between elites, or active citizen participation beyond voting, takes place within such institutional restraints.

The command features appear even more pronounced when it is understood that the act of extending or withdrawing confidence is an imperfect means of controlling the policymaking process. The voters are assured a chance to extend or to deny confidence to a party and its leaders only once every 5 years, though the authorities have the option of calling elections earlier if they think their chances of success would thereby be improved. During such a period of time, a wide variety of policies must be acted upon by any group of authorities, including Parliament. As a result, when citizens vote (in Britain or elsewhere), they can only give a very general reaction to past performance and future prospects. Their consent is far removed from the day-to-day voicing of demands and the development of issues.

The House of Commons, of course, can at any time withdraw its confidence from the Cabinet. But to vote no confidence in a government is not a means of resolving differences through compromise and accommodation. Rather, it is an action which signals an irreparable breach between the Cabinet and Parliament—a sign that negotiations between leaders have broken down. Moreover, to vote no confidence in a government controlled by one's own party is roughly equivalent to political suicide, since voters may hold the entire supporting party responsible for the Cabinet's actions when elections are held.

For this and other weighty reasons, rank and file M.P.'s (Members of Parliament) generally support their party leaders even when they would prefer not to do so. The withdrawal of confidence from a Cabinet results in prompt new elections, and it is hard to imagine a more difficult task for a party than that of appealing for votes just after its leadership has been repudiated by its own membership in the House of Commons. Taken together, these factors reduce the threat of a no confidence vote greatly; indeed no Cabinet has fallen for want of parliamentary support since World War II (except when elections have given a new party control of the legislative machinery).

CONCILIATION PROCESSES IN BRITAIN

The formal structures of the British political system might suggest that British policy processes proceed by command rather than conciliation. In practice, however, policies are made and implemented more through conciliation than through command. The conditions which support conciliation are present in Britain to a degree comparable to the United States. While a governing Cabinet usually has a secure majority of M.P.'s, it also has the concerted public opposition of the Shadow Cabinet (the leaders of the opposition party in Parliament). And while members of the governing Cabinet know they will have the support of their party rank and file when a vote is taken, they also know that party discipline does not restrict the right of an M.P. to raise questions publicly, or to apply behind-the-scenes pressures for or against a particular policy. British leaders are also praised and criticized (sometimes mercilessly) in the press, and newspapers are widely read by Britons. In short, the Cabinet faces serious opposition from other elites, and it must conciliate differences within the ranks of its supporters.

Parliamentary competition and conflict between the Cabinet and the minority party is legendary. "Her Majesty's Loyal Opposition"—the "out" party—is expected to mount a sustained attack on the Government's programs. To that end, the party in opposition has the right to determine the subject for debate for approximately a quarter of the time the House of Commons is in session. In addition, time is set aside each day when questions are put to the Government in public session by both the members of the opposition and "back benchers" from the majority party. Such questions are often probing, embarrassing, and difficult to fudge. A tenacious opposition M.P. is a much tougher interrogator than his closest American equivalent, the reporter at a Presidential press conference.

It might be argued that the opposition's right to oppose and be heard is of little consequence because it has insufficient votes to prevail in the end. This argument, however, ignores the fear—nearly universal among authorities everywhere—that they will appear to be dishonest, ignorant, or foolish in the eyes of their constituents and supporters. Thus the right and the power to subject the authorities to continuous and public criticism can be strong medicine indeed. When the authorities' political survival hangs upon future election results, their sensitivities are even more pronounced. Governments often suppress their critics, even when the opposition has no legal means to change policies (witness the imprisonment of dissenters in South Vietnam or the deportation of Alexander Solzhenitsyn from the Soviet Union).

The influence of the opposition in Britain's interparty dialogue can often be observed in actual cases. Government proposals are frequently modified because of criticism by the Shadow Cabinet, and occasionally a government bill will even be withdrawn. Moreover, when the opposition seems to be getting the better of a major debate over a period of time, friction and dissatisfaction within the ruling party is likely to increase, perhaps even to the point of forcing a change in party leadership. Thus, the debate of issues and voicing of demands and counterdemands in the British Parliament is in fact a kind of bargaining process. Though the parties to negotiation are not strictly equal, each side can bring important resources to bear.

Much negotiation and bargaining does, then, go on *between* political parties in Parliament. But *intra*party conflicts and their management or resolution are also an important feature of British public life. Earlier it was stressed that British parties are disciplined, that party members almost always vote as a bloc in the Parliament. But this does not mean that all members of each political party agree with each other easily or completely on matters of policy.

British parties have been far from monolithic, despite their voting records. Continuous struggle and debate have marked their internal relationships. Severe strains between the left-wing intellectual members of the Labour party and its trade unionists are notorious. The Conservatives have also had serious factional differences at times, though they, like Republicans in the United States, are more often internally united than their more left-leaning opposition.

It is important to note that party members and leaders outside Parliament are not required to abstain from public criticism of their leadership. They are free to form factions for the purpose of forcing a change in their party's policies. The resolution of internal differences is a continuing problem for leaders of both parties.

Even within the parties in Parliament (composed of those who are elected by each party to the House of Commons or are appointed to the House of Lords) serious differences commonly arise over policies and personalities. And, as in the national party organizations, the right to public dissent is allowed to M.P.'s so long as their votes are ultimately cast with the party. One looks in vain, for example, for a more persistent critic of the Conservative governments of the 1930s than Winston Churchill, who was a Conservative M.P. at the time (but consistently voted the party line). As in the larger party organizations, the problem of resolving differences within Parliament is always before the leaders, and their most usual means of achieving consensus is through negotiation between contending groups.

There have been times when unity within even the Cabinet or Shadow Cabinet has been hard to achieve. In choosing his Cabinet, a British Prime Minister is ordinarily expected to make that body broadly representative of all major party factions. As a result, Cabinet deliberations are an important means of negotiation and compromise. Also, since Cabinet decisions are the joint responsibility of the entire Cabinet, there is a strong incentive to reach decisions which are at least minimally acceptable to all Ministers.

Parliamentary Debate as a Check on the Cabinet

Parliamentary control is effective . . . because debates are aimed at the electorate. . . . The British Parliament is not—and has not been for almost a century—a direct restraint upon the Government, but rather the focus and the prime (but not sole) disseminator of political opinion and information to the electorate. The voter does not expect his M.P. to turn out the government he has elected; but he expects him to ask the right kind of questions and to help him know what is happening. [Bernard Crick, *The Reform of Parliament*, 2d ed. (London: Weidenfeld and Nicolson, 1968), pp. 273–274.]

In the end, then, British policies are largely made and enforced by conciliation processes in spite of the apparent dominance of the Cabinet. On the one hand, the Cabinet has authority to make decisions, to virtually control their ratification by Commons, and to implement them through their control of the bureaucracy. But on the other hand, in reaching those decisions, the Cabinet faces constant scrutiny and must answer questions from many sources: the public, the mass media, the opposition party, and their own party faithful. Each of these has leverage, whether in the form of votes in an inevitable election, or in the ability to escalate public debate and conflict. The resources of groups or individuals outside the Cabinet may not be equal to those of the authorities, but they are sufficient to be influential. While British authorities are able to decide and to command—at least in the short run—they must be prudent. If commands (in the form of laws or policies) are not worked out through broad discussion, negotiation, and compromise, the Prime Minister, his Cabinet, and many M.P.'s of his party may pay the price for failing to conciliate: removal from office and replacement by more responsive authorities.

POLITICAL PARTIES AND GROUPS

While British political parties play a dominant governmental role, they are also associations of citizens seeking to influence the formulation of public policy. In fact, they are organized into two distinct types of structure, the parliamentary groups, which are made up of the members of each party who have been elected to the House of Commons, and the national electoral organizations (with their local branches), which are composed of citizens who subscribe to the party's programs and who otherwise voluntarily participate in promoting the parties' welfare. In general, the electoral machinery serves the interests of the parties in Parliament, though on occasion, particularly in the Labour party, the mass organizations have rebelled at their subordinate roles.

The organizational division of parties into parliamentary (or Governmental) and electoral parts, of course, is not unique to Britain. In the United States, for example, members of Congress organize along party lines. Each party also has electoral organizations which are not part of the government. But unlike Britain, American parties are not cohesive and centralized; electoral machinery is decentralized and operates mostly at the state level, and elected officials are free to vote their individual preferences on most substantive issues.

Responsible parties

As in the United States, political parties in Britain provide a means whereby representative government becomes more meaningful to the average citizen. It is the parties which formulate alternative programs in the attempt to win votes, and which proffer candidates for leadership. Consequently, they give voters a chance to choose between reasonably well defined alternatives. Further, because parliamentary parties are disciplined, the party leadership is in a position to enact the party program presented to the electorate (unlike United States' congressional leaders, or even the President). As a consequence, programmatic issues are emphasized more, and personalities of individual candidates less, in Britain than they are in the United States.

An incumbent Prime Minister, of course, looks after his personal fortunes and watches the public opinion polls carefully, seeking to call an election at a time favorable to himself and his party. The Prime Minister may himself be an issue, and the opposition will almost certainly strive to put forward an individual who can convince voters that he has the stature necessary to be the head of government. But both leaderships will also put forward a program of proposed policies and actions to deal with the problems of the day.

For example, Prime Minister Harold Wilson called an election for October 1974, only 7 months after Labour had come to power in a shaky parliamentary coalition with the Liberals. He sought a clear majority of seats in the Commons. But because inflation was running at an annual rate of 17 percent, Wilson did not call the election until after he had won a promise for voluntary wage restraints from the powerful Trades Union Council. Thus he was able to tell the voters that his government would muster labor union cooperation to stem inflation—a claim the opposition could not make. Wilson's Labour party won the election.

Because British parties can and do deliver on their policy programs, political scientists label them as *responsible* parties. Responsible political parties, then, are those which make commitments to the voters and keep them. Such party politics contrast with the American two-party system, where individual candidates rely more on *local* organizational support than on national leadership, and hence take largely independent policy stands. A statement of a proposed program by a British party is thus far different from the platforms produced by presidential nominating conventions in the United States. The latter are general statements of policy tendencies to which a majority of delegates have agreed to subscribe. Elected Democrats and Republicans routinely reject all or part of their parties' platforms once they are in office. Members of Parliament do not have that option. They are committed to vote with the leadership and the leadership is committed to its campaign promises.

A two-party system

Britain's party system is essentially a *two-party* system, even though the Liberal party and some splinter parties do hold seats in the House of Commons. Currently the major parties are the Conservative party and the Labour party, Labour having displaced the Liberal party between 1900 and 1935. The Liberal party still fields large numbers of candidates for Parliament, and there is periodic speculation about the possibility of a Liberal resurgence. Nevertheless, Table 9-1 shows that the Labour and Conservative parties typically split 90 percent or more of the popular vote in a general election, and capture 95 percent or more of the seats in the House of Commons.

It is interesting to note that no party has won a majority of the popular vote in a British general election since 1935. While the Liberals

Table 9-1 Percentage of popular votes and numbers of seats in the House of Commons won by party in general elections in Britain, 1950–1974

	1950	1951	1955	1959	1964	1966	1970	(Oct) 1974
Conservative								
Percentage of votes	43.5	48	49.7	49.4	43.4	41.9	46.2	35.8
Number of seats	298	321	345	365	304	253	330	276
Labour								
Percentage of votes	46.1	48.8	46.4	43.8	44.1	47.9	43.8	39.3
Number of seats	315	295	277	258	317	363	287	319
Liberal								
Percentage of votes	9.1	2.5	2.7	5.9	11.2	8.5	7.6	18.3
Number of seats	9	6	6	6	9	12	6	13

Sources: David Butler and Michael Pinto Duschinsky, *The British General Election of 1970* (London: Macmillan, 1971), pp. 353–354.
New York Times, March 2, 1974, pp. 1, 10, and October 12, 1974, pp. 1, 10.

have not won enough to govern, they have denied the governing party a majority of votes cast. The situation would be more problematic if the Liberals held the balance of seats in Commons. They could then force concessions from the governing party and could bring down Cabinets by withholding confidence on vital issues.

The Liberals are unable, however, to win enough seats to hold this swing position because the electoral system works against minor parties. Seats are not awarded in proportion to the popular vote cast for a party. Candidates for the House of Commons each stand for election in a district. Typically, a Conservative, a Labourite, and usually a Liberal will run in each district. Election is by a plurality of votes; the winner does not need a majority. As a result, even though Liberal candidates may collectively poll up to 20 percent of the national vote, they typically win a plurality in only 1 or 2 percent of the districts and end up with only that proportion of the seats.

British parties are more sharply divided than are the American Democrats and Republicans. The Labour party was created as the working class's democratic socialist party and retains that flavor today. The Conservative party has sought to project itself as the embodiment of the nation, as an agent for all the people. While there are working-class Conservatives, however, the membership is mainly middle and upper class and the leadership is drawn heavily from the prestigious old families and privileged classes—persons with "old school ties" to Eton and

Harrow, Oxford and Cambridge. Reasonably clear lines of social class thus separate the constituencies of the two major parties.

Associational groups

Associations are intimately involved in virtually every important political conflict which develops in Britain. For example, when the demands for a government-subsidized health insurance program were incorporated into the platform of the Labour Government just after World War II, the British Medical Association waged a vigorous (but unsuccessful) campaign against the proposal, while other associations supported it.

Associational groups are sufficiently important sources of support and opposition on most political issues that in many cases the ties between them and one of the major parties have become permanent and institutionalized. This is most clearly seen in the role played by the trade unions in Labour activities. Trade unions "sponsor" candidates for seats in Parliament, contribute most of the party's campaign and operating funds, and control a sizable, and most often controlling, bloc of votes in party conferences. Though these interrelationships are more direct and complex than most other ties between parties and associations, they are unusual only in degree.

Given this active and complex involvement of associational groups in the political process, their influence is felt directly or indirectly by nearly every British citizen. Indeed, most Britons belong to some such body—a labor union, a professional association, or a local chapter of a group such as the National Society of Non-Smokers. Many belong to more than one. With their great influence and their aggregate constituencies, associational groups in Britain provide an indispensable channel through which individual interests and demands are routed and developed into policy proposals to which government leaders can respond.

In noting that Britain, like the United States, has many voluntary associations, we must not make the mistake of assuming that these groups contribute to conciliation in the same manner in both nations. American interest groups represent themselves directly to legislators and administrators. They are *advocates* of policies which favor their memberships. As advocates they are "outsiders"; they are private groups seeking to influence public agencies.

In Britain the distinction between the Government and the associations which seek to influence it is not so clear. Lobbyists seldom work to influence individual Members of Parliament. Since policy is formulated by the Cabinet or party leadership, any meaningful attempt to influence policy must be directed at the Government (which, remember, means the Prime Minister and his Cabinet). Over the years, those associations which are truly influential in Britain have developed sanctioned and recognized relationships with the Ministries. They are treated rather more as *advisers* than as advocates.

Such an arrangement does not necessarily impair the conciliation which we expect associations to produce; it does, however, institutionalize it. It is important to note that only *some* associations have achieved this semiofficial status. Those which do not advise the Government because they represent narrow or new interests or causes, do not have equal opportunity to gain attention from the authorities. Whereas a noisy, small group with a narrow concern can often gain the ear of an American member of Congress, only established and powerful groups with broad concerns are regularly heeded by the British Cabinet and Ministers.

Social elite

Britain has a heritage of aristocracy; prestigious families play an important political and social role. The premier example is the Royal Family (or House of Windsor), whose members are still considered by many Britons to personify the entire community. More important is the strong part which the aristocracy still plays in British public life, including politics. To be born a Churchill, for example, is nearly sufficient to assure an individual a successful career in public life. It is still very difficult to rise to the higher ranks of the higher civil service unless one belongs to the dominant and privileged upper 5 percent of the British population.

The British Establishment

During the late 1960s American students commonly referred to those in positions of authority here as "the establishment," implying that a privileged minority (unwittingly supported by conventional morality) exercised unwarranted power. If there is an "establishment" in the United States, it is difficult to identify with precision, and it exists by informal arrangement.

"The establishment" in Britain is more readily identified. It consists of the old families who furnish leadership for much of British industry and government plus those sanctioned institutions (e.g., the Church of England and *The London Times*) and groups (e.g., the universities and the nationalized industries) whose influence is almost universally recognized.

The British establishment has been systematically maintained. Ever since the Tudor monarchies the privileged classes in Britain have found ways to absorb challengers to their elevated station and special social advantages. As merchants garnered wealth, they were given place beside the landed gentry. As industrialization produced newly influential capitalists, the captains of industry were granted social advantages more or less commensurate with their economic power. As organized labor grew in strength, its influence in national affairs was increasingly sanctioned; later its direct role in national politics (the activity of the Labour party) was institutionalized, and some members of the party were even knighted for their services "to Crown and Country." Thus does the British political system preserve itself in the face of change.

This privileged class has maintained its favored status because its members have advocated the interests of powerful associational groups, or have taken on associational features themselves. If a family or other closed-group has become politically influential, it has usually done so by providing leadership for strong associations. This, in fact, has been the means by which leading families maintained their influence in both the civil service and the Conservative party in an era of increasing democratization. This phenomenon is not unlike a Nelson Rockefeller or an Edward Kennedy riding to power on the strength of a combination of family fame and demonstrated leadership in the United States.

Institutional groups

The several Ministries, the military, and the organizations established to run nationalized industries—such as the National Coal Board—are all examples of institutional groups which play a crucial role in the management of public conflict. The British administrative apparatus is legendarily responsive to orders from the Cabinet. The essential neutrality of the bureaucracy in political conflict is considered to be a fundamental professional tenet by British bureaucrats. It is held that civil servants should serve either Conservative or Labour Governments equally well. That they generally have done so is shown by the fact that British higher civil servants (professional administrators) just below Cabinet rank usually are not dismissed when the other political party comes into power. This is in sharp contrast with the usual practice in the United States, where secretaries, assistant secretaries, and undersecretaries of departments are appointed by a President to serve for only the duration of his term in office.

While the British higher civil service has been generally responsive to the authorities, it has been criticized for its restrictive membership. Many critics of the status quo have demanded that access to senior posts be "democratized." They want to broaden the base of the British administrative elite by opening its ranks to able people who are not fortunate enough to come from the "best" schools and families. These critics also argue that those who currently manage the bureaucracy are not sensitive enough to the needs of the masses. Their ties to important interests and associations may serve to help reconcile competing demands, and their loyalty to their superiors may be impeccable; but they may lack sensitivity to the nonprivileged and unorganized citizenry. A significant reform of the recruiting process was enacted in 1971, the effects of which remain to be seen.

Institutional groups in Britain develop vested interests just as they do anywhere else. They seek to protect and advance those interests in much the same fashion as associational groups do. And when they formulate and press demands upon authorities, they often find themselves in cooperation or conflict with independent associations. They "lobby" and they provide information to those who are a part of the policymaking group, though unlike associations they do not participate in electoral politics.

At times, cooperating institutional groups and associations pursue complementary, rather than parallel, strategies. That is, they seek a common objective through the use of different tactics. The association may conduct a publicity campaign, while the institutional group uses direct access to the authorities to gain favorable decisions. Wrote one association head—the president of the British Legion:

> When we had our own (Cabinet) Minister (i.e. The Minister was a member of the British Legion), he was something of an advocate for us with the Government. . . . It is, of course, true that, once Government policy is established, all Ministers, under the doctrine of collective responsibility, become individually and collectively responsible for the Government's

policy. But, during the months that precede decision . . . the Minister of Pensions is an advocate.[2]

Competition between groups in Britain leads to conciliation of competing demands, but it is conciliation with a distinctive flavor. For those powerful interests which have established close ties with the parties and the bureaucracy, bargaining is done through regularized procedures. Policies are derived by the meshing of mass electoral politics, aristocratic rule, bureaucratic planning, and pressure-group politics; and accommodation is managed without venom or rancorous public debate. In this process the lines between private and public, and between special pleading and the public interest, sometimes become blurred.

CITIZEN PARTICIPATION IN BRITISH POLITICS

We noted in Chapter 7 that in the conciliation model, the political process is supported by a broad range of citizen participation which affects the formulation of demands as well as the execution of public policy. On the other hand, the command structure requires only compliance by all those who are not part of the elite. As we shall see, the range of political activity available to Britons is not as great as in the United States, but British citizens can—and do—influence policymakers.

People ordinarily participate in political activities when they feel they should as part of their patriotic duty, or when they want something and think their participation will really help them get it. According to a study by Almond and Verba, most people in Britain (62 percent)[3] believe they could "do something" about an unjust national regulation. When asked what they thought they could do, most of those interviewed mentioned organizing an informal group to start a campaign, or contacting political leaders on an individual basis.[4] While such data must be interpreted carefully, they do seem to show that most Britons believe that they *can* meaningfully participate in formulating public policy if they want to. They do not believe that their sole political task is to follow orders or support the authorities.

[2]Quoted in Allen Potter, *Organized Groups in British National Politics* (London: Faber, 1961), pp. 214–215.
[3]Gabriel A. Almond and Sidney Verba, *The Civic Culture* (Boston: Little; Brown, 1965), p. 142.
[4]Ibid., p. 160.

Voting

Aside from discussing politics (which most Britons do from time to time), voting is the most common form of citizen participation in Great Britain. As shown in Table 9-2, voter turnout since 1945 averaged somewhat over 75 percent of the eligible voters (virtually all adult citizens). In these elections, the two leading parties contended quite evenly for the vote, and power changed hands several times. Moreover, as was noted above, campaigns turn much more on the party programs and the quality of the party leadership in Britain than they do in the United States. It is clear, then, that British elections are serious contests for power among contending elites who must address themselves to popular issues and formulate meaningful programs if they are to maximize their chances of electoral success. A vote for one party or the other often has a more clearly defined impact on policy formulation than a vote cast for a candidate or party in the United States. It might be fair to say that voting has a greater impact in Britain—that it is a more significant form of participation there.

Associational group participation

The other major form of political participation which is generally effective in shaping policy formulation in Britain is joining and working through recognized associational groups. According to Almond and Verba, nearly half of their national sample (47 percent) from Britain belonged to at least one voluntary association; about two-thirds of the male respondents (66 percent) held such memberships.[5] In an earlier study, Samuel Beer noted that "the big vocational pressure groups" generally have actually organized a higher percentage of their potential membership than their American counterparts, and cites as an example the fact that 90 percent of the

Table 9-2 Percentage of eligible voters casting ballots, 1945–1974

1945	1950	1951	1955	1959	1964	1966	1970	1974 Feb	1974 Oct
72.8	83.9	82.6	76.8	78.7	77.1	75.8	72.1	78.8	72.8

Source: F. W. S. Craig, *British Parliamentary Election Statistics: 1918–1974*, 3d ed. (London: Macmillan, 1976).

[5]Ibid., pp. 246–247.

farmers in Britain belong to the National Farmer's Union, while only 30 percent of all farmers in the United States belong to any of the major agriculture associations.[6]

Though group membership is common in Britain and though recognized associations have great influence in policy formation, these are "collectivist" politics which significantly limit individual options and impact. The group (or its leadership) decides collectively how its resources will be used and what policies it will espouse, and only the group's representatives have ready access to the authorities. Individual members who disagree with such decisions cannot do much, if anything, to counter them; even dropping their memberships is usually a poor option since they would then be politically isolated.

The communication system in Britain provides another important though specialized kind of political participation. The national press (read by almost all Britons) reports and evaluates the dialogue between the government and the opposition party in Parliament, and the policies of associational groups are also publicized and examined. Though control of the newspapers is in the hands of only a few, competition between them together with the tradition of a free press, has generally preserved their independence from the authorities. As a result, political leaders in Great Britain have been understandably sensitive to their press coverage.

Political participation in Britain in the command form of complying with the laws and policy decisions is also generally high, as should be expected. Most Britons are conscious of the impact of government on their lives and give generally favorable assessments of the results of governmental activity.[7] And their typical willingness to obey the laws and pay their taxes is shown in the fact that no British Government in modern times has considered noncompliance with the law to be a serious problem. Indeed, the remarkable stability of the British political system over the past several centuries, which was obtained without the widespread use of force, could not have been possible without active support for the government by the people.

BRITISH IDEALS

There is a high degree of consensus on fundamentals in Britain. Perhaps no other nation-state has had a greater voluntary sharing of ideals vital to

---

[6]Samuel H. Beer, "Group Representation in Britain and the United States," *Annals of the American Academy of Political and Social Science,* vol. CCCXIX, p. 133, September 1958.
[7]Almond and Verba, op. cit., pp. 47–48.

the support of its political system. The United Kingdom of England, Scotland, Wales, and Northern Ireland has been a remarkably cohesive political community in spite of differences between the ancient heritages of its constituent parts.

If a government is to obtain general and voluntary compliance with its policies, the great preponderance of its citizens must believe in its legitimacy—that it has the authority to make policy decisions. This elemental need has been met in Britain, for the vast majority of its citizens have agreed as to who should belong to their political community and have supported its preservation. Even preponderant majorities of the people of Northern Ireland and Scotland, where separatist movements exist, have continued their allegiance to the British political system.

Yet if even a small minority of the governed do not wish to be part of the larger community, or if they seriously aspire to political independence, the authorities may face a very difficult choice—that of using force or of granting the wishes of the secessionists. This is well illustrated by the current struggle between the government and many Irish Catholics in Northern Ireland, where violence and civil disunion have reached crisis proportions at various times. Thus far the government has opted for the use of force, combined with some offers of concessions. The result has been a deadlock, for it is hard to reconcile those who would not be part of the political community with those who insist that they must be.

The British people have shared broad agreement on the appropriate regime norms, or fundamental institutions and processes, of the political system. For example, even in the modern, "democratic" era, the British monarchy and the aristocratic House of Lords have been preserved as institutions of symbolic importance, if not as centers of decision making. Their durability stands as evidence of the commitment of most Britons to "the system." Support for the Parliament and the Cabinet is probably even greater, for public calls to bring about changes in the basic structural arrangements of the government are seldom made, and even more rarely taken seriously.

Yet disagreements over regime norms have also been present at times, and changes have resulted from these. The Labour party carried out a successful campaign to transform the House of Lords into a relatively powerless body because they could not support the previous fundamental arrangements of public authority. Today, there are some who would abolish the House of Lords outright.

Britons, first and foremost, are committed to democratic principles. There is consensus that all members of society should be given a part in shaping the demands which are converted into laws, that all members of the community should be affected by the laws in substantially the same way, and that the authorities should give serious consideration to all points of view.

Tory democracy

The values just noted are clearly democratic. But they assume a special meaning for the many Britons who believe that some individuals are "naturally" more fit to govern than others, that some are superior to others, and that such differences should be recognized and institutionalized within the political system. This point of view has been called "Tory democracy" because of its honored place in the ideological pronouncements of the Conservative party. Harold Macmillan, the Tory (Conservative) Prime Minister from 1956 to 1963, expressed it this way:

> Human beings, widely various in their capacity, character, talent and ambition, tend to differentiate at all times and in all places. . . . To deny the bold, the strong, the prudent and the clever the rewards and privileges of exercising their qualities is to enthrone in society the worst and basest of human attributes: envy, jealousy and spite.[8]

Surprising as it may seem to Americans, this view is not unique to those who feel they are part of the "natural aristocracy." Much has been written about "working class Tories" who agree with the sentiments expressed by Mr. Macmillan. Said one laborer, in comparing the Conservatives with the Labour party:

> The Conservatives have got more ideas of what they're doing than the people who come up from the working class—the mines and such like. Working class people are not the sort to run the country, because I don't think they understand it really, I'm sure I wouldn't if I got up there.[9]

We have seen that British citizens can and do participate in the choice of leaders and programs. They exercise the right to vote, and they use associations to establish close contact between segments of society and the government. Tory democracy, however, suggests that an elite class can and must represent the interests of all British subjects, indeed must embody the nation.

[8]Quoted in Richard Rose, *Politics in England* (Boston: Little, Brown, 1964), pp. 39–40.
[9]Quoted in Samuel H. Beer, *British Politics in a Collectivist Age,* (New York: Knopf, 1966), p. 100.

To the extent that the nonelite feel that its views and interests are taken into account by such a "natural aristocracy," democratic participation can support the aristocracy's governance. If the competition between parties and the representation of associational interests through parties and Ministries does in fact reconcile competing demands to the general satisfaction of the less privileged, then it can be concluded that conciliation operates for substantially all Britons. But if the apparent weakening of working-class and middle-class support for Tory democracy reflects an erosion of confidence in the ability or the desire of the old elite to protect and advance the interests of *all* Britons, then quite another conclusion seems warranted. Briton's loss of empire and international influence, coupled with hard times, has apparently led laboring people and increasing numbers of white-collar workers to vote for the Labour and Liberal parties or take direct action, such as participation in the crippling coal strike of 1974, which toppled the Conservative Government of Edward Heath.

The British system of leadership recruitment has rested upon a widespread public confidence that the elite embodied or represented the interests of the nation. Today, however, that confidence seems to be eroding badly, causing great stress on the British system. New methods of participation and of elite recruitment may evolve as a consequence.

BRITISH AND AMERICAN POLITICS: A COMPARATIVE SUMMARY

British and American politics are similar in that conciliation processes between competing elites and associational groups are prominent in both. Each nation provides opportunities for open electoral competition and for citizen participation through free elections. But Britain's politics are also strikingly different from those in the United States. Governing authority is concentrated in the hands of the Cabinet in Britain; in the United States it is dispersed between the branches of the federal government and between the federal and state governments. British political parties present a program of public policies to the voters, and the victorious party has the parliamentary means to implement its program; American parties are aggregations of local party units, and candidates run on personal policy stands. Once elected, American officials must hammer out compromises within and between parties and groups before policies can be enacted. British officials do not usually have this problem. Associational groups in the United States are "out-groups" which must continually importune the legislature, the administration, and the courts; the

British have established semi-institutional status for powerful associations, bringing them into the policy process on a regular and orderly basis.

Thus, conciliation occurs in both systems, but it takes different forms in each—and in Britain conciliation seems more structured and constrained than in the United States. Once a British party is elected, its leadership is authorized to govern. When the Cabinet proposes its program, it is enacted virtually intact. When Parliament makes a law, it stands as the ruling policy of the land. In contrast, laws passed in the United States may be challenged in the courts or ignored by the bureaucracy on the instructions of the President.

Nevertheless, it is clear that the British political system provides a framework for decision making through conciliation and compromise. Competing elites contest for the right to govern. Those who succeed must pay continuous attention to the conflicting demands of their followers, their opponents, and special-interest groups. Their right to govern is temporary and conditional.

Moreover, the underlying social and political foundations support the practice of politics by conciliation. The dominant values and regime norms legitimize the right to dissent and the right to participate in policymaking. Groups in Britain have a large measure of autonomy and often assume active political roles in the promotion of their interests. Finally, citizens participate directly and (more often) indirectly in formulating demands to which the authorities must respond.

But British politics clearly relies upon command principles as well. Once party policy is made, individual members of Parliament must vote accordingly or face (political) sanctions. And once laws have been passed, those affected must comply or face (legal) sanctions. Disagreement, dissent, and conflict are permitted and even encouraged. But they are also limited.

Overall, the British system has been remarkably well integrated. The expectations of citizens have been reflected in the performance of the elite; policy decisions by the authorities have been generally supported by the public. Individual wants and demands have been systematically refined by associations and the political elites into policy alternatives; public policies have been implemented by the bureaucracy to the general satisfaction of both the people and the governmental elite.

If Britain has reached a point in its history when fundamental changes must be made in its political arrangements, that is not surprising. The decline in British world power and influence over the last 100 years—and especially since 1945—would shake any society's confidence. The success of British political leadership has resided largely in its expertise and in the tradition of deference to the elite classes. If events have eroded public confidence in that expertise, and if a continued leveling of social-class distinctions causes some basic changes in Britain's social structure, we may expect that its political system will change too—but in what ways and to what extent, only time can tell.

SUGGESTED READINGS

Alexander, Andrew, and Alan Watkins: *The Making of the Prime Minister, 1970* (London: MacDonald, 1970). Cast in the mold of Theodore White's "Making of the President" series, this 200-page book provides an enjoyable introduction to the flavor of a British political campaign and some insights into political strategy under a parliamentary system of government.

Beer, Samuel H.: *British Politics in a Collectivist Age* (New York: Knopf, 1966). A brilliant analysis of the evolution in the style and substance of British politics and the underlying social and economic conditions which brought them about.

Butler, David, and Donald Stokes: *Political Change in Britain* (London: Macmillan, 1969). A study of electoral politics in Britain with emphasis on changes in voter turnout and preferences over time.

Crick, Bernard: *The Reform of Parliament,* 2d ed. (London: Weidenfeld and Nicholson, 1968). A readable introduction to Cabinet government and the role of Parliament with recommendations for political reform in Britain.

Jennings, Sir Ivor: *Cabinet Government,* 3d ed. (Cambridge: Cambridge, 1959). An encyclopedic analysis of the operational and organizational aspects of British government. Though it is somewhat formalistic, and it considers the government as a closed system (that is, it ignores the relationship of the government and society), it is a useful volume.

McKenzie, R. T.: *British Political Parties* (New York: Praeger, 1964). A detailed study of the organization and activities of political parties in Britain. Shares many of the strengths and weaknesses of the Jennings book listed above.

Rose, Richard (ed.): *Studies in British Politics,* 2d ed. (London: Macmillan, 1969). A series of articles on British politics which pay particular attention to the cultural and social contexts of British politics.

CHAPTER TEN

THE FRENCH POLITICAL SYSTEM

OVERVIEW In this chapter we contrast French politics with British and American. Even though these three countries are commonly thought to be "democratic," it will be apparent that politics in France is quite different.

Historically, France has not been able to establish political institutions and stay with them for long. The French people have been deeply divided over the type of government they should have. Some have demanded democracy, while others have called for rule by a privileged elite. Even democrats have been divided; some have favored a parliamentary system, while others have preferred a strong presidential office. These bitter differences of opinion over regime norms have made it difficult to select national leaders who could command widespread support. Consequently, French political leadership has tended to pass rapidly from person to person and from one coalition of parties to another. Constitutions have frequently been replaced or voided by others.

The focus of this chapter will be upon the most recent French Constitution, which established the Fifth Republic in 1958. You will note that the Fifth Republic is a unique mixture of presidential and parliamentary institutions. It was designed to remedy the instability of previous regimes by combining a strong executive with a weak but representative legislature.

Not only is the French Constitution unique, but French citizens differ markedly from British and American citizens in their attitudes toward and participation in politics. Take special note of the effect which citizen alienation and parochialism has had upon the practice of politics in France.

Be sure that you understand the following terms:

Fifth Republic	*Prefect*
Charles de Gaulle	*Department*
Referendum	*Grands corps*

LEARNING OBJECTIVES

After you have studied this chapter, you should be able to:

1. Explain why French parliamentary institutions have historically been less stable than similar institutions in Britain.
2. Contrast the presidential system of the Fifth Republic with that of the United States.
3. Identify the formal institutions of the Fifth Republic and explain how they function.
4. Explain the significance of Charles de Gaulle for contemporary French politics.
5. Explain why the bureaucracy is especially influential in France.
6. Identify the changes in the French party system which have taken place under the Fifth Republic.
7. Explain why associational groups have not played as significant a role in the politics of France as they have in the politics of Britain or the United States.
8. Compare and contrast citizen participation in France and Britain.
9. Explain how French attitudes toward politics have both inhibited conciliation and fostered personal freedom.

Over the past two centuries, the French nation has experienced frequent constitutional crises and several periods of political instability. Since the revolution of 1789 (1 year after the United States Constitution was ratified), it has had sixteen different constitutions; four of them have been in effect in the twentieth century. The present French Constitution has been in effect only since 1958, but even at that it has been more durable than most.

These repeated changes in their governmental institutions and processes reflect basic disagreements among French people over who should govern and how. A century ago, the community was divided almost evenly into republican and antirepublican camps. Their mutual antagonisms were strengthened by the anticlerical posture of most republicans and the antirepublican stance of the leadership of the Catholic Church. Republicans also saw the French Revolution as a glorious beginning, while their opponents viewed it as a disaster.

Today these divisions are less severe, though still present. The successors to the antirepublicans have mostly accepted the principle of representative government, but they support constitutional arrangements which establish a strong chief executive. Many contemporary republicans have also come to accept executive supremacy, but they would prefer a parliamentary system with a weak cabinet. Controversy over the Church has largely been reduced to debate over state aid to parochial schools, and the Revolution has become less a source of division than a venerable part of the nation's history.

But while conflicting positions on some fundamental issues have been compromised over time, others have not. New crises have erupted twice in the past two decades, one of which led to the collapse of the Fourth Republic in 1958. The more recent case came a decade later when large numbers of students and workers, together with thousands of sympathizers, went to the barricades and took over many factories in an almost successful attempt at revolution.

Thus, the French political tradition includes a strong tendency toward instability and deadlock among powerful forces over basic political issues. At the same time, there are important indications that over time many old antagonisms have become less sharp and that the prospects for political stability in the foreseeable future are relatively good. The 1958 constitutional arrangements have survived the transition from President de Gaulle to his successors with a surprising ease, and no major crises appear to be in the making.

The present French political institutions are a curious blend of presidential and parliamentary government. The Constitution of 1958 established the office of President and invested it with great authority and responsibility. But it also created a Cabinet, headed by a Prime Minister, which must retain the confidence of the National Assembly, or Parliament. This unusual combination of presidential and parliamentary institutions serves, in part, to provide continuity with the past, since during most of the past century, France had parliamentary systems similar to that found in Great Britain. But unlike the British case, parliamentary government failed to provide the basis for effective decision making in France, and so significant modifications were thought necessary and a strong presidency was also created.

PARLIAMENTARY INSTABILITY: BACKGROUND TO THE PRESENT

Since parliamentary government in Great Britain has functioned effectively for so long, it is worthwhile to consider the apparent reasons why similar institutions in France did not achieve similar results. Though the French parliamentary systems (in effect from 1870 to 1940, and from 1946 to 1958) were essentially like their British counterpart in relation to governmental structure, there were fundamental differences in the party systems of the two states. Britain, as we noted in Chapter 9, has usually had two major parties, while France had many, none of which could even come close to controlling a majority of the seats in the legislature; British parties have been *responsible* in the sense that their members in Parliament have voted as a bloc, while French parties were usually undisciplined and fragmented; and British parties have generally agreed on the regime norms or the "rules of the game," while some French parties disagreed so fundamentally that they often refused to consider issues on their merits until their preferred constitutional arrangements were put into effect.

As a consequence of the French party system, during most of the past century Cabinets were generally at the mercy of the Parliament. They could be formed only when deputies from several parties agreed to coalesce despite their differences. Moreover, the several Cabinet Ministers could not rely upon their party ties to retain the support of a majority of the assembly, since party discipline was usually weak at best. An added handicap for the Cabinet was that a significant bloc of deputies would simply cast negative votes on all questions.

Due to these several factors, French Cabinets seldom lasted more than a few months. Even during their short tenure, they were often unable to provide executive leadership. Without leadership Parliaments tended to deadlock, while stress increased because of unresolved problems.

This explanation of the failure of French parliamentary politics raises another question: "Why were French parties unable to reconcile their differences and form stable coalitions capable of formulating public policies effectively, especially when their failure to do so led to extreme stress?" An important part of the answer, it seems, is that they accurately reflected their constituencies among the electorate. The Communists were supported by about a fourth of the voters precisely because they were a permanent opposition. Anticlerical parties could not cooperate with clerical parties on questions relating to religion, nor could socialists cooperate with parties taking a conservative stand on economics without losing their popular base of support. In short, French parliamentary institutions were ineffective because they reflected uncompromising divisions in society.

The fragmented party system in France, though perhaps explainable, nevertheless fostered disillusionment and cynicism among the electorate. Whereas British voters could choose the government and its policies by voting for the party they preferred, French people had no way to predict who would govern, or to what ends, when they cast their ballots. This was so because the coalitions which established the support for a given Cabinet were constructed in the National Assembly only after the elections had been held, and in fact, several Cabinets were typically formed between one election and the next. A survey taken during one election showed that fewer than 2 percent of the voters could correctly predict who the first postelection Premier (Prime Minister) would be.[1] As a result, voters in France tended to elect representatives to protect their parochial interests from unfavorable government action rather than try to choose a Cabinet on the basis of the general policies for which a party stood.

In these circumstances, Deputies in the National Assembly could not build nationwide support for their policies, and policies to deal with severe problems were typically not formulated until matters reached crisis proportions. When the Fourth Republic collapsed in 1958 it was because no government could be formed to deal with the war in Algeria and the growing rebellion of the French military elite.

THE FIFTH REPUBLIC

The major objective of the drafters of the current French Constitution was to ensure that the government could act decisively to meet problems as

---

[1]Cited in Henry W. Ehrmann, *Politics in France,* 2d ed. (Boston: Little, Brown, 1971), p. 95.

they arose. Since they knew that the French community remained fundamentally divided and that the political parties continued to be irreconcilable on many basic issues, they believed that policymaking through conciliation and compromise was unlikely to work well; therefore they saw to it that the new Constitution gave the President and the Cabinet (which he has been able to control) substantial authority to rule by command.

Thus, though both the French and the Americans now have a Presidential system, the French President has powers which in some respects exceed those of his American counterpart. He can declare the existence of "grave and immediate" threats to the Republic and take whatever measures are "commanded by the circumstances"; that is, he can unilaterally declare a state of emergency and rule by decree if he thinks it is necessary to do so. He appoints the Prime Minister, or chief legislative leader. He has the authority to dissolve the National Assembly, though no more than once a year. When Parliament passes a law, he can return it to Parliament for "reconsideration," or submit it to the public for a direct referendum vote. Finally, the President has the authority to submit his own proposed laws directly to the public for a vote by referendum—a power Charles de Gaulle used frequently to circumvent the jurisdiction of the National Assembly. A simplified diagram of the structure of the Fifth Republic is shown in Figure 10-1.

These provisions alone place the President of France in a far stronger position than the American President, who must contend with a "coequal" legislature. But beyond these explicitly granted powers, the French Chief Executive also competes for authority with a deliberately

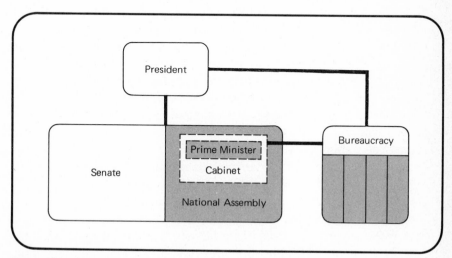

Figure 10-1. Constitutional structure of the French Fifth Republic.

weakened legislature. The Constitution provides for a "rationalized" or greatly restricted Parliament. Its regular sessions may last only 5 months each year, and its jurisdiction extends only to areas explicitly authorized by the Constitution. Excluded from that jurisdiction are all areas in which the President holds ultimate authority, such as matters related to preserving the integrity of national territory.

Presidential dominance, particularly under de Gaulle, has also been the rule because of his ability to control the Prime Minister and the Cabinet. The 1958 Constitution seems to create a dual executive. The President is responsible among other things for the conduct of foreign affairs, the meeting of emergencies, and the preservation of the Constitution. On the other hand, the Premier or Prime Minister is to "direct the operation of the Government" (Article 21), which in turn is to "determine and direct the policy of the nation" (Article 20). Even a close reading of the Constitution, however, is not sufficient to determine the respective spheres of authority of the two positions and their relationship to each other.

In practice, President de Gaulle and his successor, Georges Pompidou, effectively controlled the several Prime Ministers who served during their tenure in office. The key constitutional provision under which this control was effected is Article 8, which gives the President the authority to appoint the Premier. Both Presidents took care to select Premiers who saw their own role as subordinate to the President, even to the point of stepping down when the President called for their resignation. And while they remained in office, they agreed to permit the President to be present and to dominate Cabinet proceedings. Whether Presidential dominance will continue on the basis of the precedents set during the first 15 years of the Fifth Republic remains to be seen; it is certain, however, that the Constitutional basis for that dominance is not very precise or explicit.

Because the President has been able to exercise effective control over the Premier and the Cabinet to date, he has benefited indirectly by the constitutional provisions which assure the Cabinet control of all lawmaking in the Assembly. For example, no deputy may propose bills which would increase governmental expenditures or decrease its revenues. The Cabinet may also obtain a vote on its own legislative proposals whenever it wishes, and it can exclude unwanted amendments when the vote is taken. Moreover, the Cabinet sets the Assembly's agenda, and if the latter does not act on its budgetary proposals within seventy days, it can issue "ordinances" which have the force of law. Finally, the Cabinet can make any matter a vote of confidence, and thus threaten the dissolution of the Assembly if the vote does not carry. Since deputies ordinarily do not wish to face the uncertainty of standing for reelection, they often prefer to take an option conveniently provided—they may abstain on the vote, and so show that they disapprove of the government's position and still not bring about a defeat for the government. This happens because only negative votes are taken to show a lack of confidence; if the votes in favor of the government plus the abstentions equal more than 50 percent of all votes cast, the Cabinet retains the confidence of the Assembly.

De Gaulle: presidential dominance

As important as the formal Constitutional powers of the President and the limitations on the Assembly have been since 1958, the importance of the Presidential office can be fully understood only in the context of the unique role played by its first occupant, Charles de Gaulle, from 1958 to 1969. De Gaulle may or may not have been the dictator many of his political enemies said he was. He was probably not the sole reason for the successes of the Fifth Republic. But he clearly was the dominant French authority while he was in office. His popularity was so great (indeed he was widely viewed as indispensable) that he was able to achieve his ends in virtually every case.

Given this position of strength, he interpreted his powers broadly, and so controlled the Cabinet and its Prime Minister beyond what reasonably might have been expected from a literal reading of the Constitution. As noted above, he personally presided over meetings of the Cabinet, and established committees to control functions otherwise within the Prime Minister's jurisdiction. He also used his unmatched popularity to obtain direct public approval of his policies through referenda on specific issues; and in the campaigns before the referendum vote, he invariably threatened to resign if he failed to win the support of the majority. Finally, he encouraged the formation of a supporting (Gaullist) political party, which made loyalty to de Gaulle the basis for membership.

Perhaps the one issue which best illustrates de Gaulle's unique influence is the referendum of 1962. In it he proposed that the Constitution (still only 4 years old) be altered to permit the direct election of the President (originally he was chosen by a complicated indirect election procedure). Virtually all political parties except his own opposed de Gaulle's proposal since it was clear that the Presidential office would gain even greater authority by this modification. The opposition in the National Assembly was so great that the amendment would surely be defeated in a vote there, so de Gaulle went directly to the people. This created another serious conflict because the Constitution apparently required the involve-

De Gaulle on France

Since President de Gaulle played so great a role in the formation of the Fifth Republic, his views of his country and his hopes for it are significant. In his war memoirs he wrote:

> All my life I have thought of France in a certain way. This is inspired by sentiment as much as by reason. The emotional side of me tends to imagine France, like the princess in the fairy stories or the Madonna in the frescoes, as dedicated to an exalted and exceptional destiny. Instinctively I have the feeling that Providence has created her either for complete successes or for exemplary misfortunes. If, in spite of this, mediocrity shows in her acts and deeds, it strikes me as an absurd anomaly, to be imputed to the faults of Frenchmen, not to the genius of the land. But the positive side of my mind also assures me that France is not really herself unless in the front rank; that only vast enterprises are capable of counterbalancing the ferments of dispersal which are inherent in her people; that our country, as it is, surrounded by the others, as they are, must aim high and hold itself straight, on pain of mortal danger. In short, to my mind, France cannot be France without greatness. [*The War Memoirs of Charles De Gaulle* (New York: Simon and Schuster, 1959), vol. I, p. 3.]

Though de Gaulle is gone, his vision of France lives on. His successors, though less flamboyant, have continued his foreign policies, including the development of an independent nuclear military capability. Their justification for these policies has also been similar to de Gaulle's: France, as one of the great nations of the world, must continue to play a leading role in international affairs.

ment of the legislature in any amendment proposals. But though the President was opposed by political parties which had obtained almost three-fourths of the votes in the previous election, and though the

President could be charged with violating the Constitution he had been instrumental in writing, the people backed de Gaulle by a vote of 62 percent to 38 percent. And by that decision, as we will note below, the basis for a more permanent restructuring of the party system was laid.

Thus, the political institutions in the French Fifth Republic place the President in a very powerful position to implement his programs and policies, even in the face of widespread and organized opposition. In place of the conciliation processes which in past parliamentary systems often led to deadlock between contending political forces, the President today is able to govern largely by command if he deems it necessary.

Yet it is important to note that even with the powers they have had at their disposal, the French Presidents (including de Gaulle) have not been able to dictate at will. De Gaulle was able to dominate the French political scene because of his unmatched popularity. Although he faced serious and organized opposition (which he did not suppress) throughout most of his 10 years in power, he overcame it time and again because he could go directly to the voters for support in referenda. When his supporters dwindled and he lost a popular vote of confidence in 1969 (on a referendum over regional autonomy), he promptly resigned.

Moreover, President de Gaulle's popular support made possible the organization of a loyal political party, whose deputies in the National Assembly provided strong support for the government's programs. In 1962, the Gaullists were able to win 229 seats (and their supporters an additional 45) out of a total of 465; in the 1968 election, they became the first party ever to hold an absolute majority in a French Parliament (with 284 seats out of 487). In the last analysis, then, the French electorate has had the opportunity to veto Presidential initiatives when they have been taken to the people in referenda and when presidential or legislative elections have been held. To date, de Gaulle and his successors have maintained sufficient support to control the government and so to utilize the impressive array of powers granted under the Constitution.

The bureaucracy: technocratic rule?

Bureaucrats and institutional groups have traditionally played a prominent role in French politics. Even before the revolution of 1789, French monarchs early developed and ruled through an extensive supporting administrative structure. By 1870, the French government employed about four times as many civil servants as did the British. Historically, then, the bureaucratic structure has been the one constant feature in an otherwise changing constitutional framework. During the periods of parliamentary government, with their characteristic Cabinet instability, the French administration provided continuity and even assumed significant policymaking powers to compensate for the weak leadership of the elected authorities. Since 1958, institutional groups have remained a powerful public force, so much so that many now allege that France is ruled by "technocrats."

One major reason for the strength of the bureaucracy is that responsibility has been highly centralized. Like Britain, France has a *unitary* rather than a federal division of powers, and unlike Britain, the central government has not delegated significant authority to local governmental bodies. In fact, the key figure in local government is the *prefect* (chief officer) of each *department* (administrative district), who is directly responsible to the Ministry of Interior in Paris. Mayors and other local officials are elected, and may even play an important political role in Paris, but they do not ordinarily have sufficient influence to counterbalance the central bureaucracy in their own locale. The extent of centralization of the bureaucracy in France is also illustrated with the oft-quoted claim of a Minister of Education that he could look at his watch and a calendar and know exactly what lesson was being assigned to every student in French schools.

Though the French administrative structure is highly centralized, it would be incorrect to assume that the bureaucracy is tightly integrated and unified. In fact, the administrative elite has traditionally been divided into *corps,* each of which has had a distinctive interest and responsibility. Though reforms in 1945 abolished some of these divisions, the most prestigious *grands corps* were preserved (the departments of Finance, the Council of State, the Prefectoral Corps, and such technical organizations as the Corps of Mines). It has not been unusual for members of any of the corps to leave their own ministries or even the government bureaucracy, to take other positions of employment. But they have typically retained a sense of loyalty to their own corps, and have been expected to protect their corps' interests while on external assignment.

Recruitment to the French governmental bureaucracy traditionally has been from a small segment of the society: sons of administrators, and persons of sufficient means to permit the extensive and specialized schooling necessary to pass the examinations which provided the only means for entering government service. Though reforms were instituted at the end of World War II, with the aim of democratizing the administration, their effect appears to have been slight; the ranks of the grand corps continue to be filled largely with individuals who are from upper-middle-class backgrounds, and have had the appropriate specialized education.[2]

It seems clear that substantial additional authority has passed into the hands of persons with administrative backgrounds and training. De Gaulle and his Prime Ministers selected unprecedented numbers of civil servants to serve as Ministers in their Cabinets. Traditionally, Cabinets had been made up exclusively of members of the Parliament; but the Gaullist Constitution forbade a member of the Cabinet from simultaneously holding a seat in the Parliament. Members of the Parliament were thereby discouraged from surrendering their seats to become Ministers. Since members of Parliament no longer held a monopoly on Cabinet posts, Presidents and their Premiers were free to choose administrators or other "experts" for these positions. During the de Gaulle years, a third of the Cabinet positions were in fact filled with administrators. Though de Gaulle's successors have returned to the practice of selecting Cabinet members largely from Parliament, the importance of administrators in policymaking circles still remains great, and many technocrats have become "politicians" even to the point of winning seats in the National Assembly.

The assertion that France has recently been governed by technocrats stems primarily from resentment that command methods are used in dealing with major segments of society. Administrators have broad powers; they represent distinct and elitist grand corps; and (like bureaucrats everywhere) they are charged with being unresponsive to the needs and demands of the groups they serve. Local interests are said to be ignored and local initiative stifled because of the predominance of the prefect; students feel their interests are not considered by a distant, powerful Ministry of Education; and small merchants and farmers feel their problems are ignored or dismissed by economic planners. Whatever the merit of these charges, the fact that they are commonly made indicates the powerful role of the French bureaucracy is itself a significant political issue.

Given the power and stability of the bureaucracy, French Presidents and Premiers would ignore the technocrats at their peril. The institutional group structure in France thus provides a major source of potential competition for elected leaders. The Fifth Republic has had strong politi-

---

[2]Ezra N. Suleiman, *Politics, Power, and Bureaucracy in France* (Princeton, N.J.: Princeton, 1974), chap. 2.

cal leadership in part because the President has been able to draw support directly from the people. Cultivation of support from the bureaucracy has also enhanced the power of de Gaulle and his successors. Even though support from the electorate and from institutional groups has overcome basic social divisions for the time being, it is necessary to consider parties and groups which have not fully participated in the current regime in order to gain a full understanding of its politics.

POLITICAL PARTIES AND ASSOCIATIONAL GROUPS

French political parties

Until the mid 1960s, France had a confusing array of political parties and other loose groupings of individuals seeking public office. The more or less "permanent" political parties since World War II had included the Communists and the Socialists on the left, the Mouvement Républicain Populaire (MRP) and the Radical Socialists in the center, and the Independents on the right. In addition, several parties had brief but significant electoral successes as the focal point for protest. Seldom did any one of them control more than 25 percent of the seats in the National Assembly.

During the past decade, however, there has been a clear trend toward simplification of the party system. The Union of the New Republic (UNR) was organized in 1958 to offer the voters candidates committed to Charles de Gaulle. By the early 1960s it became the most popular party, receiving, for example, about 40 percent of the votes in the elections of 1962. In the elections of 1967, the UNR captured a near majority of the assembly seats, and in the elections held after the student revolt of 1968, the reorganized Gaullist party, Union of Democrats for the Republic (UDR), won enough seats to control the Parliament without the support of other autonomous but sympathetic deputies. The independents continued to maintain an independent existence, though they generally supported and cooperated with de Gaulle and the Gaullist party. In 1974, the Independent party leader, Valéry Giscard d'Estaing, won a narrow victory in the presidential election.

The successes of the Gaullist party and its ally, the Independents, were partly at the expense of the parties of the center and the left. One of them, the MRP, officially went out of existence in 1967, and the others were forced to enter electoral alliances in an attempt to compete more evenly with the parties of the right. In parliamentary elections, Communists and Socialists increasingly coalesced within each district to support the leading candidate of the left. In presidential elections, federations of still autonomous parties were organized on the left and in the center with the purpose of providing a single candidate a sufficiently broad base of support to have a real chance of winning a majority of the popular vote.

These changes in the French party system have largely resulted from the strength of de Gaulle, the dominant position of the office of the President, and the method by which he is chosen. Because he is directly elected by an absolute majority of the voters, and because only the Gaullists have been able to attract that level of popular support, the parties of the left and center have been forced to coalesce or suffer certain defeat. And since the presidential office has been so important, parties which cannot compete for it have been condemned to remain outside the real decision-making circles. Their Assembly seats are more honorific than powerful in the face of presidential dominance. As a result, federation among old antagonists has practically been the price of political survival.

Even though parties of the left and center have had to form coalitions, their orientations and policy positions have remained significantly different—formation of single parties on the left and in the center does not appear likely in the near future. The Communists and Socialists, for example, continue to disagree on whether to strip the President of some of his powers; they both seek greater socialization of the economy and more effective control of private wealth, but they disagree as to methods; and while the Socialists are generally supportive of a pro-Western foreign policy, the Communists oppose the continuation of the Atlantic Alliance. Parties or groupings of the center have similar continuing differences on social and economic policies.

In some respects the Presidential election of 1974 reversed the trends of the previous years. The victory, as noted above, went to Independent leader d'Estaing, thus ending the dominance of the Gaullist party for the previous 16 years. Though he was not expected to win at the outset, he and the leftist candidate, Socialist François Mitterand, far outstripped the other candidates, including the Gaullist Jacques Chaban-Delmas, on the first ballot. Then in the runoff, he won by a very narrow margin. As a result, the future of the UDR is uncertain, even though it continues to be the largest parliamentary party.

The election was also remarkable in that the leftist candidate, Mitterand, came so close to winning. The parties of the left, which for so long appeared to be in a state of decline, now can apparently look more confidently to the future, with the reasonable expectation that they may someday capture the supreme political prize.

But while the last presidential election was in some ways a break with the past, in one important respect it reflected continuity in the French party system since 1958. For while the UDR did not elect its candidate and the leftist candidate ran an almost successful campaign, the final election offered the voters only two candidates; the parties as before were forced into two broad coalitions, and the voters could choose only between the left and the right.

The party system in France, thus, is still not stable. Several parties continue to maintain a separate existence and their vote-getting ability remains substantial in parliamentary elections. However, their mutual independence has greatly declined because of the need to combine forces in order to compete for the Presidency. Their individual fates cannot now be predicted. Nevertheless, it seems likely that the continuing need to form electoral coalitions will reduce the parties' individual independence. Only if constitutional reforms restored parliamentary supremacy would the many, fragmented political parties which have been so characteristic of past French political life have much chance to survive.

Associational groups in France

French associational groups have not served to bridge the gulf between individual citizens and the authorities as have associations in Britain and the United States. Historically, French groups have been narrow in their outlooks and weak in their influence on government. Whereas American, and to a lesser extent British, political parties seek to compromise the competing interests of groups in order to attract their support, French parties have not generally sought to bring divergent interests together. Conversely, since the parties have themselves been individually unable to govern effectively, there has been little incentive for citizens to form or to use groups to influence them.

In part, French associations have been unable to perform a role comparable to their counterparts in the United States or Britain because they have typically been unable to recruit large proportions of their potential clients. For example, less than a third of the workers belong to a labor union, and the farmers' group which purports to speak for agriculture has only about 750,000 members, even though about 3 million persons (almost a fifth of the labor force) are engaged in agricultural work.

More important, however, is the fact that French groups have reflected the social and ideological divisions within the French community. Workers are fragmented into several organizations, the most important of which have affiliated directly with one or another of the parties.

Thus, instead of using their strength to influence the parties in their own interest, they have sometimes been used by the party to further party interests. Similarly, business executives, veterans, and other reference groups have been represented by competing and sometimes even feuding organizations. Farm groups have represented a single area or type of farmer, such as beet growers or meat producers, instead of farmers in general.

Fragmentation of the interest-group structure also has led to narrow memberships with minimal overlapping among groups. Workers who have voted Communist have belonged to the Communist-controlled labor union and have had little or no interaction with others outside their own tightly knit group. Small farmers and small-business executives have similarly insulated themselves from other subgroupings of society.

One reason that the French associational group structure has been so fragmented is that a relatively high percentage of French people have been involved in what might be called "traditional" or "premodern" forms of economic activity. Family-based industry has been prevalent. A high percentage of people have been employed in agriculture and most of them farm relatively small plots of land. Most merchants have continued to manage small shops, and a relatively large percentage of workers has been employed in small-to-medium-size factories. These people have proved difficult to organize, preferring to remain independent and aloof from outside groups—including government. They have also generally resisted efforts to introduce new technology or to create larger corporate economic units, which (at least in the United States and Britain) have encouraged the development of labor unions and industrywide business associations.

There are some signs, however, that the role of associations in French politics may become more important. Dramatic changes have taken place in the French economy since World War II. During the days of the Fourth Republic, the government promoted a remarkable economic recovery in which there were not only significant increases in per capita income but also a dramatic modernization of the basic areas of the economy. If the experience of other countries is repeated in France, these recent developments are likely to make associational groups increasingly important there. Indeed some observers are convinced that "modern interest groups" currently play a greater role in French political life than ever before.[3]

[3]See, for example, Jean Blondel, *The Government of France,* 4th ed. (New York: homas Y. Crowell, 1974), p. 89.

CITIZEN PARTICIPATION IN FRENCH POLITICS

In some ways, French citizens have participated in political affairs in much the same fashion as their American or British counterparts. They have turned out in good numbers to vote in open and competitive elections; they have made demands upon their legislators; and groups have represented their interests, however effectively or ineffectively. And, contrary to their reputation, the French people have generally paid their taxes and usually obeyed the law.

Nevertheless, the French have also developed very distinctive methods of political participation—methods which have made it difficult for the political elite to maintain stable government. These disruptive methods of participation stem from widespread alienation from politics among French people who are convinced that "normal" means of expressing demands or interests are ineffectual and that the authorities either cannot or will not respond to their legitimate concerns.

The indications of alienation are many. According to opinion polls, most French people do not believe they have any influence over government decisions; about four out of five feel they are treated by the state in an impersonal manner; almost three-fourths of the citizens believe the government uses a double standard in its dealings with the people.[4]

These attitudes have resulted in a variety of actions of protest. Perhaps the mildest form of protest has been simply to cast a vote "against the system." Throughout the postwar era, the Communist party has attracted most of its support (20 to 25 percent of the electorate) on this basis—it is adamantly opposed to the status quo. Voters have also "floated" from one protest movement to another in considerable numbers. The first Gaullist party (the Rally of the French People or RPF) quickly gained a large following when it was organized in 1946–1947 and won 22 percent of the vote in the 1951 parliamentary elections; its program was based on the proposition that a new constitution was needed. Then, in 1954, an obscure merchant named Pierre Poujade led a protest against tax levels on small businesses and a political party emerged, bearing his name. It had no program except protest, and it received 2.5 million votes (or 12.5 percent of the total) in the 1956 elections. Since that time, no similar electoral movements have emerged, perhaps because the level of alienation in France has been reduced, or perhaps because of the rise of de Gaulle and the Fifth Republic.

Another, more extreme, form of protest has been to call strikes for

[4]Figures are cited in Roy C. Macridis and Robert Ward (eds.), *Modern Political Systems: Europe,* 3d ed. (Englewood Cliffs, N.J.: Prentice-Hall, 1972), pp. 158–159.

political purposes. During the leftist uprisings of 1968 a student strike was called in response to the arrest of student leaders. Unions have called for 1-day shutdowns to register their support for or opposition to a particular policy. And when such strikes have struck a particularly responsive chord among the people, they have led to more general insurrections, complete with street barricades, violence, and bloodshed.

Not only have the French developed distinctive forms of protest, their leaders have also been unusual in their relatively heavy use of plebiscites or referenda to register support for themselves and their policies. These public confidence votes were first utilized by Napoleon, who contrived to obtain popular blessing for his autocratic rule. Since then, strong leaders have followed his example, and de Gaulle included provisions for referenda in the 1958 Constitution. While he was President, he called for five such votes. In each, he made it clear that he wanted a vote of confidence and would resign if he didn't get it. Since his popularity was unmatched, voters tended to support him even when they opposed the specific proposal as offered; only in 1969—when de Gaulle called a referendum, lost, and resigned—did this tactic fail.

Since de Gaulle left office, the referendum has been used only once. During that same brief time span, protest voting and politically inspired direct action has also diminished significantly. Though it is not possible to make a final judgment, there is some evidence to suggest that these developments reflect an increasingly broad belief among the French that more conventional methods of citizen participation are better able to achieve desired results. De Gaulle's presidential successors have been rather more willing than he to work with and through other public authorities. They have been less willing to take issues directly to the voters, perhaps in part because of de Gaulle's defeat in the 1969 referendum. Similarly, the relative absence of protest actions could be a function of greater citizen reliance on voting and interest-group representation to attain political objectives. But it is difficult to predict the future of either protest politics or referenda in France. Any President could decide to rely on the referendum if the National Assembly proved "uncooperative." And protest actions such as strikes could again become fashionable at the first sign of serious economic or social stress.

FRENCH IDEALS

From our previous discussion, it should be clear that French people have been deeply divided over political ends and means. At the same time, they are united by a finely developed sense of community; they almost universally express pride in their heritage and destiny. Though their feelings of pride in France have been more often based on cultural than on purely political considerations, they have responded impressively to external threats to their nation's independence. Their nationalistic spirit has been an important source of cohesion when they have come into conflict over specific issues.

But while the French have a common pride in their nation, they have been singularly unable to agree on the ordering of their public institutions and processes. They have repeatedly disagreed about regime norms and have given only limited and conditional support to the authorities who have been chosen according to constitutional provisions; since the significant elements of the public have not accepted the prevailing constitutional arrangements as legitimate, the legitimacy of those who ruled under them has also been suspect. This tenuous position of the authorities, in turn, has often weakened their capacity to deal with specific problems. Governments of the Fourth Republic, for example, were unable to deal with many problems in a decisive manner, and the constitutional system ultimately collapsed in the face of the deepening crisis in Algeria.

Because authority roles have not been legitimized by consensus on the constitutional arrangements which have defined them, and because authorities have often been unable successfully to cope with stress, French people have typically been hostile or indifferent toward politicians and government generally.

These negative attitudes are complemented by others which also tend to preserve a fragmented political order. Because the French view public officials with distrust, they have tended to be relatively uninformed and uninterested in political affairs. Only about one person in ten expresses "deep interest" in politics, while over half have "very little" or none.[5] Their low level of knowledge about political affairs is illustrated in these findings: 5 weeks before the 1967 elections 30 percent of the voters could not give the date of the upcoming elections, 61 percent couldn't name a single candidate running in their own district, and, of those who could identify a candidate, 66 percent couldn't give his or her party identification.[6]

The French, perhaps again because of their jaundiced view of government, have also been committed to individualism. One commentator has aptly explained the reasons for and implications of this frame of mind:

[5]Taken from surveys conducted by the Société Française d'Enquêtes par Sondages, and published in *Sondages,* nos. 1–2, pp. 13–14, 1969.
[6]Macridis and Ward, op. cit., p. 92.

Since the citizen feels that no one but himself can be entrusted with the defense of his interest, he is inclined to shun constructive cooperation. He fears that the discipline involved in any cooperation might put social constraints on him. When he participates in public life, he hopes to weaken authority rather than to encourage change, even when change is overdue.[7]

As befits a people who are suspicious of government, French people also tend to attach great importance to their parochial-group attachments. Their families, their local organizations, and their economic or social groups are particularly important agencies for fulfilling their individual needs and aspirations. To be sure, these groups are also important to Americans and Britons. But to an extent not found in either of these other cases, the French have tended to view public institutions and parochial groups as mutually incompatible, and they have often given greater support to their own groups when they have come into conflict with the government.

An example of this type of parochialism was evidenced in the mid-1950s when Poujade attracted his large following through attacks on the authorities and the existing political order. Poujadism was a rebellion of small merchants directed against the foundations of the Fourth Republic for narrow, parochial, economic reasons and interests.

Evidence of parochialism to the detriment of broader interests has also been identified elsewhere. The student and worker outbreaks of 1968 are recent examples. In the case of workers, they have shown a persistent determination to avoid being assimilated or "coopted" into the broader political arena:

Even though their methods are less radical than in the past, their overall attitude toward the state has not changed; too often reduced to a very minor position in national or local planning boards, they too often in turn continue to interpret efforts to integrate them or their unions into state bodies . . . as a threat to their independence and an insinuating attack against their tradition of protest.[8]

Finally, parochial interests in France tend to be not only set against public authority but also typically set against one another. Loyalty to the Church has precluded compromise with secular groups; membership in the Communist-affiliated trade union demands opposition to its socialist

---

[7]Ehrmann, op. cit., p. 12.
[8]Stanley Hoffman, *In Search of France* (Cambridge, Mass.: Harvard, 1963), p. 99.

counterpart. Such exclusivist loyalties have tended to divide French society into separate cells, making compromise and conciliation difficult.

On "Freedom" and "Conciliation"

One of the dangers in using our formulation of conciliation and command politics is that it is tempting to translate "conciliation" as "democracy," "freedom," or other such valued words from the Western and American traditions. France provides an interesting opportunity to clarify one point of potential confusion.

Our discussion has noted that (1) there is a dominant elite in France (the President) potentially challenged only by the bureaucracy; (2) associational groups do not have much effect on public policy and institutional groups are not closely attuned to their clientele; (3) participation is consequently largely confined either to elections or to protest; and (4) French consensus tends to focus on cultural rather than political things, making it difficult to compromise political differences. All of this would indicate that conciliation politics is not typical of France. Indeed, French suspicion and distrust of government leads to the conclusion that citizens view it as a command structure, beyond popular control.

Still, the French are not politically oppressed. They maintain divergent life-styles and opinions without state interference. They readily express disagreement with the government in Paris. In very important ways, then, the French are "free" even if their politics smacks more of command than of conciliation.

The explanation for this lies in the context of the problem we first encountered in Chapter 1: the line between that which is public and that which is private is hard to define, and it varies from time to time and place to place. The French have simply declared that much of their social activity is beyond public concern, reserving it to the family, the village, and other social groups more attuned to their divergent views.

And yet—despite the prevalence of political attitudes which have often been contentious, negativistic, and exclusivist—positive consensus has also been present among the French. Their devotion to the idea of France has led to the occasional willingness to set aside differences and unite behind an exceptional leader. President de Gaulle was the most recent such person. He reappeared on the political stage in 1958 after having been in retirement for more than a decade, identified himself as the personification of the nation, and won overwhelming support from almost every segment of society. Parochial interests and distrust of public authority were replaced by overwhelming support. In this case, the strong French spirit of national greatness was channeled into support for a supreme and strong authority.

Over the past several decades, the French have come to a broad agreement on the need for popular controls on public authority. Some French thinkers, of course, have long articulated this view. But until quite recently, others have contended quite the contrary, that those who govern are best able to determine society's ends and needs. But since World War II, no important voices have been raised against "democratic government." It is clear that the fiercely independent French are particularly loath to give their authorities blind obedience and support, and refuse to accept restrictions on their political rights.

Finally, though the French are often described as doctrinaire and rigid in their beliefs and commitments, there is evidence of widespread willingness to modify old ideas and biases in the face of new evidence. Since 1958, for example, their support for the present constitutional arrangements has increased. Initially, their commitment was more to the person of de Gaulle than to the Constitution. By the time of his resignation, the constitutional institutions and processes themselves were seen as essentially satisfactory. With the important exception of the Communists, no political movement now makes basic reforms in the structure of government an important part of its program. Indeed, the voters expressed no great regret at de Gaulle's resignation and indicated they preferred stable procedures to government by "heroic leadership."

Thus there is some reason to believe that a more stable consensus on the regime may be emerging in France, and that the persistent conflicts in political values which have contributed so much to political instability are becoming muted in the light of new perceptions of reality. At the same time, beliefs are not easily changed, and should a new crisis develop, the resultant stress could easily result in a reawakening of traditional differences and a loss of confidence in public authority.

SUMMARY AND CONCLUSION

The French political tradition has been profoundly different from those of Great Britain and the United States. In the latter cases institutional continuity, stability, and consensus have underlaid governmental performance, and have (with important exceptions) permitted the settlement of specific conflicts through negotiation and compromise. France has experienced deep conflict, repeated alterations of its governmental structure, and instability. As a consequence, attempts at conciliation politics in France have, until recently, typically led to deadlock, weak leadership, public disdain for the authorities, and increased stress. At times, these maladies have led to support for politics by command and (as in the case of Charles de Gaulle) the emergence of strong charismatic leadership. These characteristic features of the political system have reflected a social order in which groups have been poorly integrated into national life, ideals and values have often been parochial and mutually exclusive, and citizen participation has fluctuated from one extreme of virtual withdrawal to the other extreme of direct action. As a consequence, the stable flow of demands from the citizens to the authorities and their transformation into issues and policies has often not occurred, with the result that public support for government institutions and officials has often been lacking.

Yet two recent developments of fundamental importance suggest that the past patterns will not be carried into the future, at least not without substantial modification. First, French society has been undergoing a profound transformation over the past several decades. Old group forms are losing ground to large associations; whereas the former tended to view the government with distrust and to resist interaction with other segments of society, the latter have sought cooperative affiliation with the authorities and with institutional groups. These changes have been accompanied by attitudinal shifts and by more regularized forms of political participation. As groups (and their individual members) have obtained favorable decisions through continuing dialogue with the authorities, they have relied less and less on strikes and protests as vehicles for their demands.

Second, the constitutional changes of 1958 have permitted the effective exercise of public authority, while retaining popular participation and controls. Though de Gaulle held and utilized exceptional powers, competition among political elites for popular support has been spirited since his resignation. Moreover, the importance of the single office of the Presidency and the fact that its occupant is popularly elected has led to a streamlining of the party system and has permitted the voters to choose between national candidates and programs. Whereas voters in the Fourth Republic were faced with a confusing array of candidates for Parliament and could not in any case vote for a Premier (directly or indirectly) and his program, under the Fifth Republic voters can now choose between more meaningful alternatives in Parliament and for the highest office in the nation.

As stated repeatedly above, it is risky to make predictions about the future of French politics. Yet current controversies in France seem more mundane and less cataclysmic than in the past. Demands for better wages, elimination of graft and corruption, and control of inflation continue to be problems of great importance. But now that there appears to be a broader consensus on the constitutional basis for making public policy, the stress such demands create may be reduced more successfully than was typically the case in the past.

SUGGESTED READINGS

Ambler, John S.: *The French Army in Politics, 1945–1962* (Columbus: Ohio State University Press, 1966). A study of the politicization of the French military elite during the Fourth Republic. Particular attention is given to the role of the Army in the establishment of the Fifth Republic and to the subsequent conflicts between de Gaulle and his generals.

Aron, Raymond: *France Steadfast and Changing* (Cambridge, Mass.: Harvard, 1960). An interpretation of the events of 1958 which led to the demise of the parliamentary system and the creation of the de Gaulle republic. The author is one of the foremost students of French politics.

Ehrmann, Henry: *Politics in France* (Boston: Little, Brown, 1971). A first-rate introductory text on French politics.

Grosser, Alfred: *French Foreign Policy under DeGaulle* (Boston: Little, Brown, 1967). A survey of French foreign policies under de Gaulle. The author, though cautious and objective, concludes with a mildly critical overall evaluation of de Gaulle's record.

Hoffmann, Stanley, et al.: *In Search of France* (Cambridge, Mass.: Harvard, 1963). A collection of essays analyzing the social and political characteristics of France. Particularly valuable is the piece by the editor in which he pulls together a vast array of materials into an excellent general interpretation of French political life and its social bases.

Suleiman, Ezra N.: *Politics, Power and Bureaucracy in France* (Princeton, N.J.: Princeton, 1974). A recent and much needed examination of the French institutional-group structure, its relationships with the authorities, and its responsiveness to social needs and pressures.

Werth, Alexander: *DeGaulle: A Political Biography* (New York: Simon &

Schuster, 1966). A readable but somewhat popularized biography of the first President of France under the Fifth Republic. A useful source for anyone interested in understanding the man who brought France out of chaos in 1958.

Wright, Gordon: *Rural Revolution in France* (Stanford, Calif.: Stanford, 1964). A study of the "silent" revolution in French rural life. The social, economic, and political changes are considered and their interrelationships developed in the study of "modernization."

CHAPTER ELEVEN

THE SOVIET POLITICAL SYSTEM

OVERVIEW This chapter examines a political system which contrasts sharply with our previous three examples in that the Soviet Union functions predominantly as a command system. But note that the Soviet Union, like other countries, nevertheless has elements of both command and conciliation politics.

The relationship between the Communist party and the Soviet state should remind you of Chapter 3, where we noted that political authorities typically use commissions and watchdog agencies to control the bureaucracy. Competition between elements of the Soviet bureaucracy and bureaucratic attempts to represent their clients should also remind you of the tendency of bureaucrats everywhere to respond to their clientele and to independent organizational loyalties.

Note especially how elites, groups, participation, and ideals in the Soviet Union compare and contrast with those in France, Britain, and the United States. Note the ways in which command politics in each of these three other countries are different from, or similar to, command politics in the Soviet Union.

Be sure that you understand the following terms:

Communist Party of the Soviet Union (CPSU)
Democratic centralism
Party Congress
Central Committee
Politburo
Secretariat
　General Secretary
Supreme Soviet
　Presidium of the Supreme Soviet
Council of Ministers
　Presidium of the Council of Ministers
　Chairman of the Council of Ministers
Marxism-Leninism
Proletariat

LEARNING OBJECTIVES

After you have studied this chapter, you should be able to:

1. Identify the dominant elite in the Union of Soviet Socialist Republics.
2. Specify sources of competition for the dominant Soviet elite.
3. Identify the major organs of the formal structure of the Communist party and the Soviet state.
4. Describe the functions and operations of the Communist party and the Soviet state.
5. Discuss the ways in which Soviet institutional groups contribute to command and conciliation in the Soviet Union.
6. Describe citizen participation in politics in the Soviet Union.
7. Understand the role of intermediate Soviet elites in linking citizens to the authorities.
8. Describe the major features of Marxism-Leninism and explain how they contribute to command functioning in the Soviet Union.
9. Compare and contrast conciliation and command in the Soviet Union with conciliation and command in France, taking account of the features of elites, groups, participation, and ideals in both cases.

Many Americans seem to consider the Soviet political order to be exactly opposite to their own. Soviet citizens, they believe, are enslaved; Americans are free. The American government is controlled by its people; the Soviet government is unchecked by the popular will. The United States is a democracy; the Soviet Union is a dictatorship. Interestingly, Soviet comparisons of their own politics with that of the United States have similarly stressed contrasts between "good" and "bad," though, of course, it is the American government which suffers in the comparison.

Though there clearly are fundamental differences between politics in the Union of Soviet Socialist Republics (U.S.S.R.) and in the United States, the formulation of simple dichotomies does not contribute much to our knowledge and understanding of the Soviet Union. In fact, such dichotomies can obscure the fact that Soviet citizens support their authorities, and they ignore clear evidence that the U.S.S.R. has a stable political order which successfully manages public conflict. Perhaps the last word on moralistic comparisons was offered, tongue in cheek, by an observer who said, "In the United States with its capitalistic economic system, man exploits man. But in the U.S.S.R., where the state owns the means of production, the reverse is true."

Attempts to understand the Soviet political order are hampered by more than prejudice, however. For one thing, the kind of information available for the study of political life in Western countries is often either nonexistent or unavailable to foreign analysts. For example, there are massive amounts of survey data available concerning the attitudes and activities of citizens of Western countries, but there are virtually no survey data available on Soviet citizens. What we may think we know about the political views and beliefs of Soviet citizens is really only educated guesswork. Another problem is that Soviet decision making does not follow public, formally defined procedures—the formally defined processes are either ignored or greatly modified in practice. For example, the selection of Soviet leaders is formally by election; in practice, citizens can only ratify a list of candidates selected by Communist party leaders in secret. Because of these problems in gaining good information, it is wise to be careful not to overestimate what can be stated as fact about Soviet political life.

ELITES IN THE SOVIET UNION

The leaders of the Russian Revolution of 1917 relied heavily upon command methods both to seize power and to organize the government. Since they sought to transform their entire society, they consciously organized their people for maximum control. All citizens were assigned to quasi-military units since it was believed that the masses were incapable of organizing themselves and sacrificing their short-term interests for a longer-term ultimate good. Just as soldiers had to be ordered into battle, Soviet citizens had to be firmly directed in the economic and social battle to build socialism (and eventually communism).

By the time of Joseph Stalin's death in 1953, a massive social and economic transformation had been achieved. The economy had been centrally organized and industrialized, and it reached an average annual growth rate of perhaps 10 percent. Opponents of the Revolution had been eliminated. Foreign threats had been overcome (for instance, Hitler had been defeated) or reduced (for example, the United States no longer seemed so great a danger to the Soviet regime). The training and education of the people had advanced considerably, and they had acquired a "socialist consciousness." In the process, the use of open force to implement policy diminished, and satisfaction with previous achievements made futuristic socialist goals seem less compelling.

Yet the tradition of government by command has remained strong, and the institutions created during Stalin's rule have continued to function under his successors. Though Khrushchev and Brezhnev made some modifications designed to reduce the concentration of power in the hands of a few, power remains highly concentrated. Still, reform has broadened participation in policymaking, and differences of opinion are more often reconciled through compromise and conciliation than they were under Stalin. A broad range of influentials now has access to the formerly isolated councils of the authorities and can initiate proposals for consideration by the party and state leadership.

The key elites in Soviet politics are the leaders of (1) the Communist Party of the Soviet Union (CPSU) and (2) the Soviet government, or state. The key figures in the party and the state are directly responsible for deciding and implementing national policy decisions.

Communist Party of the Soviet Union

Political power in the Soviet Union rests ultimately in the Communist party. It controls the institutions of government through a strongly bureaucratic, hierarchical organization. Every member is a link in the chain of command, and obedience of subordinates to superiors, and of each member to the party's commands, is mandatory. Party units exist at the All-Union (national) level; the republic, regional, and district (intermediate) levels; and the primary level. Primary organs are found in such places as factories, collective farms, and educational establishments.

Though its fundamental organizing principle is said to be "democratic centralism," greater emphasis is given to "centralism" than to "democracy."

Democratic Centralism in the Soviet Union: Two Views

The rules of the Communist party stipulate:

> The guiding principle of the organizational structure of the party is democratic centralism which signifies:
>
> i.   election of all leading party bodies, from the lowest to the highest;
> ii.   periodical reports of party bodies to their party organizations and to higher bodies;
> iii.   strict party discipline and subordination of the minority to the majority;
> iv.   the decisions of higher bodies are obligatory for lower bodies.

One Soviet specialist, the late Merle Fainsod, wrote what we might call the standard Western view of this principle:

> In the slogan "democratic centralism," centralism has primary significance. Some authority must, of course, be delegated to lower Party organs, but its exercise must be consistent with the wishes of the high command. The position of the top Party leadership is sacrosanct; it cannot be subjected to challenge or criticism. The characteristic mode of selecting Party leaders is by cooption and designation from above rather than by elections from below. Party elections ordinarily represent formal devices for registering assent rather than forums of free choice. Reports are rendered by Party leaders to the mass membership, but no report which incorporates policy decisions of the leadership can be rejected or criticized; it can only be enforced. [*How Russia Is Ruled* (Cambridge, Mass.: Harvard, 1963), p. 210.]

On the other hand, Andrei Vyshinsky, a former Soviet official, says this about democratic centralism, though his focus is on the state rather than the party:

> The Soviet Union State is built on principles of democratic centralism sharply opposed to the bureaucratic centralism of the capitalist states. It takes maximum account of the singularity and the demands of separate parts of the state, it strives to unify these parts by a common conscious will, by common interests and tasks. It not only does not exclude local self-help, on the contrary, it assumes it, making it broadly possible for rural areas to utilize the most suitable means (comprehensible to the population) and ways to realize general problems. Finally it eliminates contradictions between separate parts of the state, including those between national districts.
>
> Thus democratic centralism makes real that which the bureaucratic centralized capitalist state—pursuing the opposite course of sharpening contradictions between city and country, between different regions, and between nations— could never make real. Employed to crush the weak nations (forcibly included within the boundaries of separate states), bureaucratic centralism intensifies chauvinism and nationalism, and renders international collaboration and worker class solidarity difficult. [*The Law of the Soviet State* (New York: Macmillan, 1954), p. 230.]

Formally, the supreme ruling body of the Communist party is the All-Union Congress of the Communist Party of the Soviet Union, or the Party Congress. Since the Congress is composed of representatives from party units at lower levels, an appearance of control by rank-and-file members is clearly intended. Nevertheless, the selection of these more than 1,000 "representatives" is tightly controlled by the party elite, and the deliberations of the Congresses are infrequent, brief, and formalistic. In fact, even though Party Congresses are supposed to be convened every four years, 13½ years elapsed between the Eighteenth and Nineteenth Congresses (1939 to 1952), and the system functioned without apparent difficulty. However frequently or infrequently Congresses are held, their real purposes seem to be to build support for decisions already made, and to provide an occasion for broadening public acceptance of the party line.

Although the Party Congress does not really make policy, it nevertheless "elects" a Central Committee from among its members, which is empowered to act in its name when the Congress is not in session. This smaller body of nearly 400 voting and "candidate" members meets at least twice per year and does deliberate on important matters. Yet as its size and the infrequency of meetings might suggest, the Central Committee is still a step removed from the top echelon of the party. Its independent authority becomes significant only when there is a vacuum of leadership in the policymaking agency, the Politburo.

The *Politburo* (which has sometimes been called the Presidium) is composed of between fifteen and twenty-five of the most powerful and prestigious party leaders. In spite of an almost total lack of publicity about its internal operations, sufficient information about the Politburo is available that even such a cautious observer as Merle Fainsod describes its functions with some confidence:

> It is at the Presidium (Politburo) level that the basic decisions of Soviet life are made or approved—the tempo of growth, the level of investment in heavy and light industry, military and scientific requirements, the satisfaction of human needs, the direction of agricultural policy, and the management of foreign affairs. Since resources are limited, and choices and priorities have to be enforced, the Presidium necessarily becomes a battleground on which the converging and conflicting bureaucratic interests of society seek to carve out their domain. . . . The Presidium thus offers an area of bargaining in which accommodations and compromises take place.[1]

It is here, then, that conciliation processes—bargaining and compromise between members of the elite—take place. In specific instances negotiations may occur at lower levels of the party and state organizations. But as a general rule in any such cases the Politburo either suggests the "approved" solution (that is, employs a barely disguised version of the command process) or indicates its indifference on the matter in question.

The *Secretariat,* which like the Politburo is formally appointed by the Central Committee, is the other organ at the top of the party pyramid. It is the vital center for organized control of the party itself, and therefore of society. Its key members are also on the Politburo, thus permitting the

[1]Merle Fainsod, *How Russia Is Ruled* (Cambridge, Mass.: Harvard, 1963), p. 337.

top policymakers access to the apparatus which implements the central decision. The Secretariat also controls the party through secretariats at lower levels of party organization. Secretaries at all levels are publicly held responsible for the failures and successes within their jurisdiction. It is through the Secretariats that candidates for the highest positions in party and state are recruited. Finally, the Secretariat has been a crucial battleground in the several struggles over who should become the leader of all Soviet society (e.g., after the deaths of Lenin and Stalin and the deposing of Khrushchev). In each struggle for succession it was the General Secretary of the party who triumphed, indicating that leadership of the Secretariat—a party, not a state position—is tantamount to leadership of the country.

The primary mechanism of communication and control in the Soviet Union is thus the Secretariats of the party at various levels. From the All-Union (national) level through the intermediate to the local-level secretaries, the party leadership reaches into all governmental and social organizations (factories, farms, schools, etc.) to gather information, to make its policies known, and to monitor all aspects of economic, social, and political life. The formal structure of the Soviet Communist party is shown in Figure 11-1.

The CPSU could be characterized as the nervous system of Soviet politics; it gathers information and issues commands. But if the party is the nervous system, the state is the muscle; and it takes a tremendous amount of organizational muscle to manage the affairs of the Soviet

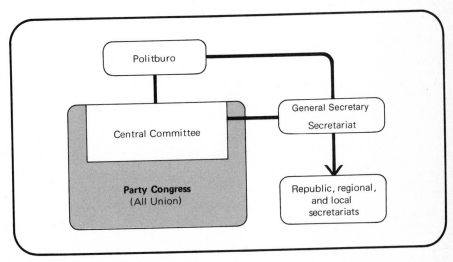

Figure 11-1. Formal structure of the Communist party of the Soviet Union.

people in the detail which the party leaders desire. As a consequence, the state bureaucracy is a potential source of competition for the party leadership.

Soviet state

The formal organization of the Soviet state parallels that of the Communist party. The Constitution of 1936 generally provides for a governmental unit parallel to each party organizational unit described above.

The governmental body which corresponds to the Party Congress is the *Soviet* or Council and at each level of government there is a Soviet as well as a Party Congress. At the All-Union level, there is a *Supreme Soviet* which is made up of two equally powerless chambers, the *Soviet of the Union* (representation in which is proportional to population) and the *Soviet of the Nationalities* (representing the several nations in the U.S.S.R.). Like the CPSU All-Union Congress, the Supreme Soviet has great formal powers: it is "the highest organ of state power." In practice, it also mirrors the Congress; each Soviet is large (over 1,000 members) and meets only briefly (about 15 days annually), and its sessions are devoted to giving ceremonial speeches and ratifying decisions made elsewhere. The real functions of the Soviets are to legitimize and publicize the party's decisions.

The Soviet Union: A Multinational State

The Soviet Union is composed of more than 100 non-Russian nationalities, tribes, or linguistic groups, many of which have resisted Russian domination since well before the 1917 Revolution. Lenin initially sought to turn anti-Russian sentiments to the Bolsheviks' advantage by promising them the right of self-determination if he and his followers came to power; when they were successful, they were as good as their promise—until their position was consolidated and the threat of foreign intervention had passed. But by the early 1920s, most non-Russian peoples (for example, Ukranians, Georgians, and Armenians) were brought back into the Soviet state, sometimes by the use of force, and "national self-determination" was permitted only if it served the socialist state.

Stalin gave this explanation of Soviet nationality policies:

How are we to make the building of a national culture, the development of schools and courses in the native tongue, and the training of personnel from among the ranks of local people, compatible with the building of socialism, with the building of a proletarian culture? Is this not an unresolvable contradiction? Of course not! We are building a proletarian culture. That is absolutely true. But it is also true that proletarian culture, which is socialist in content, assumes different forms and modes of expression among the various peoples that have been drawn into the work of socialist construction, depending on differences of language, way of life, and so forth. Proletarian in content and national in form—such is the universal human culture toward which socialism is marching. [Solomon Schwarz, *The Jews in the Soviet Union* (Syracuse, N.Y.: Syracuse University Press, 1951), pp. 38–39.]

This policy has been implemented to permit national minorities in the Soviet Union opportunities to preserve their identities and to have representation in public bodies, so long as the essential unity of the socialist state is not impaired.

There is no exact governmental counterpart to the Central Committee of the party, but parallel to the Politburo there exists a *Presidium* of the Supreme Soviet. Selected formally by the Supreme Soviet, it acts in the name of the Soviet when the larger body is not in session. In fact, it is a governmental unit which appears to be little involved in the formulation of general policy, and its real responsibilities include most of the formal and dignified functions of state such as receiving ambassadors, and so on. Though its formal powers are impressive, and its thirty-five or so members are highly placed and prestigious members of the political elite, it has not actually been an important decision-making body. Its head, the Chairman, is the ceremonial chief of state.

The most powerful state agency, however, is the *Council of Ministers,* which may be viewed as the corollary of the party Secretariat. Its subordinate units include not only the Ministries which a French or British citizen would expect in the government (like defense or foreign affairs), but also committees and Ministries which administer the entire economy (such as construction affairs, light industry, or machine building). Though these tasks are carried out under the guidance of the party, the routine and implementing decisions rest with the state bureaucracy, with the result that the Ministries and committees have an important impact on the overall success of the general party program.

The enormity of the task of administering the party program is clear. But the crucial and unique task of the Council of Ministers itself is to provide a forum in which the various administrative agencies and sectors of the economy can be coordinated. While the party Politburo is composed of men with wide experience, they are almost always generalists (whatever their educational or work backgrounds) who see problems and alternatives in broad perspective. The Council of Ministers, on the other hand, includes many technicians and others with specialized training and points of view, as well as an ample and controlling number of top party leaders. The Ministries have the expertise characteristic of bureaucracies. It is the Council of Ministers which brings these two basically different and equally necessary kinds of political actors together.

The size of the Council of Ministers (sixty to eighty-five members) is such that general deliberative sessions are barely manageable. Because of this, a *Presidium of the Council* of Ministers (not to be confused with the Presidium of the Soviet) has been established to act as a controlling "inner cabinet." In this smaller body, generalists have predominated, and its head, the *Chairman of the Council of Ministers,* is one of the two or three most important persons in Soviet politics.

Below the All-Union level, the Soviet Union has a huge governmental apparatus. There is a hierarchy of Soviets, or Councils, down to the local level, representatives to which are elected directly by the people. The local counterpart of the Council of Ministers is either a Chairman or an Executive Committee. Finally, the various Ministries extend their jurisdiction all the way down to individual enterprises and departments. Simplified somewhat, the state structure is shown in Figure 11-2.

As described above, the Soviet political system concentrates tremendous authority in the hands of a very few persons. The three key organs, the party Politburo, the Secretariat, and the Presidium of the Council of Ministers, have only sixteen, ten, and twelve full members, respectively. Moreover, the key individuals in the Secretariat and Presidium are also members of the Politburo. In 1974, eight of the ten secretaries were either full or candidate members of the Politburo, while the Chairman and First Vice Chairman of the Presidium were also on the party's top policymaking body. This overlapping of memberships provides for coordination between these powerful bodies so that once decisions are reached they will be effectively implemented.

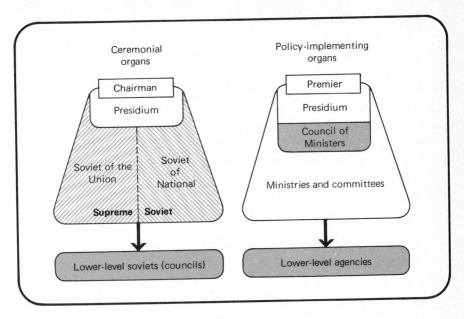

Figure 11-2. Formal structure of the Soviet state.

INSTITUTIONAL GROUPS IN THE SOVIET UNION

A few party leaders, of course, cannot govern by themselves: they require the organizational support of a huge bureaucracy. And since Soviet leaders have sought to control most aspects of social life, the institutional groups they have created form a vast network which regularly touches the lives of virtually everyone. Almost everyone works for a state enterprise (or institutional groups); trade unions, professional associations, even social groups and youth organizations are all subject to the direct supervision of the party or state apparatus. Writers cannot hope to publish their work, artists cannot exhibit their paintings, and farmers cannot work the soil unless they belong to writers' or artists' associations, or are members of collective farms. A few individuals manage to remain aloof from such bodies, but they live with the possibility of being prosecuted as "social parasites," and they must forego the professional or economic advantages of holding such memberships. Those who do belong to the officially approved groups, of course, are subject to group controls; those who refuse to be controlled, like the writer Alexander Solzhenitsyn, are likely to be expelled from the group, publicly criticized, denied the opportunity to pursue their careers, and even jailed, committed to a mental institution, or forced to leave the country.

Control mechanisms

The control mechanisms used by the authorities to obtain compliance by the institutional groups are several. In the first place, key positions in the vast bureaucracy are likely to be filled with party members. Such individuals will have shown their reliability as a precondition for entering the party ranks, and are subject to strict party supervision as long as they remain members. Their first responsibility is to the party and its directives, and they are an important source of information for higher party leaders. They also set examples of proper conduct to their nonparty coworkers.[2]

The party also exercises control through its participation in the appointment of individuals to positions of leadership. Every party unit has a list of positions under its jurisdiction, each of which can be filled only with its concurrence. In that way, even nonparty persons who fill important posts will be screened for their reliability.

A third means of control is the setting of specific goals for every organizational unit. For example, factories must achieve a planned output, and local governmental units are assigned projects which they must complete. According to Solzhenitsyn, during the great purge of the 1930s, government and party leaders were even told how many spies and counterrevolutionaries they had to arrest by a certain date—or suffer the consequences.

The advantages of setting specific goals, of course, are several. But among other things, they inform everyone of the target and permit almost automatic application of rewards or punishments. If a factory does not produce as expected (and the figures are there for all to see), the manager will not get so large a bonus and the chances of promotion are correspondingly reduced. If workers fail to fulfill their quota, their earnings will be reduced accordingly, since they work, in part at least, on a piece-rate system. In short, material rewards and deprivations can be utilized to obtain desired levels of performance when the objectives are clearly laid out.

To make certain the above controls are effective, the party and state elites have established elaborate control organs. The party has had its

[2]Approximately 15 million or 5+ percent of the Soviet Union's 240 million citizens are members of the party.

own watchdog units, such as the Party Control Commission, which have exercised internal supervisory functions. The state has both general supervisory and control organs such as the legal organs and the Secret Police, and has also relied upon direct supervision of subordinates by superior organs within a given Ministry or department, and controls which extend across ministerial boundaries. An example of this latter mechanism is found in the role of the state bank in providing loans for individual enterprises. When a request for a loan is made, the bank may refuse to provide the funds if the unit in question is expending too much of its funds for wages or is otherwise not performing according to its set norms.

Finally, the vast network of institutional groups in the U.S.S.R. is kept under control through continued transfer of personnel and reorganization of the structures themselves. The Communist party has experienced repeated periods of recruitment of new members, followed by purges of those not found to be living up to expectations. During Stalin's time this continued renewal of the party ranks reached extreme proportions, and those removed from the party were often imprisoned or even executed. But even in the last 20 years, the turnover has remained significant: in 1966, for example, more than 75,000 members were dropped from the party rolls. Turnover in state positions has also been significant, though again the trend since 1953 has been toward greater continuity. The impression clearly is that there is substantial turnover in these high positions, though not so much as to cause disruptions in production.

Reorganization has also been a continuing strategy for improving bureaucratic performance and accountability. Ministries have been added and dropped, party organs have been established and modified or disbanded, and functions or responsibilities have been shifted from one agency to another with great frequency. Sometimes, in fact, general reorganizations have been effected to meet particularly acute problems or to improve the authorities' ability to control.

Typically, wholesale reorganizations and shifts of personnel have come about as consequences of shifts in the power balance among the authorities. As Nikita Khrushchev gained in authority in the mid-1950s, those who lost in the struggle were removed from their leadership positions: the subordinate structures were reorganized, and their personnel were replaced with individuals loyal to the First Secretary (the title of the head of the Secretariat prior to Brezhnev). Though Western observers tend to see such shifts as evidence of great stress in high places, it must be remembered that changes in governmental leadership in the United

States also result in reorganizing agencies and in restaffing Cabinet and sub-Cabinet posts.

Pressure-group activity in the U.S.S.R.

Independent associations do not exist in the Soviet Union. Organizations of lawyers, workers, and other groups exist only as controlled agents of the state (or institutional groups). Nevertheless, such groups have come to play an important role in articulating needs and demands, and in defining specific issues which must be resolved. Stalin may have decided almost on his own to purge the party and state bureaucracy from the top down, or to carry out a bloody drive to collectivize agriculture in the 1930s. Today, however, such fundamental questions as foreign policy and economic planning involve many people with varying interests and professional orientations. The reconciliation of differences between these specialized elites has introduced an element of conciliation into policymaking.

Not all groups, or their representatives, have been equally effective. Some, in fact, are poorly organized or not organized at all. Others, like trade unions, have been almost totally unable to advance their members' special interests in the competition for scarce resources. Those who have had the greatest influence have been the groups the authorities needed most as they pursued their self-defined tasks. The military, for example, has benefited in resource allocation and authoritative support from the fact that Soviet leaders have wanted to develop a modern defense capability. Scientists, technicians, and others with the specialized knowledge needed to maintain and further develop the economy have been similarly rewarded, and their expertise has added to the weight of their counsel. Finally, specialists in social control—such as the Secret Police—are another category of groups whose role in the government makes them relatively influential.

At the same time, one should not overstate the ability of such groups to obtain their preferred objectives in the face of objections from the authorities. Studies of the military, literary, academic, and scientific elites have uniformly shown that they have been unable to preserve their interests when the authorities decided against them.[3] At various times, for example, the military budget has been cut, training programs have been

---

[3] See Gordon Skilling and Franklyn Griffiths (eds.), *Interest Groups in Soviet Politics* (Princeton, N.J.: Princeton, 1971).

politicized, and top military leaders have been removed from their posts, all without visible protests or opposition from military leaders.[4] Similarly, policy decisions affecting writers have oscillated. At times rigid conformity is demanded and at other times criticism of past policies has been encouraged. There seems to be no evidence that the writers themselves have initiated these policy shifts.

It appears, then, that institutional groups must present their interests circumspectly, always taking care not to force a showdown or to hold to discredited or rejected options. Their moments of greatest influence occur when they have a patron among the members of the Politburo, or when conflict among the authorities leads to a stalemate and the several contenders seek out support from other elements of the bureaucracy.

OTHER GROUPS IN SOVIET SOCIETY

Several kinds of groups—most notably the family, national minorities, and religious organizations—operate on the periphery of the institutional-group structure. As such, though they have been subject to governmental regulation, they have retained some measure of autonomy. And like such groups everywhere, they have sometimes sought objectives which were inconsistent with the goals of the authorities.

Soon after the Revolution these groups or groupings were treated with undisguised hostility and repression. Churches were turned into museums, and their members were closely observed or persecuted. National minorities were transported to alien regions, and their constitutionally guaranteed "right" to preserve their heritages was honored in the breach. The role of the family was altered by provisions for easy termination of marriage, and day nurseries and youth organizations were created.

In part because the authorities found such policies to have diminishing returns, and in part because the need for such actions has seemed less urgent as old attitudes have been replaced by more acceptable ones, the harsher features of Soviet control over these groups have been softened. As a result, churches, though not accepted as contributors to the public welfare, are permitted the right to organize. Their clergy can conduct services so long as they do not engage in "political activity," as

[4]See Roman Kolkowicz. *The Soviet Military and the Communist Party* (Princeton, N.J.: Princeton, 1967), especially chap. 10.

the authorities define the term. Since the 1920s the family has again been given an honored place in Soviet society, though its responsibilities in child rearing are still shared with public instititions, as we saw in Chapter 5. And national minorities are permitted to observe traditional holidays, speak their own language, and have representation in the Supreme Soviet, even though Russification continues by gentler means.

Limits on Religious Freedom in the U.S.S.R.

Though most of those who wish to worship are free to do so in the U.S.S.R., stories of religious persecution continue to filter out to the West, such as this report from *Time* magazine, dated January 27, 1975:

> One day a "repairman" visited the home of a pious Ukrainian Baptist in Kiev, supposedly to fix an electric meter. In fact, he was there to install a listening device so that secret police could monitor the premises. Last March 30, when the family's pastor came to the house, police pounced and arrested him for illicit religious activities.
>
> The pastor is Georgi Vins, 46, the best-known leader of 100,000 or more *Initsiativniki* (Initiators) who have split from the main body of Soviet Baptists. Stubborn and courageous, Vins is the latest in a line of Baptists from John Bunyan to Martin Luther King, Jr., who have gone to jail for defying the state on grounds of conscience. Though the plight of Soviet Jews and intellectuals is far better publicized in the West, Baptists have suffered every bit as much. At least 700 have been jailed, and one civil rights leader reports that Baptists have comprised more than one-third of the known political prisoners during the past two decades.
>
> The trouble began 15 years ago with a Communist crackdown on the 535,000-member All-Union Council of Evangelical Christians-Baptists, which is the largest body of Soviet Protestants. . . . Under pressure from the government, the All-Union Council in 1960 sent a stringent "Letter of Instructions" to its district overseers. This secret letter . . . urged church officials to be strict in their enforcement of Soviet laws against religious training and baptism for youths. It also told them to suppress

"unhealthy missionary manifestations." Convinced that their official church had become a tool of the atheistic regime, Vins and other Baptist leaders founded their own unauthorized church council. They also launched a vigorous civil rights campaign, including perhaps the most remarkable mass demonstration in Moscow since the Revolution. For his role in all this, Vins was sentenced to three years in labor camps. . . .

After release from his first jail term, he became a pastor in Kiev but was later ordered to do a year of compulsory factory labor. Fearing worse charges to come, he went underground in 1970. Till last spring's capture he led the life of a Fundamentalist Dan Berrigan, eluding government agents as he traveled about, preaching and organizing.

While Vins has been held in a Kiev jail awaiting trial, his mother Lydia, 68, herself fresh from a three-year term, has tried to rally Western support, seeking in particular a sympathetic lawyer. The Christians' response has been quiet and ineffectual. The World Council of Churches requested information and permission to send an observer, but got no reply. The Vins family approved a Norwegian judge as counsel, but he and three members of Parliament who wanted to attend the trial were refused visas. Last month Baptist World Alliance leaders—in Moscow for the All-Union Council's first meeting since 1969—asked the government for a chance to visit Vins and observe his trial but were turned down. Meanwhile, the All-Union Council's plea for amnesty for all Baptist prisoners has led to the release of 50 of them. Baptist General Secretary Aleksei Bichkov, however, plans no special appeal for Vins, whom he considers an extremist with a martyr complex: "He is the most zealous of our opponents. He has called us atheists."

A Soviet citizen who viewed the government as alien and hostile could hope for very little autonomy. In contrast to France, where (as we noted in Chapter 10) large numbers of alienated citizens nonetheless seem to conduct their family and group life without substantial state interference, the Soviet government exercises a much higher degree of social control. The Revolutionary reshaping of Russia into a socialist-communist society has required that any religious, national, family, or other value which conflicts with the achievement of party objectives be suppressed or altered. Only those practices deemed compatible with the party program are allowed to persist. Consequently, very few aspects of group life are free of state control.

CITIZEN PARTICIPATION IN THE U.S.S.R.

In our discussions of the United States, Britain, and France we noted that in each country some citizens were more effective in influencing public policy than were others. In particular, some groups have close ties to the authorities in each country, while other groups have been largely excluded from affecting policymakers.

Some Soviet citizens also have more effect on public policy than do others. The major difference is that *most* Soviet citizens are unable to influence the authorities in any direct way. In fact, fundamental policy decisions have sometimes directly contradicted popular preferences. Major past reforms such as the collectivization of agriculture have been carried out over widespread and violent public resistance. And the selection of such supreme political leaders as Lenin, Stalin, Khrushchev, and Brezhnev has been the province of a small group of high party leaders and Ministers.

To be sure, Soviet citizens participate in frequent elections and belong to a wide variety of groups which play a role in the political process. In each case, however, the purpose is to build popular support for the authorities and the governmental system, not to influence policy or to choose leaders. Elections (which result in turnouts of more than 99 percent of the eligible population) permit no choice between competing elites; only one candidate is listed for each office, and the person nominated is chosen under the direction of the appropriate party organization. Moreover, popular elections are only for representatives to the various Soviets; the selection of the members of the Presidium, Secretariat, and Council of Ministers is controlled by a handful of men. The purpose of elections is to provide a demonstration of support and to publicize the programs of the political elite.

Similarly, groups such as trade unions and professional organizations are more a means of exercising control than a vehicle of expressing policy preferences or demands. Membership in them is a prerequisite for employment, and with membership comes the obligation to live by their norms. Within carefully determined limits, groups such as trade unions are allowed to advance the ends of their members—social welfare benefits, for example, are basically administered by unions. Nevertheless, in the first years of the Soviet regime it was decided that workers could not strike in a workers' state, and the limits on the autonomy and bargaining power of organizations representing groups of employees have been stringent.

Virtually All Citizen Activity Must Support the State

Citizen participation is encouraged to take the form of active support in the Soviet Union. As a result, most social and even individual activities tend to become politicized. Working is not seen merely as a means to earn a livelihood; it is a way to serve the ends of the state. A 1962 statement by a high party leader about the proper role of Soviet artists illustrates the point:

> The talent of a true artist is the property of the people. To the young creative intelligentsia we are compelled to state the following: You no longer belong to yourselves. If your creative abilities have been recognized by the people, they have become the people's property and their wealth. You are at the disposal of the people and must serve them loyally. . . . Those in literature and the arts must check their ideological and aesthetic position against the party program. No other "program," no matter how it is expressed in prose, verse, or memoirs, can be adopted by people working in socialist culture. [*Sovetskaya Kultura (Soviet Culture*, a periodical publication), Jan. 10, 1963.]

Most sanctioned activities are held to serve the higher purposes of "the people." Those who excel at them are often given state awards. Leading workers are called *Stakhanovites*, after a worker who in the early days of industrialization performed a prodigious amount of labor. Others are awarded the Lenin Prize. Conversely, those who do not or will not work are not just lazy; rather, they are "social parasites" who are subjected to legal penalties. But whether the authorities are praising the *Stakhanovites* or condemning the parasites, the point they are stressing is that what each person does demonstrates his or her degree of support for the political system.

A number of activities, of course, are specified as especially suppor-tive of the regime. Voting, fulfilling the economic plan, obeying the law, following the leadership of the party, and reporting those who do not do these things, are all emphasized in the Soviet press and in the schools as duties of all citizens. Moreover, voting or working to fulfill the plan is not an isolated act for the Soviet citizen. Rather, he or she is expected to participate in organized discussions of party policies and needs which are held regularly in factories, or farms, in schools, and elsewhere. These discussions, held under the supervision of party members, are a means of encouraging great numbers of people to voice their support of the regime publicly; indeed, they make it difficult to remain aloof.

Finally, Soviet men and women have been called on to show their support of the party and state leaders by making a special effort in time of particular need. Teams of young people are recruited to go out to the countryside and help bring in the harvests. Workers have been asked to work overtime without extra pay for the good of the fatherland. Though such appeals to patriotism are not unique to the Soviet Union, they are probably more common there than in most other countries. They also are apparently successful.

Participation by intermediate elites

The gap between the authorities and the masses is bridged in the U.S.S.R. by a network of lower- and intermediate-level elites. Included in this category are Communist party members and persons in positions of some responsibility in government. As a crude estimate, they comprise about 10 percent of the population, and they are rewarded with status, relatively high salaries, and other perquisites.

In several significant ways, such intermediate elites participate in formulating the issues which are considered by the authorities. They speak out for their constituencies, often with forcefulness. Regional party Secretaries demand money for local projects. Rural leaders call for better schools, and so on. These are the persons who act as agents of institu-tional groups, and their demands can hardly be ignored by the authori-ties. They also may actually formulate policy to the extent that authority is delegated to them.

But while their activities are partly directed toward formulating policy, much is also demanded of them in the form of active support for the regime. They must lead the masses by example, whether in the factories, on the farms, or in special social or political activities. They are also most strongly encouraged to attend schools operated by the party, where the regime's expectations are taught. And if they do not show sufficient support or if their performances are not satisfactory, their promotions will be denied, and they may even be removed from their positions of influence. In the past there have been periods of "renewal," when all membership cards were called in and each individual record examined and approved before a new card was issued. Many members have been expelled in such purges, and during Stalin's era, expulsion was sometimes followed by more severe punishment.

Overall, citizen participation has been more in the form of supporting and complying with authoritative decisions than in the application of political pressures on the government/party leaders to obtain desired ends. While this condition might be considered intolerable to many Americans, the limited evidence available does not suggest that most Soviet citizens find it so. Indeed, one study of the attitudes of Soviet refugees to the West concluded that most of them thought that governments should be authoritarian.[5] After all, according to their prevailing view, who knows better what is good for the country than the people who are best informed and trained in public affairs?

Limited popular participation does not mean that citizen desires are totally ignored. At least since 1953 Soviet leaders have voiced concern for the needs and desires of their people, even though they have been relatively free to make policy decisions for whatever other reasons they might have found most weighty. When Stalin died, his successors quickly and surely moved to enact a variety of popular measures; they thought they knew what the public wanted, and they sought to secure their positions by responding. Since 1953, both the Khrushchev and Brezhnev governments have adopted consumer policies which suggest a serious commitment to improving the material conditions of the people.

SOVIET IDEALS

As we discussed the United States, Britain, and France, we noted that in each case potentially troublesome social divisions are usually subordinated to unifying ideas and symbols. In Chapter 6 we called such unifying frames of reference *national ideologies* and pointed out that they can facilitate communications for political leaders as they seek to gain com-

---

[5]Raymond Bauer, Alex Inkeles, and Clyde Kluckhohn, *How the Soviet System Works* (Cambridge, Mass.: Harvard, 1956), p. 119.

pliance with and build support for their politics. In the three countries previously discussed, the national ideology was neither so explicit, comprehensive, exclusivist, nor official as is the case in the Union of Soviet Socialist Republics. Soviet authorities must have a comprehensive official ideology which leaves little room for competing ideas and values. When policies which seem to contradict the national ideology are adopted (or might be so interpreted), every effort is given to show that they are fully compatible with "Marxist-Leninist" principles.

Marxism-Leninism

The Soviet ideology is, of course, Marxism-Leninism, supplemented frequently by the "creative" interpretations of such political leaders as Khrushchev and Brezhnev. This belief system is an extraordinarily complex world view, and only a few of its major propositions can be outlined here.

Fundamental to the Marxist-Leninist ideology is the proposition that there are scientific laws of history which can be determined and interpreted by people who have the proper methods of analysis. From there it is only a short, though important, jump to the assertion that only Marxist-Leninists have the correct method of analysis, and that only they can properly interpret humanity's past and predict its future. In short, Marxist-Leninists are convinced that they know the "truth." As is often the case with persons of deep conviction, they are not very tolerant of those who disagree with them.

Marxism-Leninism holds that humanity is progressing inevitably toward "communism," which is a shorthand term for a society in which conflict and economic need will be eliminated and people will finally be "free." That happy human condition, however, will be reached neither easily nor quickly, for social organization began at a very primitive level, and "progress" has been resisted by privileged groups in all precommunist societies.

Because progress has been resisted by those who stand to lose the most, the improvement of the human condition can only be achieved through struggle, often violent struggle. This takes place between classes of people who are grouped together because of their common economic condition. In the present historic epoch, class conflict takes the form of struggle between capitalists and workers. In earlier phases of human development, slaves fought slave owners and serfs opposed aristocratic landholders. In each of these periods of human history, the class destined by history to be destroyed has forcefully resisted its passage into the "dustbin of history." As a consequence, class struggle between "progressive" and "reactionary" groups has been a constant feature of human history.

Marxist-Leninists are, naturally enough, particularly concerned with the current historic epoch. They hold that the present class struggle is between workers and capitalists, and the workers are destined to triumph. Since Marxist-Leninists are the leadership of the workers (the "vanguard of the proletariat"), they believe they are in a desirable and pivotal position—they are on history's side. They are, so to speak, the leaders of history's "chosen people" (the proletariat).

Finally, this world view includes the proposition that while the final victory of the working class is certain, human effort can hasten that end. That is, the working class, or more properly its vanguard, *can* and therefore *should* help history, since it serves their fundamental interests to do so. Of course, since they know the "laws of history," Marxist-Leninists can best decide what strategies to follow.

These, then, are the basic tenets of Marxism-Leninism. Those who speak in its name hold an enviable position, for (1) they know the "truth"; (2) that "truth" literally promises them the world; and (3) it also encourages them to move actively and decisively to take what is "rightfully" theirs in the name of the workers.

On each of these points, of course, it is possible to take a contrary view. Someone might say that Marxist-Leninists do not have the truth, or that history is not on their side. To such assertions, the Marxist-Leninist has two characteristic responses. On the one hand, the critic might be viewed as ignorant. Or contrary views might be dismissed as the ideology of a reactionary class. In either case, Marxist-Leninists deny the legitimacy of the criticism, and thereby remove the need to answer in specifics. They are consequently free to act on their own knowledge and according to their own perceptions of the interests of the working class.

Armed with this basic rationale, Soviet Marxists have developed and institutionalized many supplementary propositions. The Communist party early became the organized body of true believers which speaks for the real interests of the workers, and its actions have been placed beyond outside control or even criticism. In our terms, Soviet Marxist-Leninists, who control the Communist party, have justified an elaborate command structure as necessary to further what they hold to be the ultimate condition of human development—communism.

The Marxist-Leninist ideology is the exclusive orthodoxy of the entire society: no other ideology is permitted. It is regularly presented in the mass media and taught in the schools. Even professional artists, writers, and scientists make at least token public attempts to relate their personal and professional concerns to its principles. As such it is a national ideology which seeks to relate each distinct person and activity to a unified central purpose.

Public support for Marxism-Leninism

Soviet leaders claim that their people are nearly unanimous in their support for and commitment to the orthodox ideals of Marxism-Leninism and to the political order it legitimizes. In ideological terms, this claim is based on the proposition that all Soviet citizens—bureaucrats and artists as well as all other "workers"—belong to the working class, and therefore have the same common interests. Only a few counterrevolutionary holdovers of the old Russian Czarist period (or fellow travelers of the bourgeoisie) are admitted to be unwilling to support the authorities in word and deed. As evidence, Soviet leaders point to the tremendous accomplishments of the Soviet Union over the past several decades, to the virtual absence of public dissent, and to the nearly universal participation in realizing planned objectives.

Westerners, on the other hand, have often assumed that most Russians and other Soviet peoples have been on the verge of insurrection ever since the Bolsheviks took control of the Russian government in late 1917, and that only the widespread use of force and terror has kept them in check. As days and months have passed into years, and the Soviet state has continued to maintain itself, and as the use of terror has been greatly reduced, if not nearly eliminated, most Western observers have become more willing to concede that the regime has great public support and that reports of its impending collapse have been premature, to say the least.

Though the evidence is elusive in any case, it seems to suggest that the support of the masses for the regime is deep-rooted and that the major difference between the official claims of public support and reality is one of degree. That is, most Soviet citizens are supportive of the system, but their support is more conditional and less intense than the authorities expect and demand. As a consequence, when individual choices are between an alternative which would advance personal interests (but would be adverse to the "public interest") and another which would foster the needs of the state (but which would run counter to one's self-interest), Soviet people often choose the former. Rural citizens, especially those with needed skills, continue to leave the collective farms for the cities, despite party exhortations to stay where they are most needed. Similarly, parents continue to encourage their children to seek positions in the professions, despite the fact that the regime glorifies the lot of the worker.

Several elements of the population seem to be most likely to criticize the authorities, or at least some of their policies. Among the most obvious of these are national minorities, certain religious groups, and artists and writers. Yet despite the widespread attention given in the West to such dissenters as Pasternak, Solzhenitsyn, and Sakharov, it would not be correct to assume that most "intellectuals" (or Baptists or Lithuanians) are anti-Soviet. Rather, only a relatively few can be confidently described that way, at least on the basis of their overt statements and actions; the great majority comply with state expectations and policies. It may be that this compliance is a result of the systematic efforts by the authorities to command obedience and support. Those who have dared to call for greater religious or artistic freedom, or more national autonomy, have sometimes lost their position or otherwise been harassed, or even tried in court for anti-Soviet behavior; in the face of such threats, those who oppose the regime might well feel that publicly voiced dissent gains little besides trouble for the dissenter.

The fact that opposition to the authorities is strongly discouraged and that evidence of dissent is suppressed makes it impossible to determine the attitudes of Soviet citizens with any precision. It is clear, however, that the authorities expend considerable effort to control criticism of the system and that support for the regime has been sufficient to permit the achievement of ambitious programs.

SUMMARY AND CONCLUSION

The Soviet political system has developed a comprehensive command structure, and it rests upon social and political foundations which support that mode of conflict management. A single, relatively homogeneous elite has a near monopoly over positions of authority; its dominant position is legitimized by a single, comprehensive and exclusivist ideology; its decisions are implemented by a controlled, institutional-group structure; and citizens participate in the political process by showing their support for the regime.

At the same time, conciliation processes are also in evidence, though only to a limited extent. The party leaders have often disagreed over policy matters, and since Stalin's death these differences have often led to compromise. In addition, speakers on behalf of important groups, though formally a part of the institutional-group structure, have often played meaningful roles in the formulation of public policy. Finally, even the preferences of the masses are taken into account by those who make the decisions. It should not be thought, then, that the Soviet authorities make wholly arbitrary decisions or that they could totally disregard their people's needs and wants even if they wanted to.

As different as the Soviet Union might appear to be from the states we considered in earlier chapters, its viability as a political system is beyond serious question. It has generated widespread public support, and it has developed effective methods of identifying and solving problems. Command-style politics tempered by some elements of conciliation can be a successful means of managing public conflict.

SUGGESTED READINGS

Brzezinski, Zbigniew, and Samuel Huntington: *Political Power, U.S.A./ U.S.S.R: Similarities and Contrasts, Convergence or Revolution* (New York: Viking, 1964). A comparison of the United States and the U.S.S.R. which moves beyond the obvious, formal contrasts. Emphasis is placed on such issues as elite recruitment and value systems, and the validity of the theory of "convergence" is also analyzed.

Fainsod, Merle: *How Russia Is Ruled,* rev. ed. (Cambridge, Mass.: Harvard, 1963). A textbook classic which has been the standard work in classes on Soviet politics for many years. It is comprehensive, balanced, and thorough, though it has become dated with the passage of time.

Kassof, Allen (ed.): *Prospects for Soviet Society* (New York: Praeger, 1968). A large collection of essays covering a wide variety of topics on contemporary Soviet social and political life. It is particularly useful as a source of factual material.

Meyer, Alfred G.: *Communism,* 3d ed. (New York: Random House, 1967). A useful analysis of Soviet ideology, the role it plays in Soviet politics and the ways it has evolved.

Shapiro, Leonard: *The Communist Party of the Soviet Union,* rev. ed. (New York: Random House, 1971). A comprehensive history of the Communist party from its beginning up to the late 1960s. It is particularly valuable for its treatment of the party during the Stalinist era.

Tatu, Michel: *Power in the Kremlin: From Khrushchev to Kosygin,* trans. by Helen Katel (New York: Viking, 1968). A detailed analysis of Soviet politics for the period 1955 to 1967. Its focus is on the top-level political elite.

Ulam, Adam E.: *Expansion and Coexistence: The History of Soviet Foreign Policy 1919–1971,* rev. ed. (New York: Praeger, 1973). A comprehensive history of Soviet foreign policy. It is cautiously interpretative and balanced in its assessment of Soviet objectives and achievements.

Wolfe, Bertram D.: *Three Who Made a Revolution: A Biographical History* (New York: Dial, 1964). A classic biography of Lenin, Trotsky, and Stalin. It is particularly interesting reading, though the author scarcely conceals his disgust with Stalin.

CHAPTER TWELVE

THE CHINESE POLITICAL SYSTEM

OVERVIEW

This chapter discusses the distinctive politics of the People's Republic of China. Though China and the Soviet Union are both governed by Communist parties, politics in China contrasts markedly with Soviet politics in several ways.

China's development in the twentieth century can be understood only in the context of China's ancient imperial tradition and its disruption by Western powers. China's present leaders and institutions emerged from a bloody struggle for control of the country and restoration of Chinese national dignity.

Chinese communism is based upon Mao Tse-tung's adaptation of Marxism-Leninism. Note that Mao has moved the proletarian revolution from the city to the countryside (where his successful drive for power was based). This Maoist adaptation is in direct contrast to Soviet doctrine, which emphasized the role of the urban masses as against rural peasants.

Take particular care to contrast the massive and powerful Soviet bureaucracy with personalized command politics in China. The People's Republic of China is dominated by the leaders of the revolution. It will be apparent that this personalized politics makes formal institutional structures less important than they might otherwise be.

In fact, our discussion of institutional groups and "campaigns" should make clear that Mao has tried to ensure that the kind of vested interests which typically appear in bureaucracies do not develop in China. Periodic disruption of the party and state structures has been used to keep revolutionary fervor alive and avoid bureaucratization.

Finally, the Chinese emphasis upon education and resocialization as a means of gaining compliance contrasts with Soviet practice. Virtually nowhere else in the world can one find intensive state-directed socialization activities to compare with the "consciousness-raising" programs of the People's Republic of China.

Be sure that you understand the following terms:

Kuomintang
Chinese Communist party (CCP)
The Long March
Marxism-Leninism-Maoism
Politburo of the CCP and its Standing Committee
State Council and its Standing Committee
People's Liberation Army
"Campaigns"
Great Proletarian Cultural Revolution

LEARNING OBJECTIVES

After you have studied this chapter, you should be able to:

1. Describe the nineteenth- and twentieth-century historical background of the People's Republic of China.
2. Explain the importance of Mao Tse-tung in contemporary Chinese politics.
3. Describe Mao's adaptation of Marxism-Leninism to Chinese circumstances.
4. Describe and explain the prominent role of the People's Liberation Army in Chinese politics.
5. Explain how "campaigns" change the part which institutional groups might otherwise play in formulating public policy.

6. Explain how the education and resocialization programs of the Chinese regime enhance its ability to gain compliance.
7. Contrast command politics in the Soviet Union with command politics in the People's Republic of China, particularly noting differences in elites, groups, ideology, and citizen participation.

We have seen that politics is different in style and form from one state to the next, that French politics is quite unlike that found in Britain or the United States, and that Soviet politics also is unique in important ways. These differences, however, are relatively insignificant when they are compared with the striking contrasts between most of the states previously considered and the People's Republic of China. Even Soviet politics, though it was an early source of inspiration and expertise to China's present leaders, is different from China's in several very important respects. In short, politics in China is particularly distinctive.

This distinctiveness derives in part from the non-Western traditions of Imperial China, which according to legend dates back about 2700 years before Christ. During the Han dynasty, which began about 200 B.C., the imperial system developed more fully, and its basic character remained relatively unchanged until the nineteenth century. Contemporary Chinese politics has also been influenced greatly by the events of the past century: the disintegration of the traditional system, the increasing contacts with the West, and the intense struggle for political power by numerous political forces.

Traditional Chinese society was composed mostly of peasants who were organized into extended families and clans. The Emperor, in fact, had contact with individuals only through the heads of these familial groups. Though traditional society had survived and even prospered for centuries, it was seriously undermined by the intrusions of Western traders, missionaries, and gunboats in the late nineteenth and early twentieth centuries. China was never made a colony, but the concessions forced upon its imperial government by Britain, France, Russia, and even the United States deeply humiliated the proud Chinese people. Consequently, by the early twentieth century, the major concern of most politically conscious Chinese was the reestablishment of Chinese control over China and the restoration of their people to a place of honor in the international community. This required the reestablishment of a strong Chinese state to force the unwanted foreign intruders out of their territory.

Various factions competed in attempts to seize power and reunify the country. The traditional imperial government was replaced by a republic in 1911–1912, under the revolutionary leadership of Sun Yat-sen. In fact, however, the republic was unable to consolidate its position, and most of the country continued to be ruled by local warlords in the provinces. During the 1920s and 1930s, the Kuomintang movement (or Nationalists), in which Sun Yat-sen had played a leading role until his death in 1925, appeared to be the faction most likely to reunite the country. After Sun's death, it was led by Chiang Kai-shek. As a military man with considerable organizing ability, he succeeded in gaining nominal control over most of the country by 1930, and was able to abolish some of the more flagrant Western abuses of China's sovereignty.

Chiang's successes, however, were short-lived; he had to contend with local warlords and the Communist party within, and after 1931, with invading Japanese troops. Though he tried repeatedly, he was never able to fully destroy the Communist party and its army. When Japan occupied first Manchuria and then most of Northern China, Chiang was forced to divide his attention between his communist rivals and the foreign threat. This gave the Communists time to reorganize and to increase their capabilities.

Moreover, the ineffectiveness and corruption of the Kuomintang increased markedly (and became more obvious) during the Japanese invasion. By the time the Japanese were defeated in 1945, alienation from Chiang and his Nationalists was widespread. By 1947, the country was torn by civil war. In that struggle the Nationalists, despite their better equipment and larger numbers of troops, were defeated by the Communist People's Liberation Army. The Communist regime, *The People's Republic of China,* was formally established on October 1, 1949, and Chiang Kai-shek was forced to retreat with his followers to the island of Taiwan off the mainland's coast.

The victorious Chinese Communist party had first been organized in 1921, and its success in seizing control from the Nationalists came despite unfavorable odds. Their commitment to Marxist ideology, which stresses the need for a revolution led by an industrial working class, seemed inappropriate for China's peasant society. Their opponents, the Nationalists, were vastly superior in numbers and in strength of arms. They had few identifiable political or military resources: their only source of weapons was their enemies, and they had no funds or exchangeable goods with which to purchase food and other necessities. Their only source of outside support came from the Soviet Union, which contributed almost no material aid.

Despite these handicaps, the Chinese Communist party persevered under the leadership of Mao Tse-tung, and eventually came to power. Mao withstood Nationalist military attacks by retreating into the hills of the northwestern province of Shensi. That fighting retreat, now called "The Long March," lasted for more than a year and covered 6,000 miles; understandably, it was an ordeal which has since been described and redescribed to show the heroic commitment and resourcefulness of Chairman Mao and his followers. Marxist-Leninist ideology, which had been adopted from the Soviets, was reinterpreted by Mao to fit Chinese conditions. Lack of resources forced the Communists to rely upon peasant support and to develop a highly effective guerrilla style of warfare. The isolation of the movement from external support forced them to be self-reliant.

The pre-1949 experiences of the Chinese Communists have had a lasting impact upon their views and practices. The tremendous odds which they overcame have made them confident in spite of the severe new problems they have confronted. The leaders who brought the party through the impossible early years, particularly Mao, have been venerated to the point of sainthood; it is they, not the organizational base they formed, who are given primary credit for the victory over Chiang. And the procedures and methods by which the civil war was fought have been relied upon again and again in domestic as well as foreign affairs since Mao came to power.

CHINESE POLITICAL ELITE

When communist rule was established in China in 1949, the men who had led the revolutionary movement to success became the new governing elite. Men like Mao Tse-tung, Chou En-lai, Liu Shao-chi, Lin Piao, Chu Teh, and Chen Yi had experienced the near disasters of the 1920s and 1930s as well as the later successes, and their attitudes and methods were developed in those crucial years. At the time of the 1975 convocation of the National People's Congress, two of that group—Mao and Chou—were still in the top positions of authority. The others, and most of their generation, had died or been the victims of public denunciations and dismissals. Nevertheless, the Chinese political system since 1949 has continuously been dominated by those who conceived and founded the movement and developed its strategy; the consequences of this fact are significant, as can be seen by examining the roles played to date by Mao Tse-tung and Chou En-lai.

Mao Tse-tung

Though according to some reports Mao Tse-tung no longer plays an active role in day-to-day policymaking, he clearly has been the key political figure in China for the past 26 years. Before that, he was the undisputed leader of the party from about 1935, and had gained considerable experience as a political organizer as early as 1927.

Mao's authority rests upon a truly remarkable series of accomplishments in the years before 1949. He successfully wrested control of the Chinese Communist party from those who were willing to be the puppets of Soviet Communist leaders. Once in control, he cultivated ties with Stalin while he built his own movement largely untouched by external interference. He was convinced as early as 1927 that the peasantry would be the necessary force for revolution, and despite an initial reprimand from his party for his views, he ultimately demonstrated that his strategy would work. He led his beleaguered supporters on the famous Long March and lived in austerity with them in the caves near Yenan. He developed a military strategy—guerrilla warfare—admirably suited to his army's capabilities. Perhaps most important, he was able to create a movement which was highly motivated and sensitive to the needs of its members and to those who were seeking alternatives to the Nationalists. Even without the fanfare and exaggeration which customarily accompanies all official Chinese descriptions of Mao's exploits, his record has been extraordinary.

Mao on the Peasantry

Mao Tse-tung was the first of his party to believe that the peasantry could become the agent of revolution in China. In 1927, while the Chinese Communist party was engaged in organizing the workers in the cities, he was busy in the rural areas of the province of Hunan; the following is an excerpt of his report on that experience:

> During my recent visit to Hunan I made a first-hand investigation of conditions in the five counties of Hsiangtan, Hsianghsiang, Hengshan, Liling and Changsha. . . . I saw and heard of many strange things of which I had hitherto been unaware. . . . All talk directed against the peasant movement

must be speedily set right. All the wrong measures taken by the revolutionary authorities concerning the peasant movement must be speedily changed. Only thus can the future of the revolution be benefited. For the present upsurge of the peasant movement is a colossal event. In a very short time, in China's central, southern and northern provinces, several hundred million peasants will rise like a mighty storm, like a hurricane, a force so swift and violent that no power, however great, will be able to hold it back. They will smash all the trammels that bind them and rush forward along the road to liberation. They will sweep all the imperialists, warlords, corrupt officials, local tyrants and evil gentry into their graves. Every revolutionary party and every revolutionary comrade will be put to the test, to be accepted or rejected as they decide. There are three alternatives. To march at their head and lead them? To trail behind them, gesticulating and criticizing? Or to stand in their way and oppose them? Every Chinese is free to choose, but events will force you to make the choice quickly. ["Report on an Investigation of the Peasant Movement in Hunan," in *Selected Works of Mao Tse-tung*, vol I (Peking: Foreign Languages Press, 1967), pp. 23–24.]

Like his Russian counterpart, Lenin, Mao's great successes have resulted in his being accorded almost religious deference. Most successful revolutions have produced their legendary, heroic figures; Mao is that individual in the Chinese instance. Authority based on such considerations is, of course, personal and nontransferable; only he is viewed as the virtual personification of the revolution. As a consequence, his prestige has allowed him to dominate all other political leaders; his pronouncements and policy positions have not been publicly scrutinized or debated, though they have no doubt been questioned from time to time. To a great extent, then, his decisions have taken the form of commands: conciliation and compromise have generally taken place only when he has given specific approval.

Given Mao's ability to command and obtain compliance, his goals and hopes for the Chinese nation have typically been the bases for making policy, and the methods and procedures he has preferred in their implementation have also commonly been used. As might be expected, he has opted since 1949 for methods and procedures which were successful in previous years, and he has similarly relied on his experiences in defining China's goals.

Chou En-lai

The basis of Chou En-lai's authority has been more conditional than Mao's in that it has depended on the continued support of the Chairman. Mao over the years has relied heavily upon him because of his great organizational talents, his capacity for uninterrupted hard work, and his willingness to play second fiddle, that is, to never threaten Mao's position as party leader.

Like Mao, Chou's work in the Communist party also extends back to the 1920s. He became a party member while he was a student in France, and he there gained invaluable experience and knowledge of the West. When he returned to China in 1924, he worked together with many Nationalist leaders for a brief time until Chiang Kai-shek first moved to crush the communist movement in 1926. In all his activities he showed an uncommon talent in the arts of mediation and negotiation.

These abilities and contacts have made Chou an indispensable lieutenant for Chairman Mao. He was the principal figure in negotiations with the Nationalists which took place in 1936 and then again a decade later. He has also been the main architect of, and spokesman for, China's foreign policy. And, as Premier or head of the government, he has been a major arbiter in the settlement of disputes between the organs of state. He has been Mao's conciliator, the person who has been able to reconcile differences without eroding Mao's authority.

After Mao, who—and what?

Over the past two decades, both Mao and Chou have been challenged by other Chinese leaders. In both the mid-1950s and the aftermath of the Great Leap Forward movement, criticisms were directed at Mao (1) because of his radical policies and (2) because he allegedly sought to be elevated above public criticism and party controls. Chou En-lai, who has consistently been a "moderate," was relegated to a relatively less important governmental position during the cultural revolution, and was thought by many at the time to have lost the confidence of Chairman Mao. Nevertheless, both Mao and Chou have overcome all challenges, and at the time of this writing, are clearly the dominant figures in Chinese politics.

Both Mao Tse-tung and Chou En-lai are nearing the ends of their respective careers: Mao was born in 1893 and Chou in 1898. Neither is likely to be replaced by persons with equal personal prestige and authority, since within a short period of time a postrevolutionary generation of leaders must necessarily come to power. As a consequence, the personalized style of leadership and authority which has been so important up to now will almost certainly be modified. This modification may take the form of attaching authority to specific formal roles or positions at the apex of the state or party organization. Almost certainly, control of public policy will remain in the hands of a few top party officials who will use the legend of Mao Tse-tung to bolster their authority.

MARXISM-LENINISM-MAOISM

Like the Soviet Union, the national political ideology of the People's Republic of China is an adaptation of the doctrines of Karl Marx. In fact, since the Soviet Union and the Chinese authorities came into open contention in 1960, the Chinese have held that only they have remained true to the great revolutionary tradition which Marx began. The most important point, however, is that the People's Republic officially subscribes to the same major tenets of Marxist ideology outlined in the previous chapter. These are that (1) there are scientific laws of history which can be understood through the methods discovered by Marx and later elaborated upon by Engels and Lenin; (2) as Marxists-Leninists, only they fully understand these laws (which, happily for them, inform them that history is on their side); and (3) these laws describe history as successive clashes between economic classes which will continue until communism triumphs because workers will successfully revolt against capitalist oppression.

In its original form, Marx's theory did not describe conditions either in the Soviet Union or in China. Lenin had to interpret Marx "creatively" to fit the Russian situation; Mao Tse-tung had to do the same with respect to his own society. In particular, he had to define "workers" to include all persons who share proletarian values, whatever their occupations might be. For a time, even capitalist business executives could qualify as "workers" in Mao's China.

Two particularly troublesome problems confronted the leadership of the Chinese Communist party as it sought to win and exercise power, and these problems dictated that revisions in Marxism-Leninism be made. First, the Chinese revolution was occurring in a country which had not been industrialized, and Marx's theory held that it was the oppression of industrial workers which would cause the proletarians to arise against their bourgeois exploiters. Second, they had to unify and mobilize a society which, while it had a long tradition of political identity, was not organized to compete successfully with other nation-states in the twentieth century. Neither Marx nor Lenin had developed ideological tenets to deal with the parochialism characteristic of traditional China.

Mao's reinterpretation of Marxist-Leninist ideology stressed and expanded Lenin's theory of imperialism—that capitalist countries had been able to postpone the revolution by exploiting non-Western states and using the fruits of that exploitation to "buy off" their own workers. Since, according to the theory, the troubles of China could be attributed to the greed and intervention of capitalist Western states, it seemed to Mao to describe the Chinese situation accurately. But nonindustrialized countries like China had no urban proletariat to fight against the "imperialists and their lackeys." As a result, said Mao, successful revolution had to begin in the countryside, with the exploited peasants acting as its agents. This major revision of Marx was all the more necessary since the cities of China were controlled either by foreigners or by the Kuomintang. Mao thus developed a theory of peasant-based revolution which has become influential not only in China, but also in other parts of Asia (e.g., Vietnam), Africa, and Latin America.

Mao's second problem was how to transform a nation of villages into a major world power. While the Chinese people had a long history of cultural unity, they had not had strong, active loyalties to central authorities. Imperial politics had been the concern of the Emperor, his court, and the professional, Confucian civil servants (or Mandarins). Ordinary people were involved in family and village affairs, not with the affairs of state. The Emperor was far away, and his local representatives controlled individuals only indirectly. In fact, it was considered inappropriate even to discuss political topics, as the report of a Catholic missionary from the nineteenth century cited in the comment below clearly shows.

This indifference to national political goals and aspirations presented Mao with the need to radically reorient the traditional values of the Chinese people. Maoist doctrine, therefore, came to stress the need to "reeducate" the masses, including enemies of the revolution. Translated into practice, this emphasis upon creating a new basis for society has meant that the Chinese Communists have developed sophisticated psychological and social techniques for obtaining apparently voluntary and uniform compliance with the commands of the authorities. Of course, the

fact that material conditions in China are much better now—no one
starves, disease is pretty much under control, and people are well
clothed—makes voluntary support much easier to obtain.

Traditional Chinese Attitudes about Politics

In Imperial China, peasants viewed the Emperor from afar. In
fact, they typically were unwilling to reflect upon affairs of state,
as the following report illustrates:

> In ordinary times, and when they are not under the influence
> of any revolutionary movement, the Chinese are not at all
> inclined to meddle with affairs of government: they are a
> delightfully quiet people to deal with. In 1851, at the period of
> the death of the Emperor Tao-kuang, we were traveling on the
> road from Peking, and one day, when we had been taking tea
> at an inn in company with some Chinese citizens, we tried to
> get up a little political discussion.
>
> We spoke of the recent death of the Emperor, an impor-
> tant event which, of course, must have interested everybody.
> We expressed our anxiety on the subject of the succession to
> the Imperial throne, the heir to which was not yet publicly
> declared. "Who knows," said we, "which of the three sons of
> the Emperor will have been appointed to succeed him? If it
> should be the eldest, will he pursue the same system of gov-
> ernment? If the younger, he is still very young; and it is said
> there are contrary influences, two opposing parties, at court—
> to which will he lean?" We put forward, in short, all kinds of
> hypotheses, in order to stimulate these good citizens to make
> some observation. But they hardly listened to us. We came
> back again and again to the charge, in order to elicit some
> opinion or other, on questions that really appeared to us of
> great importance. But to all our piquant suggestions, they
> replied only by shaking their heads, puffing out whiffs of
> smoke, and taking great gulps of tea.
>
> This apathy was really beginning to provoke us, when
> one of these worthy Chinese, getting up from his seat, came
> and laid his two hands on our shoulders in a manner quite

paternal, and said, smiling rather ironically, "Listen to me, my friend! Why should you trouble your heart and fatigue your head by all these vain surmises? The Mandarins have to attend to affairs of State; they are paid for it. Let them earn their money, then. But don't let us torment ourselves about what does not concern us. We should be great fools to want to do political business for nothing."

"This is very conformable to reason," cried the rest of the company; and thereupon they pointed out to us that our tea was getting cold and our pipes were out. . . . [Regis-Evariste Huc, *The Chinese Empire* (London: Longman Brown, Green, and Longmans, 1855). Reprinted in Franz Schurmann and Orville Schell (eds.), *Imperial China* (New York: Random House, 1967), pp. 28–29.]

Mao's Marxism-Leninism can thus be seen to differ from the Soviet version in some remarkable ways. Most particularly, the Soviet version insists that revolutions will succeed first in the cities. Mao, on the other hand, argued that revolution would begin in the countryside and envelop the cities at a later stage in the struggle. Mao's emphasis upon reeducation without overt displays of brutality also contrasts with the extensive Soviet use of terror as a means of social control.

These differences should not, however, obscure the fundamental similarities between Chinese and Soviet ideology. The elites of both countries have been pragmatic in their interpretations of Marx, molding his doctrines to make them applicable to the particular problems they have faced. Moreover, whatever the differences in technique, both governments have attempted to transform the attitudes of citizens and the character of the societies they rule. As a result, both have used Marxist ideology to legitimize extensive command systems of politics.

CHINESE COMMUNIST PARTY AND STATE STRUCTURES

Though the flavor of Chinese politics has been set largely through Mao Tse-tung's highly personalized political leadership, the formal party and state organizations have also played a crucial role. In fact China has been so highly organized that virtually each of its 800 million people has a form of contact with the political elite.

Communist party structure

The key organization in China is the Chinese Communist party (CCP). Like its Soviet counterpart, the CPSU, it provides the core of leadership for all other organizations; it provides a communications network to convey policy decisions throughout society; it is the single agency which coordinates the vast array of public activity; and it provides the top leaders with the cadres who exercise subordinate leadership roles. In an earlier era, it was the political arm of the revolution.

Initially, the Chinese Communist party was organized to mirror the structure of the Communist party of the Soviet Union: until the 1930s, in fact, Stalin made the key personnel and policy decisions for the Chinese party organization. As a result, structural similarities between the Soviet and Chinese parties have been considerable. According to the 1969 party Constitution, the supreme organ of the CCP is the *National Party Congress.* Like its Soviet counterpart, it meets briefly and infrequently and delegates all real responsibility to the *Central Committee.* The Central Committee, in turn, elects the key bodies: the *Politburo,* the *Standing Committee of the Politburo,* and the *Chairman and Vice Chairman of the Central Committee.* As important as these bodies are, however, the key fact is that Mao Tse-tung is recognized as the leader of the party in the Constitution itself (he is also the Chairman of the Central Committee). It is he who "has integrated the universal truth of Marxism-Leninism with the concrete practice of revolution."[1]

Again as with the Soviet party, the organizational, bureaucratic functions rest with a Secretariat, though the Constitution merely states that "under the leadership of the Chairman, Vice Chairman and Standing Committee . . . a number of necessary organs, which are compact and efficient, shall be set up to attend to the day to day work of the party."[2] Finally, subordinate party structures are established from the provincial level down to the primary group in a fashion similar to Soviet practice. The Chinese party structure is shown in Figure 12-1.

One distinctive characteristic of the Chinese party structure should be noted. The Chairman and the Standing Committee have had formal authority to supervise the Secretariat. This has curbed that body's powers so that it has not developed the predominant influence which its Soviet counterpart did under Stalin.

[1]See Chapter 1 *(General Programme)* of the Constitution. *New China News Agency,* Apr. 28, 1969.
[2]Article 10.

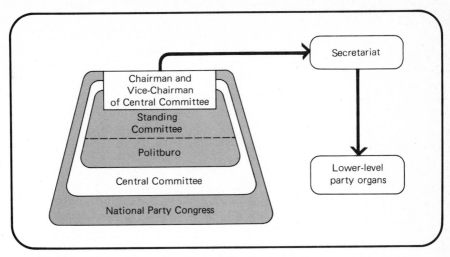

Figure 12-1 Formal structure of the Chinese Communist party.

State structure

Chinese governmental structures also parallel the Soviet example. In the early years of the People's Republic, many government agencies were established with powers and responsibilities identical to Soviet state organizations. At the national level, the Chinese *National People's Congress* is the counterpart of the Russian Supreme Soviet. The Congress, like the Supreme Soviet, meets infrequently at best (it did not meet between 1965 and 1975), has had a large membership, and has performed the function of legitimizing decisions made elsewhere. It is not, however, bicameral, as is the Supreme Soviet. Perhaps this is because China has no significant national minorities and has no formal federal structures which would parallel the Soviet Republics. There is a *Standing Committee* of the National People's Congress, similar to the Presidium of the Supreme Soviet, which acts when the larger body is not in session. The Committee, though at times it has met often, has not had an important role in policymaking.

The chief organ of state has been the *State Council.* Like the Soviet Council of Ministers, its members include both top-level party leaders (such as Chou En-lai) and specialists from the various elements of the bureaucracy. The State Council, then, has been the agency in which both political generalists and specialists have come together. Since it has been a sizable body, it has been managed by its own *Standing Committee,* which in turn is headed by the Premier, Chou En-lai. A simplified diagram of the state structure is shown in Figure 12-2.

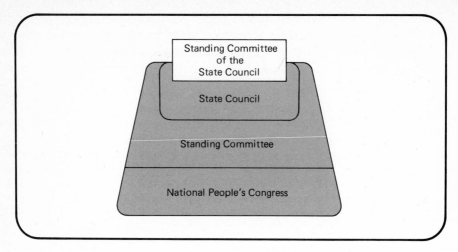

Figure 12-2 Formal state structure of the People's Republic of China.

GROUPS IN CHINESE POLITICS

Institutional groups

Since the ultimate authority to decide and govern in China has rested more with individuals than with organizations, even the key party and state structures outlined above could seemingly be considered institutional groups. That is, even though the Politburo of the Communist party and the State Council have had formal policymaking authority, they have generally acted more to implement the general decisions of Chairman Mao and, to a lesser extent, Chou En-lai, than to shape them.

Still, however extraordinary Mao and Chou may be, two individuals cannot possibly make all policy without involving others. Thus, even though we have little direct knowledge of how decisions are reached in China, it is nearly certain that the key governmental and party bodies have influenced and decided important public policy matters. This ambiguity of the roles of other members of the elite in decision making illustrates the dilemma we noted in Chapter 2: it is often difficult to tell who decides as against who merely influences decisions. The influentials are sometimes hard to tell from the authorities and vice versa.

Over the period of communist rule in China, the bureaucracy has increased in size and scope as new areas of social activity have been brought under Peking's control. In the early years, the task of establishing a new social order required dramatic reforms which generated great resistance, especially among those who were previously privileged. This placed great demands on developing strong organs of social control, particularly the Army and the public security forces. As attention later turned to economic development—to the collectivization of agriculture and industry—organizations to meet those purposes were found to be necessary. Further, since Mao has sought to drastically reeducate or resocialize all the people, an elaborate system of controlled social and cultural groups down to the primary-group level has been developed.

People's Liberation Army   The People's Liberation Army merits special mention. Since Mao and his lieutenants came to power through success on the battlefield, the Army was the chief organized and loyal agent of the new revolutionary government in 1949. Moreover, even during the struggle prior to 1949, its purposes and functions had been defined broadly; they included such tasks as "educating the masses," harvesting crops, and flood control, as well as engaging in battle. As a consequence, the Army played a key role in policy implementation from the beginning of the communist regime. In 1967, for example, the Army became a major force in checking the excesses of the Red Guards (groups of pro-Maoist young people who called for a return to revolutionary values and methods). Then, in the succeeding months, Army cadres served prominently on the "revolutionary committees" which governed in place of the regular administrative agencies.

The great responsibilities entrusted to the People's Liberation Army reflect, in part, the authorities' confidence that the Army can be effectively controlled and that it will remain responsive to directions from above. In fact the Army has remained responsive, and for several reasons. One important factor is that most of China's leaders have had military backgrounds and experience. Many were active participants in the long years of the civil war. They are familiar with military ways and have maintained their ties with the military elite. This is especially true of Mao Tse-tung and Chou En-lai. Mao formulated the strategy used in the civil war and supervised its implementation. Chou was an instructor at the Whampoa Military Academy in the 1920s, and many of China's later military leaders were his pupils.

Another important reason why the Army continues to be responsive is that military needs and interests have consistently been given high priority in policy and budget decisions. Given the primitive state of the economy, the costs of maintaining a large, well-equipped army have been enormous. The fact that the authorities have been willing to pay a high price for military preparedness has no doubt been a source of satisfaction to China's generals.

Chairman Mao on Using the Army to Build a New Order

As the Communist People's Liberation Army was taking control of China, Chairman Mao Tse-tung emphasized the importance of the Army in the postliberation phase of the revolution. In a declaration of February 8, 1949, he asserted:

> The army is not only a fighting force, it is mainly a working force. All army cadres should learn how to take over and administer cities. In urban work they should learn how to be good at dealing with the imperialists and Kuomintang reactionaries, good at dealing with the bourgeoisie, good at leading the workers and organizing trade unions, good at mobilizing and organizing the youth, good at uniting with and training cadres in the new Liberated Areas, good at managing industry and commerce, good at running schools, newspapers, news agencies and broadcasting stations, good at handling foreign affairs, good at handling problems relating to the democratic parties and people's organizations, good at adjusting the relations between the cities and the rural areas and solving the problems of food, coal and other daily necessities and good at handling monetary and financial problems. In short, all urban problems, with which in the past our army cadres and fighters were unfamiliar, should from now on be shouldered by them. [*Selected Works of Chairman Mao*, vol. IV (Peking: Foreign Languages Press, 1961), p. 337.]

Finally, the Chinese authorities have effectively used the strategies and resources outlined in Chapter 3 as they try to control the PLA. They have not been reluctant to reorganize the Army, to alter its responsibilities, or to dismiss its leaders when such steps have appeared necessary. For example, in 1965 the entire officer's corps was reduced in status in a move to curb too narrow a concern with Army matters at the expense of commitment to "the people" and ideological purity. To that end, all outward indications of rank, on uniforms or otherwise, were forbidden.

Earlier, in 1959, General P'êng Têh-huai was purged for advocating excessive professional autonomy in the military.

Bureaucracy and "campaigns"   Institutional groups may have played a crucial role in implementing the policies of China's political elite, but they are also viewed with suspicion—particularly by Chairman Mao. He has been committed to a revolutionary transformation of society through mobilization of the masses. Institutional groups, with their tendency to develop vested organizational interests, are thought to hinder this transformation. Bureaucrats become concerned with preserving their own status and that of their organizations. Mao holds that they tend to look down on "the masses" and to seek independence or autonomy from their superiors. Though they may continue to express support for revolution, they actually come to look at problems as technicians rather than as revolutionaries. As we noted in Chapter 3, bureaucrats do tend to develop such viewpoints; Mao's concerns are justified, at least to a point.

To counter the undesirable consequences of bureaucratization, the Chinese have repeatedly used "campaigns" to keep revolutionary fervor alive and to circumvent institutional-group interests. This is a radical political device, intended to generate enthusiasm and involvement similar to that found in religious revival services. Temporary groups are formed with memberships drawn from the masses. The members have no special expertise, other than a fanatical commitment to the goals of the revolution. Their specific task, whether it be to seize land from landowners or to suppress "counterrevolutionaries," is outlined by the central elite and is executed under the supervision of trusted cadres. Their purpose is to achieve a specific goal, but in addition they are thought to heighten the revolutionary consciousness and increase the involvement of the masses.

Campaigns usually circumvent institutional groups. They transfer responsibilities—normally the province of established government agencies—to these special groups, which are unrestrained by procedural and professional niceties. Sometimes they not only circumvent, but are directed against institutional groups themselves. In the early 1950s, for instance, the "three-anti" campaign was designed to stamp out "bureaucratism," "corruption," and "waste"—vices found in the institutional groups normally charged with policy implementation. Later campaigns were used to attack "improper attitudes" and practices among intellectuals, government and Army officials, and even party cadres.

While campaigns have been a useful device, they also have posed distinct and serious problems, as Chairman Mao no doubt has understood very well. They are weak precisely where the bureaucracies are strong: they permit no specialization or regularization; they encourage decision by emotion rather than rational judgment; they require concentration on one crucial objective or problem area to the exclusion of others; and they permit excesses in the name of a higher purpose.

The Great Proletarian Cultural Revolution (1965–1969) was the last great campaign, and it illustrates the weaknesses just noted. Red Guards and other "revolutionary groups" were organized to root out bureaucratic practices and "anti-Maoist reactionaries." As a consequence, specialists of all sorts were either obstructed in their efforts to carry on their normal responsibilities or pressured into joining the ranks of the revolutionaries. Such mundane but important tasks as maintaining diplomatic missions or harvesting crops were given only secondary consideration at best, and China's international interests and its economic performance suffered as a consequence.

From Mao's perspective, no single organizational structure or procedure has been totally satisfactory. Bureaucratic organization offers the advantages of specialization and rationality, but it can threaten the future of the revolution because of its conservative bias. Campaigns, on the other hand, are ideal revolutionary instruments, but they ignore the advantages of expertise and stability. Because of Mao's suspicions, and because bureaucracy is needed in spite of them, policy implementation in China has alternated between periods when the emphasis was upon bureaucratic organization and stability, and those when policy implementation was brought about through campaigns. The result has been that Mao has achieved his objective; institutional groups have apparently played a lesser role in policymaking than is the case in the Soviet Union. But the price of campaigns has been periodic civil disruption.

Will this pattern of alternate "normalcy" and disruption continue beyond Mao's lifetime? It is impossible to say. However, if the experience of other states is any guide, China is likely to become increasingly bureaucratized as it becomes more industrialized. The costs of relying on campaigns will become much greater as the country's industrial and technical capacities develop: specialists are needed to plan and supervise an industrial economy. While revolutionary fervor may generate a sense of national purpose, it does not qualify anyone to design an aircraft or a production line (as Chinese leaders, of course, know). Further, the costs of civil strife tend to become harder to bear as a society becomes more dependent on machine production: the complex social organization involved has many crucial decision points, which are bottlenecks if they are disrupted. The performance of the whole industrial and distribution network suffers accordingly. This is why campaigns would cause greater havoc in a developed, industrialized society than in a more rural, less-industrialized one.

Other groups in Chinese politics

The Chinese system of centrally controlled groups, including the special ad hoc bodies utilized in campaigns, has been so comprehensive as to involve virtually every citizen. Some organizations are large and complex bureaucracies, but others are small primary groups in which the members must periodically discuss political topics. As a consequence, it would seem that little opportunity has been given for independent or autonomous organizations to be formed (except perhaps on an informal basis). Professional groups are an example. Even in the Soviet Union, groups of professionals have been important in introducing an element of conciliation somewhat parallel to that introduced by professional associations in Britain, France, and the United States. But such groups have been relatively unimportant in China since 1949.

Noncommunist parties In the early days of the regime, several noncommunist parties were permitted to exist. They were even allowed to play a role in Chinese political life, though this role was largely honorific. Their leaders held seats in an assembly called the Chinese People's Political Consultative Conference, which acted as a legislative body before the Constitution was drafted in 1954. A few such party leaders held high positions (such as the Minister of Justice) in the state structure. They were, of course, expected to support the revolution, its leaders, and its objectives. They were permitted to function (1) in order to demonstrate that the new regime had a broad base of support and (2) because their members had expertise in areas where it was sorely needed.

This tolerance largely ended, however, in 1956. A movement named the One Hundred Flowers Campaign was inaugurated, in which noncommunist intellectuals were encouraged to criticize the system. When they did so, often with very serious charges, the authorities quickly reversed their policy of tolerance. They punished many of their critics and removed them from university and government positions. Many have argued that the campaign was just a trap set to lure the intellectuals into saying things which could be used against them. Others assert that Mao was actually surprised at the harsh attacks on Communist party rule. Whichever view is correct, intellectuals have not since been permitted to speak out on political matters (except to express unquestioning support for the regime and its leaders).

The family The family is perhaps the only important noninstitutional group in contemporary China. In traditional China the family was the key social unit. It was the foremost object of individual loyalty, and it also was ordinarily the center of economic activity. The head of the family had great authority over its members' conduct. The state did not ordinarily infringe upon its internal autonomy—although the family head was responsible to the state for the social actions (such as violent crimes) of the members of the household.

The traditional role of the family in Chinese social life thus posed a significant problem for the communist political elite as it took power. It claimed intense loyalties from its members and was an obstacle to revolutionary change. As a consequence, the new government moved quickly after 1949 to reduce the scope of familial controls over the lives of individuals. For instance, family control of marriage was undermined by a 1950 law which permitted divorce and made mutual consent the basis for entering a marriage. In the mid-1950s, the state imposed central control over agriculture, and economic functions which had largely rested with the family were thus assumed by state agencies. During the Great Leap Forward of 1958–1959, when communes were established, attempts were made to further socialize familial activities through the creation and use of mess halls and nurseries.

But although the family is no longer as important an institution as it once was, it still plays a significant social and political role in China. It provides for the early socialization of children, and it provides its members with stable emotional attachments. And, despite its diminished role, it probably still is a vehicle for the transmission of traditional non-Socialist values.

CITIZEN PARTICIPATION IN CHINA

It should now be clear that China has, on the whole, been organized to function by command. The political elite is committed to the transformation of society; it has developed a comprehensive ideological orthodoxy;

and an impressive array of controlled groups have been created to accomplish the aims of the authorities. Since the goal is clear, and the means developed are adequate for that purpose, differences over strategy are not legitimate and therefore need not be conciliated.

But while China is governed largely by command, the authorities make strenuous efforts to obtain mass support by persuasion rather than coercion. The point is important, and too often ignored. In our initial illustration of a command situation in Chapter 7 we described a soldier who played no part in deciding whether he would enter into battle, but was nevertheless subject to his superior's command. It should be noted that he could obey either because he would otherwise be punished, or because he agreed that the order was necessary to achieve a goal he shared. Chinese political leaders want obedience from the masses for the latter reason—though they are willing to use coercion when they must. They believe that the great majority of the Chinese people will actively support their programs if they can be made to understand the purposes of the revolution.

Raising mass consciousness

This view has been responsible for a truly remarkable effort at "raising the consciousness" of the masses. This effort has been so pervasive, in fact, that it is fair to say that the most common form of citizen participation in China has been in programs aimed at resocialization of the citizenry. Virtually all political actions are used or are justified as necessary to "educate" the people; sufficient activities have been designed for that purpose to involve virtually every citizen on a continuing basis.

One widely used form of political participation which illustrates this is the study group. Composed of from ten to fifteen persons, such groups meet regularly in factories, on collective farms, in communes, or elsewhere under the leadership of a party member. They discuss prescribed study materials and practice "criticism and self-criticism," in which participants express their views, criticize themselves, and submit to the criticism of others. One student of China describes the basic advantages of study-group activity:

> First, by assigning to cadres and activists responsibility for the guidance of small units of specified membership, it enables group leaders to verify by personal observation the transmission of Party policy to the citizenry. . . . Second, the small group makes politics more vivid and memora-

ble by placing it in a setting where face-to-face discussion is possible. . . . Finally, since the small group normally consists of people who live or work together, it brings formidable social pressure to bear on its members.[3]

In addition to participating in small groups, Chinese citizens also have been frequently mobilized for mass activities such as parades, rallies, or public trials of "counterrevolutionaries" or other enemies of the state. In the early and mid-1950s, for example, public trials were sometimes attended by 50,000 or more persons, some of whom were encouraged to contribute their evidence against the defendants on the spot. More recently, such mass rallies were used frequently during the cultural revolution.

Though such mass activities no doubt have been important in promoting a sense of personal involvement in nationwide drives, they are of limited value in some respects. They are a poor vehicle for eliciting and stimulating discussion, and, of course, they provide no means to check on the attitudes and behavior of individual participants. In China, as well as elsewhere, it is relatively easy to get lost in the crowd. As a consequence, the use of mass meetings is important, primarily as a complement to small-group activities.

The Chinese political elite has also sought to involve the masses politically by encouraging them to participate in elections for the various levels of the state congresses. As in the U.S.S.R., elections are a means of publicizing party policies and generating popular support for them rather than a means by which public authorities are chosen. Party cadres play a dominant role in choosing candidates, and the number nominated equals the number of vacancies to be filled.

Though political participation in China is highly controlled and is intended primarily to promote support for the authorities and their policies, Chinese authorities have also stressed the point that political leaders are "responsible to the masses." However, this does not mean that policymaking is carried out in response to pressures from below. Rather, responsibility to the masses permits popular checks on public officials at all levels to assure their strict compliance with central policy, and to check any tendencies on the part of the cadres to act in an arbitrary or improper manner. In fact, cadres are supposed to provide an example:

[3]James R. Townsend, *Political Participation in Communist China* (Berkeley: University of California Press, 1967), p. 176.

they are to participate in production like the lowliest worker and live as austerely as everyone else.

Overall political participation in China is high and is tightly controlled from above. It may not retain its current revolutionary style beyond the period of control by Mao and the other veteran leaders of his generation. But for those looking for convincing evidence that Mao's control of China has been virtually complete, the high degree of observable citizen participation in conformity with his directives should provide it.

CONCLUSION

We have seen that the Chinese political system has rested ultimately upon the authority of Chairman Mao. He developed the strategy which provided for the successful seizure of power and the consolidation of that power in the hands of a highly centralized political elite. Though he drew heavily upon the ideas of Marx and Lenin, he adapted those ideas to Chinese conditions, and relying upon them in their altered form, he was able to impose a political system that has involved virtually every citizen in the process of transforming Chinese society.

Mao's remarkable successes have not gone unnoticed by leaders of other revolutionary movements and by governing elites whose problems seem similar to those faced by the Chinese. If Maoist strategy has been successful in bringing a nation of peasants together into a centralized and integrated political order, and in enabling that nation to successfully reassert its independence from foreign interference, why would it not work elsewhere, in other parts of the world where Western colonialism and its consequences have been so directly felt? Indeed, Mao himself and his followers have repeatedly claimed that their example can and should be emulated.

Nevertheless, Maoism has not had the broad application elsewhere that some have desired. Perhaps the reason for this is that others have not made the adaptations of it necessary to fit the peculiar conditions in which they find themselves. China has had much in common with such countries as India, Brazil, or Ghana, but it is also unique in important ways, and Mao accounted for those areas of uniqueness when he devised his strategy and carried it out.

While Maoism has been successful, two problems remain on the horizon for the People's Republic of China. First, of course, is the matter of succession. The system has developed so much around the person of

Mao that when he dies or is no longer able to govern, significant adjustments must necessarily be made. No heirs apparent are clearly visible, at least beyond the also aged Chou En-lai. When they are gone, a struggle among the lower echelon of younger leaders seems almost inevitable.

Second, the clash between bureaucratic and campaign methods of governing is likely to continue, and perhaps even to worsen. The goal of industrialization, which is of high priority, seems to dictate increased reliance upon bureaucratic organizations and upon "experts." On the other hand, preserving the Maoist vision of the revolution seems to require periodic use of campaigns to develop and maintain "redness" or a proper revolutionary mentality. Compromising these seemingly incompatible approaches to politics would appear to be increasingly difficult in the days ahead.

A prudent evaluation of the Chinese system would balance recognition of past accomplishments against skepticism about the permanence of its key features. To date, Mao's vision of "permanent revolution" has not been achieved elsewhere—and in the long run it may not prove to be "permanent" in China either.

SUGGESTED READINGS

Barnett, A. Doak: *Cadres, Bureaucracy & Political Power in Communist China* (New York: Columbia, 1967). A comprehensive analysis of the organization and principles of the Chinese state and the manner in which it has functioned. The book is now somewhat dated, since it was published as the cultural revolution just began.

———: *Uncertain Passage: China's Transition to the Post-Mao Era* (Washington: Brookings, 1974). An analysis of the problems and prospects for the Chinese system when the current leaders are no longer on the scene.

Fairbank, John K.: *The United States & China,* 3d ed. (Cambridge, Mass.: Harvard, 1971). An excellent introduction to the evolution of Chinese society and politics from the traditional setting to the present. It also includes an analysis of America's interests and involvement in China, past and present.

Ho, Ping-ti, and Tang Tsou (eds.): *China's Crisis* (Chicago: University of Chicago Press, 1968). A series of incisive, analytic essays on various aspects of contemporary China, written by many of the world's foremost sinologists.

Schram, Stuart: *Chairman Mao Talks to the People* (New York: Random House, 1974). A useful anthology, with analysis, of Chairman Mao's talks and letters from the period 1956–1971.

Snow, Edgar: *Red Star over China* (New York: Random House, 1938). An early first-hand account of the organization and activities of the communist movement before it came to power. It includes evaluations of China's current leaders, Mao and Chou, based on interviews and direct observation.

Townsend, James: *Politics in China* (Boston: Little, Brown, 1974). The best, and almost the only, general textbook on contemporary Chinese politics.

CHAPTER THIRTEEN

POLITICAL CHANGE
Past Reality, Future Prospect

OVERVIEW   In this final chapter we discuss the complex
topic of political and social change. The phenomenon of change is poorly understood, and
there is much disagreement about it. Some of the
basic differences of opinion center on whether or
not there is a *direction* to change; other fundamental arguments concern the degree to which it
is thought that change can be *controlled.* Note
that even though we commonly assume that governments have the power to promote progress,
there is not agreement on the proposition that
control is possible or even on what progress is.

As we discuss the dynamics of political
change, you will note that there are some things
about it which can be observed without necessarily taking sides on the issues of control and direction. New ideas and practices can be seen to
spread through imitation and adaptation; and
change is easier to produce when people want it,
and harder when it is thought to be threatening.
Such observations may seem obvious, but both
citizens and officials often overlook their implications for the effectiveness of proposed policies.

Finally, we look at the question of how political systems differ in their approaches to change. Note that we use the terms "democracy" and "dictatorship" in this section, not to replace "conciliation" and "command," but to indicate clearly that in the real world governments are mixtures of our models. In discussing differences between systems it is only possible to note tendencies such as: dictatorships seek to control change more completely than do democracies, and parochial groups make centralized control of change difficult.

Be sure you understand the following terms:

Progress	Diffusion
Cyclical	Adaptation
Confucianism	Vulnerability
Development	Rising expectations
Marxism	

LEARNING OBJECTIVES

After you have studied this chapter, you should be able to:

1. Contrast the Confucian view of change with the idea of developmental change.
2. Discuss the relationship between democracy and industrial development.
3. Describe the Marxist theory of change.
4. Explain why tradition and progress come into conflict.
5. Describe the processes of diffusion and adaptation.
6. Identify conditions which foster or impede change and explain why they do.
7. Compare and contrast patterns of political change in democracies and dictatorships.
8. Identify the major instruments which dictatorships use to control change.
9. Explain why attempts to "modernize" usually produce frustration for the authorities.
10. Discuss whether conciliation or command politics is most likely to be successful in producing economic development in the less-industrialized countries of the world.

Upon his appointment as Secretary of State, a teasing reporter asked "Doctor" Henry Kissinger, "What will we all call you now?" The good

Doctor replied that he wasn't very concerned, but that "Excellency" would be fine. That response provoked laughter in 1974. But 60 years earlier, before World War I, the title would have been most appropriate for a ranking official, and the open and jocular banter between such officials and the press would have been unthinkable in most of the world. Within the lifetimes of millions of Americans, the political divisions of the globe and the modes of governing nations have changed drastically. In 1914 the "great powers" were Britain, France, Germany, Austria-Hungary, and Russia. European nations dominated Asia and Africa under competing empires, including systems of colonies and domination of Imperial China by gunboat diplomacy. Today the Russian Czar and the German Emperor are gone, and the spread of European-inspired nationalism, democracy, socialism, and industrialization have spurred the creation of more than 150 "sovereign" nations on the globe of the 1970s.

Were we to look at the world 200 years ago, at the time of the American Revolution, the contrast with today's world would be even more striking. The powerful monarchies of that age are no more. "Divine right" to rule is gone from the Western world and waning almost everywhere else. Royalty is either largely powerless and honored symbolically, as in Britain, or the pet of jet-setters who enjoy having an aristocrat in exile as a party guest or weekend companion. Power comes dressed in metal tanks, planes, and rockets rather than in the flesh of horses and wood of sailing vessels. Elections, bureaucratic maneuvering, and military muscle elevate leaders to power, in place of accident of aristocratic birth.

Indeed, we need not look beyond the last few years in the United States to note how political issues and events undergo rapid change. In the 1960s riots, civil rights, and an Asian war dominated political debate. They have been replaced by recession, inflation, ecology, and energy.

Rapid changes in leadership, policies, issues, and institutions of politics are the rule rather than the exception in today's world. We will examine here (1) some widely held perspectives on political change, (2) the dynamics of change, and (3) systemic patterns and problems of change.

PERSPECTIVES ON POLITICAL CHANGE

There are many attitudes toward, and explanations of, political change. Some pertain to perceived *directions,* or patterns of change. One common view sees change as *progress* from "lower" to "higher," or "primitive" to "advanced" forms of organization, and from "baser" to "more civilized" ways of life. A countering perspective views change as *decline;* departures from past practice are thought to lead to social decay. Still another viewpoint is that change is *cyclical* and that history continuously repeats itself. Finally, it is possible to reject the notion that political and social change has any pattern or direction at all—to hold that changes are *random.*

Other perspectives on change focus on the degree to which humankind can *control* it. Those who believe that events are governed by *immutable* (unchangeable) *laws* discount the ability of humans to alter a predetermined course of events; such people might be called "political fatalists." Others hold that individual and collective efforts can be used to shape the future; they could be called "political activists." The view we have advanced in this book—that political authorities attempt to formulate policies to cope with social stress—presumes that public policy decisions *do* make a difference in the way things turn out. It presumes that human choices influence change to at least some extent.

These perspectives on change have practical implications as well as theoretical interest. The attitudes of leaders and followers toward change partly determine their political action—or inaction. Fatalistic attitudes encourage leaders to ignore political problems and choices in the belief that their actions make no difference. Believers in progress, the activists, are more apt to press for change than are those who view history as cyclical. And the idea that change produces social decay is apt to produce resistance to it.

Cyclical change: Confucianism

Most peoples of the past have been aware of change as nature presents it to all living things—in the form of death and renewal. Most of our ancestors viewed change as cyclical. Those who must rely for sustenance upon the weather, migration patterns of animals, and other natural phenomena, develop traditions, rites, and rituals which center upon such cyclical phenomena as the change of seasons or the hardships of dry years followed by the joys of bounteous years. Reliance upon natural cycles produces social institutions which attempt to regulate human behavior to take advantage of natural change, in order to ensure the well-being of the group.

It would be easy to focus upon so-called primitive peoples and their traditions relating to harvests, hunting seasons, floods, and drought when discussing such cyclical views of change. The risk in this is that we might thereby be tempted to dismiss cyclical perspectives too easily. Cyclical views might appear not to take "higher" achievements and civilizations enough into account. To avoid the danger of discounting the utility of a cyclical view, it is helpful to consider Confucian ideas of change, which underlay one of the highest and most persistent of human cultures.[1]

Confucian philosophy—a profoundly influential "cyclical" view of humanity and nature—provided principles of civic and social behavior for the Chinese people and their rulers from the fifth century B.C. into our own. Confucianism thus demonstrated its capability to provide the philosophical basis to govern masses of people spread over large territories. Further, it proved capable of surviving conquests and revolutions, and has assimilated once-alien cultures and peoples while maintaining its own basic character. Such a philosophy must be presumed to provide a satisfying mode of social life, and an effective basis for governmental authority, since so many generations chose to maintain the social patterns it advocates.

Confucius held that societies do not progress, and that change is not necessarily good. Goodness is constant and unchanging, and therefore change is only good if it brings society closer to perfection. Human beings, though good, are capable of evil. All societies, therefore, are capable of departing from the ideal, which is to be in harmony with nature. Such departures result in suffering, and lead to decisions which redirect us toward a state of natural harmony.

Pointing to the long history of China, Confucianist historians depicted their ancestors as having gone through a series of cyclical changes. Each involved the rise and fall of a dynasty, a process which may have lasted as much as 300 years. In the golden eras, when Emperors ruled wisely and the people prospered, change was not desirable, for it would only lessen the tranquility of life. At such times, when things went smoothly and well, Emperors were said to enjoy the "Mandate of Heaven." On the other hand, when Emperors governed badly, this mandate was withdrawn and the people suffered (sometimes for generations) until a nonheavenly savior appeared with heaven's renewed mandate to lead the people again into harmony. In practice, the mandate was as good as an Emperor's ability to maintain control and to stifle attempts at resistance or rebellion. When he lost his powers, he also lost his authority. Thus, the social history of the empire was interpreted to reinforce the

---

[1] Cf. Lin Yutang, ed., *The Wisdom of Confucius* (New York: Modern Library, 1943).

basic Confucian philosophy, and the cyclical view which it incorporated enabled the people to endure hardship in the sure hope that it would eventually end in social restoration, as it had in the past.

The future of Confucianism as an influential social doctrine is uncertain. It was unable adequately to provide for the control of modern technology. Confucius did not consider wealth and material considerations to be proper social and political goals. Rather it was the moral state of rulers and subjects which was of primary concern. Since moral goodness was the aim of human beings and their institutions, the ability to wage war or to produce goods had to be viewed as means, rather than as ends. The intrusion of technology, with its accompanying materialistic ideologies, has changed Confucianism beyond recognition in contemporary China.

Progress: development and democracy

The advent of modern technology and industry has spawned a great emphasis upon human ability to increase economic production, raise living standards, provide leisure in place of drudgery, and to give all individuals opportunities for education and cultured living. Industrialization has thus done much more than increase per capita income; it has encouraged the belief in human progress.

Much of the claimed evidence for progress, apart from judgments about whether the world is actually becoming more egalitarian, libertarian, or democratic, rests upon the consequences of industrial development. Societies equate progress with increased affluence or more comprehensive and universal formal education. Even where progress is asserted to have taken place in the improvement of human character (we are becoming more peace-loving, or we are becoming better citizens), technology is seen as the vehicle which permits the liberation of the best in human character.

If the idea of progress does not appear in a single guise, it can nevertheless be seen as pervasive in our time. We commonly believe that science and technology can solve problems which plague us, problems such as hunger, overpopulation, disease, and poverty. We expect and aspire to better educational and employment opportunities for each generation. Many of us believe that conflict and strife can be reduced, that individual freedom can be advanced, and that equal opportunity and status can be extended to previously excluded groups (such as women and blacks in the United States, or newly independent nations).

The *credibility* of the idea of progress is usually based upon the tangible benefits of technology and industry. Many of the world's governmental authorities subscribe to the idea of progress in its guise of "development"—meaning industrialization, education, and attendant increases in material goods and the comfort of life.

From a Western, and particularly from an American, perspective, progress has also been associated with movements toward "democratic" values. Changes from despotism to democracy, from colonial subjugation to self-rule, from slavery to equality have been viewed as indicators of human progress. Within Western nations, the increasing general standard of living has helped to narrow extreme differences in status and privilege between individuals, and the role of the average person in public affairs has been expanded.

Though the ability of the West to produce more goods and services and the promise of control of disease and hunger has helped to spread democratic ideas, "democratic" progress is not *logically* dependent upon industrialization and technology. The eighteenth-century intellectual movement toward social equality, individual liberty, and popular government was not predicated on the affluent society. The philosophical godfathers of the American Revolution of 1776 and the French Revolution of 1789 did not foresee the Revolution in the average standard of living made possible by modern technology. They believed that both nature and society could be controlled through rational thought, and that basic human nature, not brutalized by corrupted social institutions, would construct rational governmental institutions. Their contention was that existing social institutions in Europe were based upon unnecessary fear, superstition, and suffering. If reason replaced privilege as the basis for law and individual rights, they argued, then the ordinary individual might be trusted to care for his or her own social fate.

The emergence of industrial economies in Western Europe and the United States during the nineteenth century was accompanied by expanding political participation on the part of the emerging middle classes. Further, the demise of aristocracy in the twentieth century led some to suppose that industrialism and democracy develop hand in hand—an obvious mistake. What has happened is that the rhetoric of democracy has been generally adopted, and as nations have sought the progress of "development," they have often done so in the name of "democracy." But states have found it difficult to use massive popular participation to industrialize their economies; they tend to use institutional groups to control participation. They typically rely more on command than upon conciliation.

Immutable progress: Marxism

The relationship of technology to the idea of progress was firmly grasped by Karl Marx. But he formulated a theory of change and progress quite different from that of Western democrats. While he, too, embraced technology as a tool for human improvement, he was unconvinced that moral improvement and self-government could be produced through the application of eighteenth-century scientific reason to human affairs. Social progress would lead to the ideal communist society regardless of thoughtful human efforts. Whereas the eighteenth-century democratic tradition stressed human beings' ability to control history, Marx proclaimed us to be in its unbreakable, if benevolent, grip.

Marxism holds that change takes the form of progress, and is governed by immutable economic laws. Marx held that while humankind began its social existence in a state of primitive communism, the development of commerce and of technology permitted some individuals to control the means of production at the expense of others. Thus classes of haves and have-nots developed with an inevitable struggle between them resulting. In feudal society the aristocratic class controlled the land—the means of production in that economy—thereby allowing them to enslave and deprive the peasant classes. As industrialism developed, Marx held, an alternative means of production came into being, and with it the capitalistic class, or *bourgeoisie*, which controlled money and factories at the expense of the working class, or *proletariat*.

In Marx's view, the class struggle will inevitably end in the triumph of the proletariat and the abolition of the system of private property which gives the bourgeoisie social control. Marx held that if the working classes owned the means of production, a classless society in which all would be equal would come into being. Though they are convinced that this end is inevitable, Marxists hold that the process of history can be helped along by right-thinking people who speed progress toward an unavoidable, violent working-class revolution. This can be done by making the proletariat aware of its oppression, or in Marxist terms, by raising "class consciousness."

The bulk of Marx's writings develop and elaborate these laws, explain how they have governed history, and predict how they will determine future change.[2] His basic ideas have been modified by others,

[2] Cf. Lewis S. Feuer, ed., *Marx and Engels: Basic Writings on Politics and Philosophy* (New York: Doubleday, 1959).

preeminently by Lenin and Mao, but his basic explanation of change has seemed so comprehensive and adequate to Marxist adherents that they have had a remarkably confident belief that history is on their side— much to the discomfort of those not sharing their beliefs. Not including nations governed by less-radical versions of socialist thought, over a third of the earth's population lives under governments which inculcate the Marxist view of change as prescribed ideological orthodoxy. This perspective on political and social change has had, and continues to have, profound effects on the political behavior of the world's people.

Tradition and change

We have noted that the widespread acceptance of change as progress is relatively recent in human history, and is probably linked to the growth of scientific rationalism and industrial technology. Everywhere that Western science, technology, and economic development have spread, there has been resistance to the displacement of older, traditional ways by the demands of mining, manufacturing, urbanization, and "rationalization" (bureaucratization). Older ideals which did not embrace the notion of progress, but which viewed change as cyclical or destructive, have been rejected or set aside, first by colonial administrations and then by new national governments whose priorities will not allow traditional values to impede economic development. This is as true of Ghana and Egypt as it is of the Soviet Union and China.

There are ample signs that traditional ideal patterns which resist the notion of progress survive, and that at some point they may displace the belief in progress. When we focus upon morality or human nature, rather than upon productivity or affluence, sanguine judgments about the "progress" made by the industrial world are not easy to accept. Fundamentalist Christians, for instance, continue to believe in the impending apocalypse of a world growing ever more decadent, even if richer in material goods. Humanist scholars and recent Western converts to Eastern mysticism alike are asking with the Christian, "What shall it profit a man if he gain the world and lose his own soul?" Though leaders of hungry nations embrace economic development as a tool for nation building, their fellow citizens often remain in physical, linguistic, and philosophic isolation from attempts to induce them to leave old ways in search of progress. While the riches of industrial life remain prized, the doctrine of progress and even the ideals of science have won somewhat more tenuous acceptance.

Tradition Is "Something of Value"

While the material advantages of industrialized society are evident, the costs of abandoning old ways are more subtle. In his book *Something of Value* Robert Ruark quotes a Basuto proverb:

> If a man does away with his traditional way of living and throws away his good customs, he had better first make certain that he has something of value to replace them.

A Kikuyu elder in the novel laments his loss:

> Since the white man came things have changed. Old magic has thinned out its strength. . . . The white man has a greater magic than I, in many respects, because he can drive an iron bird through the skies and he can heal in his white huts the ills that used to destroy our people like the Masai once killed our old people and children.

A British administrator admonishes a police officer who has come to arrest an old Kikuyu who allowed his newborn son to be smothered in accordance with tribal law:

> What in the name of God Almighty are you trying to do with these people? You tell them to quit killing the Masai and not to dance the big dances and don't circumcize the women. You teach 'em to read and write and don't give 'em anything to use it on. The men who used to be warriors are spivs in Nairobi. The wenches want lipstick and jazz-dance halls. On the very few shambas that try to operate in the old way, there's a Government howl every time they slaughter a goat for a powwow. You take away all the old stuff and you don't give them anything to replace it with. [Robert Ruark, *Something of Value* (Garden City, N.Y.: Doubleday, 1950), pp. 64, 87.]

In Europe and North America, where experience with industrialism and rationalism is the longest, as well as in the parts of the world most newly exposed to science and industry, many are

> reluctant to abandon older, more mystical beliefs, even while they want to share in a more abundant economy and an increasing standard of living.

Part of the danger to the preeminence of scientific rationality and the idea of progress stems from the consequences of its success. As we have seen, technology's influence reaches well beyond mechanics, into mores, and beyond wealth, into the realm of human values. Technology has helped to control disease and consequently the world is becoming crowded. The earth's resources are being devoured by the appetites of the newly affluent masses of industrialized states. The natural balance of forces which regulated human life before human beings controlled so much of nature has become upset. Having created the problems of pollution and overpopulation, technology is asked to provide their solutions. But the solutions strike further at traditional values. If family size is to be restricted, religious strictures against birth control, abortion, and sterilization must yield; cries for the "right to life" for the unborn must be answered by authorities attempting to deal with overpopulation. If wildlife is to be preserved and air and waters cleaned, resources must be diverted from consumer goods and the standard of living must suffer. Current yearnings for older, more serene, cleaner life-styles are thus both made possible and provoked by industrialization. Surely wisdom, if not traditional moral values, is needed for the world's secular leaders to cope with the issues which successful industrialization has produced.

DYNAMICS OF POLITICAL CHANGE

Our knowledge of why and how political change occurs is not precise enough to allow us to predict the future. We do, however, understand some of the basic means by which changes occur, and some of the factors which foster or impede it. In discussing perspectives on change above, we noted that some views and attitudes help, while some hinder, the receptivity with which particular societies greet prospective change. Further, the policy process is a means whereby societies make adjustive changes through governmental institutions. In addition, anthropologists have described general processes of diffusion and adaptation which account for intersocietal transfer of changes, and we can identify a number of additional factors which either foster or inhibit political change.

Diffusion and adaptation

When changes are introduced into a society, they are more often copied than invented. This is not strange since it is generally easier to learn and understand ideas than to invent or create them; it is less difficult to make the second spear, rifle, automobile, or power plant than the first.

Anthropologists refer to the process whereby new social practices and technologies spread from one society to another as *diffusion*. This process is as old as humanity, and it is accelerated as intersociety contacts increase. As people of different societies interact more frequently, they hasten the borrowing of elements of each others' cultures. Some scholars have claimed to discern the emergence of a single world culture in the not-too-distant future as the result of high levels of intercultural interaction in the electronic/jet age. They think that our propensity to borrow from each other is so strong that we may be becoming essentially alike, culturally.

Two examples of change through diffusion should provide ample illustration of the process. In 1945, the United States exploded the first atomic bomb. Since that time, Britain, France, the Soviet Union, China, and most recently India have also joined the "nuclear club." Most observers expect the "club" to become less and less exclusive with the passage of time. The technology each nuclear power has developed is similar to that of the others; in fact, the desire to borrow technology has been so intense that spy networks have been employed. And, even though the United States and other states with the know-how have sought to prohibit the dissemination of such information, diffusion has taken place on a worldwide scale.

Diffusion also occurs with ideas, and the intangible aspects of a political culture. Lenin, the great Russian Bolshevik leader, developed and expanded the ideas of Marx in order to explain and organize a new political order suited to Russian needs. Today only a few decades after Lenin's death, his ideas are not only known worldwide, but political leaders on all continents consciously or unconsciously draw upon his organizing principles or use his analysis of imperialism to criticize Western domination of the world's economies.

Diffusion, of course, does not ordinarily take the form of exact replication. People not only adopt the practices and beliefs of others;

they also *adapt* them to their own purposes and needs. Lenin not only explained Marx's teachings; he also modified them. Soviet nuclear technology is *very similar to,* not *identical with,* that of the United States. Leninist ideas in Algeria are similar to, but not identical with, Leninist ideas in Moscow.

Though it seems sensible to expect people to modify innovations as they assimilate them, we have often been surprised when adaptation takes place. Most ex-colonies were granted independence on the condition that they would establish constitutional arrangements similar to those of their "mother" country. Thus, British India and Nigeria established parliamentary systems on the British model, while the former United States colony of the Philippines established a presidential system similar to ours. In each case, however, the transplanted system was adapted to fit the local traditions, and all have had difficulty in surviving as originally instituted.

Conditions fostering change

The causes of change are hard to identify with precision. But we know that changes seem more likely to occur in some times and places than in others. For instance, the Japanese state adjusted to the impact of Western expansionism more easily and successfully than did the Chinese. Britain modified and liberalized its colonial policies in time to avoid the intractable difficulties which the French encountered in their colonies of Indochina and Algeria. Women's rights became a major issue in the United States in the 1970s rather than in the 1960s. Explanations for these examples can, of course, be offered, but they would be incomplete and open to criticism from many sides.

Dissatisfaction with the status quo   People who do not like things as they are, are more likely to want or to accept change than those who are satisfied. An individual unhappy with a job or spouse is more likely to consider changing employment or divorce than one who is happy. Unpopular political leaders and regimes, too, are more likely to be replaced. This proposition and the examples may seem obvious, but they highlight the way in which *stress,* in the form of social dissatisfaction, can foster political change. Richard Nixon's plunge from 61 percent of the popular vote in 1972 to 77 percent approval of his resignation in 1974 did not in itself remove him from office, but it had a large bearing upon the decisions taken by key authorities, including Mr. Nixon himself.

The creation of dissatisfaction and demands is a common tool of the demagogue and the revolutionary. The problems of the state and the poverty of the people are the fault of Communists and Jews, declared an outraged Adolph Hitler, or of counterrevolutionary forces, denounced Stalin. To eradicate such evil forces, the personnel and institutions of government can be totally altered, as they were under Hitler and Stalin. Programs of propaganda and resocialization of the populace can be mounted, and vast changes in the distribution of wealth and status result. A ruthless elite with a receptive population can use the creation of dissatisfaction, or the diversion of existing dissatisfaction to different objects, as a powerful tool for changing the polity.

Previous political and social change Because social phenomena are intricately interrelated, the introduction of one change tends to trigger others. As we noted in discussing the development of policy issues in Chapter 4, a policy has both intended and unintended consequences. These consequences are themselves a form of change, and they provoke the need for further policy adjustments. This can be seen in the personal as well as in the political realm. In changing jobs, a person may find it is also necessary to move the household, change the transportation used to get to and from work, enroll children in new schools, adjust to new neighbors, and possibly adopt a very different life-style.

In the sociopolitical realm, the effects of previous changes are clearly apparent where industrialization has occurred. Industrialization brought an increase in the range of opportunities for gainful employment. Men and women could increasingly find jobs in factories and in offices rather than on the land. Many chose, or were forced, to move into the cities to take up such positions. As a consequence, life-styles have changed dramatically. City dwellers required new services from their governments; some found the church and their neighbors no longer relevant to their daily needs. What initially could be viewed as a change in economic opportunity brought about a transformation of social, political, community, and religious practices.

One notable consequence of the introduction of change is that receptiveness to further change is likely to be enhanced. One salary increase leads to the expectation that others will follow. One economic disaster will probably lead to remedial action to ensure that another will not occur. As soon as constancy is disproved as the "natural" or necessary state of affairs, and change can be seen as improvement, indifference or resignation in the face of adversity is apt to give way to dissatisfaction and hope.

Whether or not change occurs because of specific conditions or even because of specific levels of dissatisfaction can depend upon a variety of factors. An unhappily married person may avoid divorce if a depleted pocketbook or religious prohibitions will not allow it. Many dissatisfied people stay on their jobs for lack of an alternative. Unpopular leaders can be changed with relative ease where they are subject to election, but may not be removed at all if their tenure is backed strongly by military force and terror, or if they are thought to rule by divine right. If the average British worker earned $400 per year, a revolution might result; if that were the average wage in India, the government would be acclaimed. Poverty and even despotism are only agents of political change when those who are "oppressed" feel that they should have a better life or social order. Thus, as in the case of the attitudes and resources of decision makers, levels of popular dissatisfaction will be more or less likely to produce change, depending upon other social values and upon the perceived availability of alternatives. In short, a "rising level of expectation" does not develop in a vacuum: it depends on what the people of a society have been led to expect.

Relative dissatisfaction by elites can also affect the likelihood of change. There is little evidence that Charles de Gaulle responded to popular demands in his decision to develop an independent atomic capability for France. He seemed personally concerned that Britain and the United States enjoyed status and potential influence superior to France, apparently because of their nuclear capability. Demands and dissatisfaction with the status quo had thus to be generated in the name of protecting the glory of France: France must take its "rightful place" among nations. It was apparently de Gaulle's aspirations, then, which triggered moves to gain popular support for a French nuclear weapons program.

Social and political vulnerability We have stressed the purposive, or intentional, change anticipated by policymakers as they make decisions and by members of society as they express preferences. We have noted that dissatisfaction is the handmaiden of change, provoking conscious attempts to relieve it. A person may change jobs because he or she wants to, leaders may be deposed by popular vote, and programs may be instituted by deliberate choice. At times, however, such changes come about because individuals and societies become vulnerable to forces beyond their control. Jobs may be lost because a firm goes into bankruptcy, leaders may be forced to resign, and nations may be forced to react to external threats or to internal calamity beyond immediate control.

There are numerous external sources of political and social vulnerability. Natural disasters and climatic changes have forced tribes to migrate and to modify their social patterns in the past. More commonly, peoples have been victimized by others. The enslavement and deportation of Africans by Western nations disrupted the lives of individuals, villages, and whole societies. Colonization of Africa, Asia, and the Americas led to subjugation of many native peoples and the imposition of alien norms upon their social and political practices. The threat of an Axis victory and the Japanese attack upon Pearl Harbor forced a drastic military mobilization program upon the United States in 1941. Change may thus be forced upon a system by external events which force reaction or adaptation.

Internal conditions may also be interpreted as vulnerabilities which force unwanted choices upon governments. As societies have become more technologically complex and interdependent, they have acquired new, internal vulnerability. While they may seem to have acquired greater protection from external threat, internal dangers in the form of potential social and economic maladjustments have substantially increased. Maladjustments such as a breakdown in the production and distribution of goods and services are man-made in the sense they are the consequence of human organization, but they are not the intended consequences of policy choices. The great depression of the 1930s "happened"; it was not the conscious objective of anyone. Yet that dismal experience changed the lives of millions of powerless citizens and led to sweeping reforms of political and economic policies of Western nations. Further, increased social interaction between conflicting subcultures can produce internal frictions which might be avoided if different ethnic, tribal, religious, and social groups were more isolated.

Impediments to change

Change, in the guise of progress and problem solving, seems to be an accepted value in contemporary society. There are, however, occasions when preservation of the status quo is pursued fiercely, even in the face of conclusive evidence that all the benefits are on the side of "progress." For example, the need for strict gun-control legislation is so manifest, the effectiveness of such laws is so certain, and the dangers they would pose to sportsmen are so minimal that foreigners with a knowledge of America would likely express astonishment that firearms are readily available for any purpose in the United States. Yet strict, effective gun-control laws have not been passed by Congress and are not likely to be in the near future. The persistence of cold war perceptions and values despite evidence of their flaws might be another example of the point. Why do such attitudes and/or policies persist?

Change as a threat to values Most of us live by the axiom that the good should be preserved. Architectural masterpieces should be renovated, not destroyed; the family as a social institution should be honored; the Constitution (if not all its provisions) should be protected and followed. But what should be done if something good stands in the way of "progress"? Should the most beautiful building in the city be razed to make room for a mass-transit system or a new expressway? Should accepted ideas of the family stand in the way of the liberation of women? Should the Constitution be honored even if the safety of the nation is at stake? There may be no objectively correct answer to these or similar questions. Rather, subjective preferences might be decisive— and because they might, honest differences are at least likely if not inevitable.

Change very often affects our subjective assessments of what is good. Welfare benefits, though they might be "good" in themselves, might carry bad consequences with them; some of their recipients might forsake the "work ethic" for a life of indolence. The taxpayer will lose some increment of control over the utilization of hard-won earnings; he or she might also lose the incentive to earn a higher income.

In most instances, resistance to change is partly a function of the desire to preserve something seen as good, as we saw in our discussion of tradition and progress. Gun-control laws are seen as a reduction of our "freedoms," and a threat to the ability of the individual to defend himself or herself. Public medical insurance is seen as a threat to the free-enterprise system or the doctor-patient relationship. But more importantly, the good to be preserved is present and real, while the alleged good which might result from a change is viewed as problematic at best and foolish dreaming at worst; it may or may not be an improvement, and we fear things might be made worse. Perhaps the *first* gun-control law would be reasonable, but "before you know it, they would . . ."—and a catalog of horrors is then introduced into the debate. Thus, the proponents of the status quo make the valid point that desirable change often leads to unforeseen, undesirable change.

Change as a threat to institutions Pressures for change do not build up in a vacuum. Change, though it may be beneficial in some general way, can work to the real disadvantage of some individuals or groups. In fact, it is generally true that in our change-oriented society, proposed modifications will usually be implemented if no politically important segment of a society feels threatened. Conversely, when important institutions may be or are likely to be damaged by proposed changes, they ordinarily will champion the status quo. It is significant that resistance to abortion or Medicare or gun-control laws is effective because influential groups such as the church, the American Medical Association, or the National Rifle Association bring their resources to bear in the struggle.

This is not to say that the AMA and the NRA base their cases in public debate on the interests of their associations or their members. To do so would assure defeat, for the general welfare is held to be more important than the rights of "special interests" in our hierarchy of values. Thus, they will cite loss of freedom or something similar. For instance, the NRA sometimes invokes the Constitution's provision ensuring the citizen's "right to bear arms" (often neglecting, however, to note that this provision concerned the need for "a well-regulated militia . . . necessary to the security of a free state"—a need many feel is now adequately met by the Army and by National Guard units). But the fact remains that *interests,* as well as *values,* are often the basis for resistance to change, even in change-oriented societies.

One example of the tendency of groups to resist change when their interests would be adversely affected was the struggle over equality of representation in the United States. As Americans became more urban (and suburban), rural interests sought successfully to preserve their dominance in state legislatures and in the U.S. House of Representatives by creating and maintaining rural legislative districts with disproportionately small numbers of voters. The urban districts were drawn so as to include as many as ten times the people found in some rural districts in the same states, with the result that some urban leaders complained that pigs were better represented in the legislatures than city folks. Their demand became "one man, one vote," which indicated that they were calling for the implementation of the important democratic value of "equality" in representation.

The rural response stressed the argument that the American system was not exclusively democratic, but rather "republican." That is, it was not based upon equalitarianism alone, but rather on fair participation and representation in all segments of society. States, after all, were not given representation in the Senate on the basis of population. Their stand, in other words, stressed their identification with the principles of the Founding Fathers.

Thus, neither side rested its case on the effect a change or its lack would have on its own interests, but rather, each urged arguments identifying their cause with some generally accepted public good. The Supreme Court in the case of *Baker v. Carr* found in favor of the "one man, one vote" principle, and a significant shift in the balance of legislative power has since taken place, though feared shifts in policy disadvantageous to rural voters have perhaps not materialized.

CHANGE AND POLITICAL SYSTEMS

Political systems play varying roles in the process of social and political change, depending upon the mix of conciliation and command processes which characterizes them. The role of any particular system in the change process will also depend upon its own peculiar internal and external circumstances, and the orientation toward change of its citizens and leaders. In general, as we saw earlier, some systems (such as the Soviet Union and China) strive for control of change processes, and others (such as the United States and Britain) allow policy to be made in a less-controlled, give-and-take manner. Where policies are designed to impose changes counter to the values of significant ascriptive groups and traditional values, or where communication is segmented and implementation resources are inadequate, politically directed change is difficult to achieve. Neither command nor conciliation is developed easily.

An interesting sidelight on the role of political systems in the process of social change can be found in the contention that governments do not make a difference. Research on American state governments has found that in some policy areas, such as the level of spending on welfare services, the important determinant is not the political structure of government, but the relative affluence of the society. While this research should not be taken as definitive (political scientists are still arguing its validity and import), it does suggest that the impact of decision makers in shaping policy may be less dramatic than we sometimes imagine. Karl Marx, of course, would applaud. He held that economic reality and the class struggle determined change. Politics was merely a tool of the ruling class—a reflection of the class struggle.

Political change in democracies

We can characterize democracies as political systems in which many institutions, groups, and individuals compete for and cooperate in the exercise of influence. That is, numerous governmental organs and nongovernmental organizations participate in formulating and implementing public policy. Given this dispersion of political clout, no single individual or institution can consistently either preserve the status quo, or introduce change. Rather, in different circumstances, first one "change agent" and then another might provide the impetus for, or obstacle to, innovation.

Change may be introduced by a particular agency of the government itself. A new foreign policy may be announced, governmental offices may be reorganized, or a new tax levy may be imposed. For example, Franklin Roosevelt declared a "good neighbor" policy toward Latin America and created the Office of the President. In international affairs he was able to bring about a decisive change from the previous policy of isolationism. The reorganization of the President's immediate subordinates, and the creation of the Office of the President, was the first important step toward making the President preeminently powerful in the American system of government (and, we might add, resulted in structural changes which would later permit and even encourage the attitudes and behaviors which could lead to the isolation from public opinion and the abuses of power which culminated in the Watergate tragedy).

Alternatively, forces for change in democratic systems can originate with some segment of the people, or with nongovernmental groups. The current drive for women's rights in the United States has not been governmentally inspired. In fact, at times, the authorities have strongly opposed the efforts of Gloria Steinem, Kate Millett, and others; only when pressures for change have threatened the authorities with loss of support have they (often reluctantly) supported "affirmative action" and an "equal rights" amendment for the Constitution. (Of course, the feminist movement now has its champions—such as Congresswoman Bella Abzug—among the authorities themselves.) In Britain, efforts of blue-collar workers to gain access to top-level governmental positions and officials were similarly resisted by the authorities in power. Nevertheless, the Labour party has emerged as a governing body several times in the twentieth century; a fundamental change was effected by pressures from below.

Finally, political change in democratic, as in other, systems can derive from foreign sources. The energy crisis, at least in the short run, hit democracies (and nondemocratic states as well) when the Arab oil-producing nations placed an embargo on the shipment of petroleum to "pro-Israeli" countries in 1973. Just how significant the resulting changes will be is still not known. But in the United States, consumer preferences for smaller cars have forced a significant reassessment of markets on the auto industry; environmentalist groups face new resistance to their efforts to require cars and power plants to stop polluting the air; and

Conciliation, Command, and Change

As we have seen in Chapters 8 through 12, all actual political systems have elements of both conciliation and command. Democracy and dictatorship are not the same as the conciliation and command models.

The contrast between change in the pure models of conciliation and command is easily drawn. Since decisions are made through accommodation of competing interests in the conciliation model, change would logically occur as the interests of different groups changed in a society. In the command model, change would be imposed by the political elite, since autonomous demands are not permitted.

Projecting the models to national governments, it would be logical to expect that the stimulus for change under conciliation would come from decentralized portions of society, and under command it would come from the political elite.

In the conciliation model participating citizens, associational groups, and competing elites would all contend to promote or to resist various changes in policy. In the command model the dominant elite would use institutional groups and controlled participation to achieve its own goals for change.

increased costs for petroleum have played an important part in disturbing the economy.

In many, if not most, instances, change is introduced by some combination of these forces. Though President Johnson decided to escalate the war in Vietnam, his calculations were based in good part on his perceptions of external forces and the options they imposed. The Vietcong and the North Vietnamese, at least in his view, simply gave him no acceptable alternative. Forces at home, however, led him to escalate the war gradually rather than quickly and decisively (against military advice), and eventually the unpopularity of the war drove him from the Presidency.

Several words of caution are in order when political change in democracies is discussed and examples are drawn primarily from United States experience. As we have seen, the United States, like Britain and

France, is not governed solely according to conciliation. Some groups, most notably blacks and the poor, have had limited impact on the policy-making processes and so are typically not able to effect change or to effectively oppose it. And, in some instances, the authorities appear to be beyond the control of nongovernmental individuals and groups. President Nixon conducted a secret war in Cambodia for months, and the activities of the Central Intelligence Agency are not subject to popular review. In these cases, policies were made in essentially the same fashion as they are in systems whose political processes more closely fit the command model.

Moreover, democracies vary greatly in ways which affect the processes by which changes take place; not all are replicas of the United States. India, for example, is much less developed technologically and is much less affluent. Democracies are more similar in the ways they reach decisions than in the substance of decisions reached, which is reflective of different values and circumstances.

Democracies thus vary in the extent to which the government itself is an agent of change. The Indian government has actively sought to develop the national economy in spite of the portentous consequences of increased urbanization and the erosion of caste distinctions and other traditional values. By contrast, the Australian government, which does not have to deal with the severe economic problems of India, has been more committed to nonintervention.

Finally, democratic societies differ in the extent of their complexity and degree of social interdependence. More complex and interdependent societies are apt to conciliate contesting factions through giving something to each, and consequently to face problems of coordinating one policy with another. It has often been noted that in the United States we have often failed to devise solutions for our problems simply because we have delegated an objective to one governmental agency which is at cross purposes with the responsibilities assigned another. The result has been that we often not only have failed to correct a problem, but also have created another one in the process. We have built interstate highways to improve our transportation network, and in doing so, we have created immense problems for the people whose land and communities are disrupted by that "improvement." Complex democracies which permit broad participation in decision making (because they are democratic), and which face problems of integration (because they are highly complex), seem peculiarly vulnerable to the unintended consequences of the changes they permit. In less-diverse, smaller societies (such as Sweden) efforts to implement "progressive" reforms have often been more successful.

Still, democratic political systems do face the problems and opportunities of change similarly in important respects. They all permit change to originate from numerous sources; they all view change as legitimate and even desirable; and they see the acceptance of change by affected groups as preferable to the imposition of innovation by a dominant group or institution.

Political change in dictatorships

There have been many varieties of dictatorships, and their postures on political change have differed widely. Some have sought to isolate their people from outside influence, while others have encouraged comprehensive borrowing of foreign ideas and/or technologies. Some have been rather simple in organizational form, while others have been highly complex and differentiated. And some have sought to preserve the status quo, while others have promoted drastic change to reach a desired final goal.

Whatever the specific structures, policies, and goals of dictators, however, they have one characteristic in common with respect to political change: dictatorships seek to control which innovations will be permitted and which will be prohibited. If they are committed to maintaining existing institutions and social organizations, they will isolate their peoples from foreign influence and permit only those changes which they believe will strengthen their own positions and their government. The Imperial Chinese government of the eighteenth and nineteenth centuries, for example, wanted neither trade nor other contacts with the West. Emperor Ch'ien Lung responded to a request for diplomatic contact from King George III of Britain in a manner which reveals attitudes resistant to change:

> As to your entreaty to send one of your nationals to be accredited to my Celestial Court and to be in control of your country's trade with China, this request is contrary to all usage of my dynasty and cannot possibly be entertained. . . .
>
> Swaying the wide world, I have but one aim in view, namely to maintain a perfect governance and to fulfill the duties of state; strange and costly objects do not interest me. . . . As your Ambassador can see for himself, we possess all things. I set no value on objects strange or ingenious, and have no use for your country's manufactures.[3]

---

[3]Harley F. McNair, *Modern Chinese History* (New York: Paragon, 1967), pp. 2–4.

Contemporary dictatorships are more typically committed to change than was Imperial China, but only to change which they control. Modern dictatorships commonly employ *planning* processes in order to establish goals and priorities and to allocate tasks to various agencies and citizens in order to control change. These comprehensive sets of policies and goals would not be worth the paper they were written on if the command structure were reluctant to implement them. It is for this reason that dictatorships such as the Soviet state seek comprehensive controls over the socialization and communication processes of society. If influences which would undermine the willingness of bureaucrats and citizens to obey commands can be excluded or controlled, if the formation of personality traits and attitudes toward society and the state can be managed, the implementation of centrally drawn plans can be more fully assured.

One means of control is to limit citizen communication and contact with foreign societies and cultures. In the current Soviet regime, the authorities scrutinize and restrict contact with other societies by their citizens. Visitors are greatly restricted in their movement while in the U.S.S.R.; citizens cannot easily travel to foreign countries; foreign books and other publications are censored; and foreign trade and other economic contacts are regulated in accordance with the centrally controlled domestic economic plan.

It is true, of course, that Soviet citizens who have had chance contacts with foreigners are no longer executed summarily, and it is also the case that Western broadcasts in Russian are no longer "jammed." But controls remain, as the noted Soviet dissidents Medvedev, Solzhenitsyn, and Sakharov have so often found out. Their attempts to publish their writings in the Soviet Union have been uniformly unsuccessful because they have been "infected" with Western bourgeois interpretations and values.

Changes promoted internally by nonofficial sources also are typically discouraged in dictatorships. In the Soviet case, we earlier noted that curriculum, textbooks, lesson plans, and teaching methods are centrally determined in order to control the socialization process. Organizations of all types obtain their legitimacy by being integrated into (and controlled by) the political elite. Perhaps most important persons whose skills make them sensitive to the needs and opportunities for change are the most thoroughly politicized; scientists, technicians, engineers, and military leaders are especially encouraged to become members of the Communist party, where they can be used and watched.

It is understandable that Americans and other peoples from the

Western tradition view these dictatorial practices with dismay. Nevertheless, the logic behind them is not so alien to our ways as might be supposed. Soviet leaders have a vision. They are progressing toward a utopian end, and so have a point of reference against which policies can be measured, including policies of development, which involve change. As a result, they cannot logically permit changes to be introduced by persons who do not share the vision, or who see it imperfectly; football coaches and even some corporation executives are sometimes similarly single-minded and dictatorial within narrower spheres.

Try as they might, however, dictators cannot entirely control change. The Chinese Emperors were unable to stop the advance of Western influence and penetration. The resulting changes were so severe that the regime itself was destroyed. Even the powerful and efficient Stalin and his successors have been unable to check the flow of *kolkhozniks* (collective farmers) to the cities, with the result that agricultural specialists have long been in short supply, while urban centers have been seriously overcrowded. More generally, the impact of the drive to industrialize has enhanced the status of new groups, encouraged the use of material rewards, and required the population to be highly trained. Some observers foresee these trends as leading the U.S.S.R. down a path converging with that being followed by the United States in spite of the objectives of the party leaders. Unintended consequences of policy occur in dictatorial as well as democratic systems.

Nevertheless, dictators are more able to control the "progress" of their systems, and they can more effectively mute the pressures for change from foreign and domestic sources than democratic leaders can. Soviet Russia illustrates the point well, for a truly revolutionary (but controlled) transformation has taken place there in the years since the Bolshevik takeover of 1917.

Political change for communal societies

Most of the nations in the non-Western world have a mixture of the characteristics of democratic and dictatorial change patterns, and their authorities find stability to be an elusive goal. The central elites of these nations do not, typically, command the popular support or even the compliance of all those they govern. Their authority is markedly limited by groups with strongly defended local traditions—those groups we have earlier called "parochial." Thus, whether the patterns of government more closely fit the conciliation or command model, centrally coordinated attempts to direct change will meet with limited success. In fact, vigorous programs intended to change ancient and traditional village or tribal ways can lead to resistance, rebellion, warfare, and general instability.

Leaders in such states are similar to some contemporary dictators in their commitment to change, and in their belief that they can oversee the transformation of their states into "modern" and stable entities. They further are convinced that they cannot permit decisions regarding change to be made freely by foreigners or by tradition-bound, indigenous political, social, and economic groups. Foreigners are viewed as exploiters of the human and natural resources of their former colonies. They are, in the thoughts of much of the developing world, colonialists or imperialists. Domestic groups, on the other hand, tend to resist the kinds of innovation that might collectively be labeled "modernization." The leaders feel they alone know what is best in the way of progress for their peoples and their governments.

But while they might think they know, they typically are limited in the extent to which they can implement their knowledge. They require foreign assistance of one kind or another to develop their economies and to establish security forces, and they risk grave conflicts if they choose to ignore traditional elites completely. Moreover, many of them are committed in some degree to democratic institutions. As a result, they are forced to compromise their policies with dissenting groups if they are to achieve any substantial degree of progress.

India, until recently one of the most democratic modernizing systems, serves as an illustration. It has been ruled since 1947 by a fiercely nationalistic political elite who understand the pitfalls that accompany foreign investments and other involvement in their country, and who have nevertheless accepted American and Soviet contributions to modernization, which have been valued at more than $10 billion in the past decade. And though economic development and modernization have been the consistent goals of the regime, tradition and traditional institutions continue to dominate local affairs throughout the country.

The usual result of this combination of conflicting tendencies is uneven development and persistent tensions between poorly integrated groups within the nation. India has been developing a nuclear capability; it has modern steel plants and a modernized military force. At the same time, average per capita annual income is still only slightly higher than it was years ago. Other countries which have modern airports, government buildings, and other symbols of development, also remain nations of peasants.

The tensions which result are partly a function of frustrated "rising expectations." Unemployed and underemployed city dwellers see evidence of "better" things, but have no share in them and little hope for an improvement in their material conditions. Those in the countryside, too, become aware of the affluence of others, and come to want a share in modern economic conveniences. Over time, hope can turn to despair or cynicism, and a potentially explosive situation can develop as dissatisfaction is directed against the authorities and the regime.

Frustration over unsatisfied wants is only part of the dilemma facing modernizing elites today. In order to become more affluent they must industrialize and raise levels of education—they must "modernize." But the process of modernization challenges the adequacy of existing social and political institutions. Ancient tradition must be asked to give way. To accept that proposition is not easy, for it means that time-honored ways of life as well as traditional institutions must be considered to be flawed. In a very real sense, it means that one must break with one's past.

Not only is it necessary to deny tradition, it is necessary to do so despite the fact that the future is not well charted. Old patterns of allocating status and of granting legitimacy to political leaders must give way to new, only dimly perceived models, for cultures, even political cultures, do not come into being spontaneously and instantaneously. The end result is that peoples in modernizing societies are in the difficult position of having no satisfactory world view which can order their lives and justify their political and social acts and beliefs.

Finally, the limited resources of political elites in these poorly integrated states, together with the terribly difficult problems they face internally, make them particularly vulnerable to foreign intervention. In many cases, this intervention has taken the form of economic penetration— foreign investments in the mining of ores and the extraction of petroleum, and the exporting of raw materials. Though the foreign investors tend to see their activity as beneficial (they pay taxes and provide jobs, after all), the fact remains that considerable disruption has resulted, and little "progress" toward industrialization has been registered over the past century in those places where foreign investments have been important. In recent years, such investments have been much more zealously controlled by exporting states, and expropriation of foreign capital has become more common.

In some cases, foreign penetration has taken the form of wars or of military assistance. Vietnam, of course, is the most extreme illustration here. The introduction of 500,000 American troops was a tremendously disruptive force even without consideration of the damage and dislocations caused by bombings and military ground action. Foreign intervention did not achieve its intended goal, but the social and economic consequences which have resulted from American, Soviet, and Chinese technology will have an impact on the ability of the Vietnamese to control their development.

Taking all these considerations into account, the prospects for measured progress toward stable and affluent political entities in many of the non-Western states are not good. Rather, future change will likely continue to be uneven, disjointed, and insufficient, with political instabilities an important consequence.

POLITICAL CHANGE AND THE FUTURE

Throughout this book, we have focused on the nation-state as the main unit of analysis. Underlying this focus is the assumption that nation-states will persist for the immediate future. Neither the emergence of a worldwide government nor the general disintegration of states into smaller units seems likely since most nation-states seem capable of successfully resisting change in either direction. Few people see disintegration as a real possibility except as an outgrowth of a worldwide nuclear holocaust. Though world government is a more popular (and some perceive a needed) "solution" to persistent problems inherent in a world system of nation-states, no one has satisfactorily shown how such a transformation can be accomplished by conscious design or will be accomplished because of inexorable forces. In fact, calls for world government have greatly diminished over the past two decades.

If world political change of so fundamental proportions does not seem likely, the prospects for stasis, or the prevention of further change, seems even less probable. Change will be a constant in future decades. The precise forms change will take, or even the general trends which will materialize in the next decades, are not easily predicted. Political scientists are poor prophets, perhaps even poorer than most. Just a decade ago, conventional wisdom in the political science fraternity held that, internally, the United States was experiencing an "end of ideology," and the beginning of an era of tranquility. Indeed, these sanguine voices were being heard even as political assassinations shocked the people, as Watts went up in flames, and as civil strife over our involvement in Vietnam was about to drive an incumbent President into forced retirement. Only a foolish person would attempt to predict social and political developments with much confidence.

And yet the past can tell us something of the future. It appears likely, first of all, that the level of interaction and interdependency between nation-states will continue to increase. Opportunities for greater contacts are increasing as transportation and communication networks expand. The benefits of imitation and reproduction of new technologies are consequently greater than ever before. Complex contemporary technology leaves all nations dependent on others for expertise, raw materials, and capital.

The implication is that differences between nations and cultures may well diminish. It might even be appropriate, if futuristic and presumptive, to anticipate the development of a single world culture. This is not to suggest that conflicts between countries will necessarily diminish. Conflict may result from familiarity as well as mutual ignorance, as many who have experienced an unsuccessful marriage know only too well. In fact, it may be that change will cause heightened tensions, for as old patterns are discarded, those who stand to lose by new developments may choose to resist what others seek to establish. And problems of economic inequality seem certain to persist, providing a basis for resentment and fear.

The future also seems to present us with some intractable, perhaps insoluble problems. Overpopulation, depleted resources, limited food supplies, and pollution seem certain to plague us for years to come.

How these dilemmas will affect our political institutions and processes is anyone's guess. That we have the political means to solve them is far from certain. Whether democratic or dictatorial political systems can better cope with them will probably continue to be a matter of debate. And whether the nations "in transition" which seem particularly threatened can establish effective democratic or dictatorial systems cannot be determined.

We cannot see the future, and we do not know if it will work. Our technologies are unmatched in their sophistication; our collective knowledge is staggering. But maybe our problems are unmatched and staggering too. Perhaps the ambivalence of our situation is best captured by the old adage from the days of the cold war: we don't know whether we should be dying of curiosity or scared to death.

SUGGESTED READINGS

Apter, David E.: *The Politics of Modernization* (Chicago: University of Chicago Press, 1965). An examination of the problems and strategies of modernization; Apter also evaluates the state of our knowledge of modernizing processes.

Black, C. E.: *The Dynamics of Modernization* (New York: Harper & Row, Publishers, 1966). The problems and processes of modernization are explored from the perspectives of a historian.

Johnson, Chalmers: *Revolutionary Change* (Boston: Little, Brown, 1966). A brief analysis of rapid and violent change, its causes and its consequences.

Kahn, Herman, and B. Bruce-Briggs: *Things to Come* (New York: Macmillan, 1972). A controversial attempt to predict the likely political and social consequences of the continuing technological revolution.

Pye, Lucian W.: *Aspects of Political Development* (Boston: Little, Brown, 1966). A short but comprehensive analysis of the problems of development in the non-Western, formerly colonial world.

INDEX

347

Ladd, Everret C., Jr., 146
Langton, Kenneth P., 117n. 119, 122
Lasswell, Harold D., 5, 154
Laurence, Joan E., 117n.
Legitimacy, 155–156
  authority and, 20
Lenin, Vladimir I., 21, 299, 327
Levine, Robert A., 118n.
Liberty:
  John S. Mill on, 13–14
  religious, 16–18
Lindblom, Charles E., 50
Lipset, Seymour M., 77
Long March, The (in China), 294
Love, John, 78
Lowi, Theodore J., 81

McCarthy, Eugene, 50
McClosky, Herbert, 118
McGovern, George, 49
MacMillan, Harold, 231
McNair, Harley F., 336, 338
Macridis, Roy C., 252
Mao Tse-tung:
  on authority and force, 23–24
  campaigns and, 308
  importance of, 295–297
  on the peasantry, 295–296
  on role of People's Liberation Army, 305
Maoism, 298–301
Marbury v. Madison, 188
Marshall, John 188
Marx, Karl, 11, 324, 327–328
Marxism and change, 323–324
Marxism-Leninism, 284–285
  Soviet public support for, 286–287
Marxism-Leninism-Maoism, 298–301
Mass media in Britain, 229
Messages in communications, 135, 137
Middle class in United States, 199–202
Military-industrial complex, 37
Mill, John S., on liberty, 13–14
Mills, C. Wright, 37n.
Mitterand, Francois, 249
Models:
  Kaplan on, 166
  uses of, 166
Montesquieu, Charles de, 187
Mouvement Republicain Populaire (MRP) in France, 248
Multinationalism in Soviet Union, 270–271

National ideology and communications, 154–156
National Party Congress (in China), 302
National People's Congress (in China), 303
Nationalist Party (Kuomintang), 293
Niemi, Richard G., 117n.
Nixon, Richard M., 50–51, 78, 137–139, 176, 328
  China visit, 35–36
  Archibald Cox and, 76
Non-decisions, 56–57
Non-institutional groups in China, 309–310

Opposition party in Britain, 217
Overlapping group memberships, implications of, 172
Overstreet, Gene D., 153

Parkinson's Law, 99
Parliament, British, 212
  conciliation in, 218
  question time, 217
Parliamentary government in France, 239–240

Parochialism:
  in France, 255
  problem of, 179–181
  support and, 179–181
Participation:
  in Britain, 227–229
  in China, 310–313
  in command model, 175–176
  in conciliation model, 175
  exclusions in United States, 200–203
  in France, 252–253
  in Soviet Union, 280–281
  in United States, 198–203
Parties:
  in Britain, 220–223
  in China, 301–303, 309
  in France, 248–251
  objectives of, 96–98
  responsible, 220–221
  in Soviet Union, 265–270
  in United States, 195–196
Party Congress:
  in China, 302
  in Soviet Union, 267
Party discipline:
  in Britain, 216
  in Soviet Union, 266–267
Party system:
  in Britain, 213–214
  in France, 248–250
  in United States, 195–196
Peer groups and political socialization, 118–119
People's Liberation Army (PLA) in China, 305
Politburo:
  in China, 302
  in Soviet Union, 268
Political change:
  communal societies and, 340–343
  in democracies, 334–338
  in dictatorships, 338–340
  differing perspectives on, 318–319
  dynamics of, 326–334
  future and, 343–344
Political participation (see Participation)
Political parties (see Parties)
Political socialization (see Socialization)
Political system, model of, 28–29
Politics:
  definitions of, 5–6
  popular attitudes toward, 3–5
Pompidou, Georges, 242
Potter, Allen, 227n.
Power, 22–23
Power elite, 37
Predictability and decision-making, 52
Prefect in France, 246
Presidential dominance:
  in France, 241–245
  in United States, 192–195
Presidium:
  of Soviet Central Committee (see Politburo in Soviet Union)
  of Soviet Council of Ministers, 272
  of Supreme Soviet, 271
Presthus, Robert, 120
Primary groups and socialization, 117–119
Progress:
  democracy and, 321–322
  immutable, 323–324
  industrial development and, 321–322
  resistance to, 324

Public conflict, 12–17, 19
Public interest and politics, 7
Public officials (*see* Authorities; Bureaucrats)

Reference groups and socialization, 125–128
Referenda in France, 244–245
Regime norms:
    decision-making and, 44–46
    definition of, 44
    policy implementation and, 79–80
Reinforcement of attitudes, 142
Reiss, Albert J., Jr., 21
Religious freedom in Soviet Union, 278–279
Representative government:
    in Britain, 212
    in United States, 201–202
Rodriguez, Richard, 201–202
Roelofs, H. Mark, 133
Roosevelt, Franklin D., 21, 72
Rose, Richard, 231*n.*
Ruark, Robert, 325
Rusk, Dean, 78–79

Schools and political socialization, 119–125
Scoble, Harry M., 117*n.*
Screening in communications, 147
Secondary groups and socialization, 119–125
Secretariat:
    of Chinese Communist Party, 302
    of Soviet Communist Party, 268–269
Selective attention, 141
Selective perception, 141
Selective retention, 141
Separation of powers, 187
    figure, 189
Shadow cabinet (in Britain), 217
Silent majority, 50–51
Skilling, Gordon, 276*n.*
Smith, Adam, 10
Socialization, 178
    of the authorities, 46–48
    childhood, 111–116
    civics courses and, 122
    political, defined, 110–111
    political orientations and, 113–115
    primary groups and, 117–119
    reference groups and, 125–128
    schools as agents of, 119–125
    secondary groups and, 119–125
Social conflict, sources of, 10–12
Solzhenitsyn, Alexandr, 273–274
Soviet Union:
    artists in, 281
    authorities in, 264–272
    bureaucracy in, 273–277
    command model and Soviet politics, 264–265, 274–276
    Communist Party (CPSU) in, 265–270
    conciliation model and Soviet politics, 268, 276–279
    dissent in, 287
    elections in, 280
    formal institutions, 265–272
    groups: control of, 274–276
        influence by, 276–277
        institutional, 273–277
    ideals in, 283–287
    Marxism-Leninism in, 284–285
    participation in, 280–283
Specialization in bureaucracies, 257
Stakhanovites (in the Soviet Union), 281

Stalin, Josef, 21, 302
    on Soviet nationalities, 270–271
Stennis, John, 50
Stevenson, Adlai E., 78–79
Stilwell, Joseph, 72
Stokes, Donald, 127
Stress:
    authorities and, 41
    causes of, 42–43
    definition of, 41
    issue definition, 90–91
Sun Yat-sen, 293
Support, 28–29
    in Britain, 229–231
    in China, 310–313
    in France, 257
    popular expectations and, 178–179
    socialization and, 111
    in Soviet Union, 280–282
    in United States, 204–205
Supreme Soviet, 270
Symbols, ideological, 156
Systems model, 26–30

Technocratic rule in France, 245–248
Thieu, Nguyen Van, 48
Torney, Judith V., 111*n.*
Tory democracy, 231–232
Townsend, James R., 312
Tradition and change, 324–326
Truman, Harry S:
    on Eisenhower, 73
    health insurance and, 92–94
Two-step flow of communications, 143

Unions in Britain, 223
Unitary government:
    in Britain, 212
    in France, 246
United States:
    associational groups in, 196–198
    authorities in, 187–195
    bureaucracy in, 192–195
    command model and American political system, 200–203
    conciliation model and American political system, 186–192
    Congress in, 187–188
    federalism in, 189
    formal structure in, 186–192
    ideals in, 203–206
    political parties in, 195–196
    Presidential dominance in, 192–195
    separation of powers in, 187
    Supreme Court in, 188
    voting in, 191

Verba, Sidney, 20, 124, 196*n.*, 205, 212, 227, 229*n.*
Votes of confidence:
    in Britain, 215–216
    in France, 242–243
Vyshinsky, Andrei Y., 39*n.*
    on democratic centralism, 267

Wants and demands, 91
Ward, Robert, 252
Warlords, Chinese, 293
Weber, Max, on bureaucracy, 66
Wilson, Woodrow, W., 21

Zhukov, G. K., Marshal, 49